D1602244

A HALFWAY HOUSE FOR WOMEN

Gail A. Caputo, *A Halfway House for Women: Oppression and Resistance*

Walter S. DeKeseredy and Martin D. Schwartz, *Male Peer Support and Violence against Women: The History and Verification of a Theory*

Chitra Raghavan and Shuki J. Cohen, editors, *Domestic Violence: Methodologies in Dialogue*

Karen G. Weiss, *Party School: Crime, Campus, and Community*

Claire M. Renzetti and Sandra Yocum, editors, *Clergy Sexual Abuse: Social Science Perspectives*

Taryn Lindhorst and Jeffrey L. Edleson, *Battered Women, Their Children, and International Law: The Unintended Consequences of the Hague Child Abduction Convention*

Edward W. Gondolf, *The Future of Batterer Programs: Reassessing Evidence-Based Practice*

Jessica P. Hodge, *Gendered Hate: Exploring Gender in Hate Crime Law*

Molly Dragiewicz, *Equality with a Vengeance: Men's Rights Groups, Battered Women, and Antifeminist Backlash*

Mary Lay Schuster and Amy D. Propen, *Victim Advocacy in the Courtroom: Persuasive Practices in Domestic Violence and Child Protection Cases*

Jana L. Jasinski, Jennifer K. Wesely, James D. Wright, and Elizabeth E. Mustaine, *Hard Lives, Mean Streets: Violence in the Lives of Homeless Women*

Merry Morash, *Women on Probation and Parole: A Feminist Critique of Community Programs and Services*

Drew Humphries, *Women, Violence, and the Media: Readings in Feminist Criminology*

Gail A. Caputo, *Out in the Storm: Drug-Addicted Women Living as Shoplifters and Sex Workers*

Michael P. Johnson, *A Typology of Domestic Violence: Intimate Terrorism, Violent Resistance, and Situational Couple Violence*

Susan L. Miller, editor, *Criminal Justice Research and Practice: Diverse Voices from the Field*

Jody Raphael, *Freeing Tammy: Women, Drugs, and Incarceration*

Kathleen J. Ferraro, *Neither Angels nor Demons: Women, Crime, and Victimization*

Michelle L. Meloy, *Sex Offenses and the Men Who Commit Them: An Assessment of Sex Offenders on Probation*

Amy Neustein and Michael Lesher, *From Madness to Mutiny: Why Mothers Are Running from the Family Courts— and What Can Be Done about It*

A HALFWAY HOUSE FOR WOMEN

OPPRESSION AND RESISTANCE

GAIL A. CAPUTO

NORTHEASTERN UNIVERSITY PRESS | BOSTON

Northeastern University Press

An imprint of University Press of New England

www.upne.com

© 2014 Northeastern University

All rights reserved

Manufactured in the United States of America

Designed by April Leidig

Typeset in Garamond by Copperline Book Services, Inc.

University Press of New England is a member of the Green Press Initiative.
The paper used in this book meets their minimum requirement for recycled paper.

For permission to reproduce any of the material in this book, contact
Permissions, University Press of New England, One Court Street, Suite 250,
Lebanon NH 03766; or visit www.upne.com

Library of Congress Cataloging-in-Publication Data

Caputo, Gail A., 1965–

A halfway house for women : oppression and resistance / Gail A. Caputo.

pages cm. — (Northeastern series on gender, crime, and law)

Includes bibliographical references and index.

ISBN 978-1-55553-841-5 (cloth : alk. paper)

ISBN 978-1-55553-842-2 (pbk. : alk. paper)

ISBN 978-1-55553-843-9 (ebook)

1. Female offenders — Rehabilitation — United States. 2. Halfway houses —
United States. 3. Prisoners — Deinstitutionalization — United States.

4. Corrections — United States. I. Title.

HV9304.C3195 2014

365'.430973 — dc23   2013048989

5 4 3 2 1

For my daughter, Gia

CONTENTS

PREFACE

I DID NOT SET OUT to write about how a halfway house reproduces patriarchal oppression in women's transition from incarceration to community and how women manage this domination. My research aim was quite different. I wanted to explore how women are able to exploit a criminal labor market despite sexism and other types of exclusion in that setting to make crime profitable. A central assumption in that research was my understanding that even though women involved in criminal and deviant activities may have lived difficult lives characterized by victimization and oppression, they nonetheless maintain a steady attitude of responsibility and determination consistent with the idea of human agency, the ability to act on one's own behalf. While my research topic changed over the course of my research, my understanding of women's agency did not.

The planned research took me to a halfway house, otherwise known as a residential reentry center, for women leaving incarceration and transitioning back to community life. The house was the same location where several years earlier I had conducted ethnographic research. I was familiar with the physical environment of the house, its management, and the population of women it served, so I knew I would be able to interview women with histories of different types of crimes and deviance. After being welcomed back by administrative staff, I arranged a first visit in the fall of 2010.

At this point, things took an unpredicted turn.

As I approached the house from the city street, I began to notice things I had not paid attention to before. The building's stone architecture, strikingly different from the surrounding brick storefronts and inner-city row homes, seemed to fit a past time, invoking a sense of seclusion. The tiny front-door window reflected my image rather than offered a view inside. I rang a buzzer for entry and announced my name into a door-mounted microphone as instructed by a woman's voice that came through a nearby speaker. The woman herself, revealed as a "monitor" clad in medical scrubs, instructed me to sign the visitor's log on a small entryway table. Noting as well the current time and my purpose for visiting, I saw that the last visitor had signed in seven days earlier. *This is unusual,* I thought, recalling that criminal justice agencies and institutions are generally frequently visited. A second log, this one for residents to sign in and out, showed that only two women had left the house on this refreshing November day. I thought it odd that so few women were outside for work and activities because halfway houses had been developed years before to facilitate the reintegration of men and women into community living after having served periods of incarceration.

After a brief meeting with the administrators of this comparatively small facility, I headed toward the women who lived there—but paused as an intercom sounded a directive: "All residents report to the living room. Ladies, go to the living room for a mandatory class." The voice over the intercom reminded me of a prison environment; it was impersonal and firm, and oddly formal given that the monitor making the announcement was just steps away from the women and could have easily introduced me personally.

As I stepped into the "living room" and through what seemed like an invisible barrier into the women's space, I noticed five women dressed in loungewear, slouching in old and worn couches and gazing toward a very loud television. I introduced myself as Gail, shook hands with each of the women, then sat on the edge of a chair among them. One of the women started the conversation: "What your class? We gotta take your class?" Some of the other women stiffened up at that question and waited for my response. "No," I told them. "I'm not here for a class. You don't have to do anything for me. I don't work in the [criminal justice] system. I'm a researcher. I write about women's lives. I spent a lot of time here before with women who lived here. I want to know more about you guys; I want to learn from you. I want to tell your stories." I explained that I had been here before and spent time with many other women who had shared this space. At this the women seemed to relax and began asking me questions about my prior research; some even asked for a copy of that work. I explained to the women that most people outside these walls have no conception of what life is like for women in high-crime and poor urban areas like this one. I told them that life challenges faced by women who are addicted and involved in the criminal justice system, who are incarcerated, or who are in a reentry center such as this one are foreign to most people. I told them that I wanted to share their world.

Other women entered the room, and the talk became livelier. Some described experiences in the criminal justice system; others complained about "classes" at this house and were happy to know I was not giving them one. They talked about being a particular "level" of stay at the house, about their past crimes and how they earned money on the "street," about rules of this reentry center that they opposed, and about the two "new girls" in "Blackout" arriving the day before. One woman said she would like to participate in my research but would be "graduating" in the morning. As the minutes turned into an hour, I realized that we, the women narrators and the researcher of the reentry experience, were connecting. We carried on conversation with ease, as if we were in a different place, away from the surveillance that surrounded us.

As I prepared to leave, the women invited me to return, and I promised I would. On the drive home, I realized I had never before paid close attention to what was happening around me when I was inside the house. I had failed to notice just how idle the women seemed as they carried on "reintegration," their styles of dress, the argot spoken at the house, and the feeling of distance between monitors and residents who went about their days in close proximity. I now felt the reentry center very much as a domestic space, but at the same time it remained a custodial and highly controlled environment filled with troubled yet determined women with internal struggles, such as drug cravings, and external constraints, including both the world outside that seemed to be so far away from them and restraints on their behavior inside the house. It was then that I knew my research topic would have to change. I needed to learn more about the women's lives inside this space and give voice to their experiences in a reentry center geared to "changing lives." After having obtained necessary approval, I returned to the women for a period of about eighteen months with a simple agenda: to learn from the women what it was actually like to progress through the phases, or levels, of stay in this reentry halfway house and how the women demonstrated their agency when defining and caring for their needs.

Ethnographic Method

The book is built on ethnographic research. Sometimes called participant observation or fieldwork, ethnography is the study of groups as they go about their everyday lives. Ethnographic research characteristically involves "participating in people's daily lives for an extended period of time, watching what happens, listening to what is said, asking questions—in fact collecting whatever data are available to throw light on the issues" (Hammersley and Atkinson, 1995, p. 3). The participant observer's task is to describe a scene or culture—here the everyday experience of women progressing through phases of reentry for community reintegration—from the emic, or "insider's," perspective (Fetterman, 2010). My goal as ethnographer was to convey for the reader what it was actually like to be inside the house for reentry. As Geertz (1988, p. 16) writes, ethnographers have to do more than simply establish they have "been there"; they must also convince us readers that "had we been there we should have seen what they saw, felt what they felt, concluded what they concluded." Thus, ethnography requires a deep physical and psychological immersion into the new world under study, not as a genuine member of the group—because that cannot ever be achieved—but as participant or witness to everyday activities and relationships. This participant observation is approached, as Goffman (1989) explains,

> by subjecting yourself, your own body and your own personality and your own social situation, to the set of contingencies that play upon a set of individuals so that you can physically and ecologically penetrate their circle of response to their situation . . . so that you are close to them while they are responding to what life does to them . . . to subject yourself . . . to their life circumstances . . . the desirable and undesirable things that are a feature of their life . . . and you're empathetic enough—because you've been taking the same crap they've been taking—to sense what it is they're responding to . . . [by doing this] you're artificially forcing yourself to be tuned into to something that you then pick up as witness—not as an interviewer, not as a listener, but as a witness to how they react to what gets done to and around them. (p. 125)

The physical immersion into the residents' world was accomplished by living with the women as they went about their reintegration. My past relationship with the center worked in my favor. Having maintained a professional connection with the house after the end of my previous research project, I was given open access to the building and the women inside. I was welcomed during weekdays and on weekends at any hour, with the only restriction that I could not reside in the house itself. An administrator said to me, "You're family here. Come and go as you please. The women need you." I was given access to all areas of the house, including the residents' bedrooms and the "Blackout" room, used to isolate newly admitted residents, and I was permitted to attend residents' classes and treatment programing in the house, complete chores and eat meals with the residents, and travel with the women outside of the house.

Such physical immersion at a site of study coincides with the psychological immersion to which Goffman refers, requiring constant focus and commitment to the research no matter how inconvenient or tiresome it may become or how much it invades the researcher's primary social world. Ethnographic studies of deviant populations vary widely in terms of time a researcher spends in the field.

Sometimes the researcher is involved on a part-time basis or on weekends when the researcher's schedule permits; other times the researcher's presence is much more sustained, nearing full immersion in the world under study. As it happened, I had the opportunity to relocate near the house just months before the start of the project. This move proved invaluable because I was able to physically submerge myself in the cultural and economic setting of the house, a neighborhood known for high crime, poverty, open-air drug sales and use, high rates of unemployment, and urban decay. To fully appreciate the area's culture and become part of it, I traveled on foot and by bicycle, and used public transportation. I also ran the streets every day for exercise—past drug users on stoops of abandoned row homes and across discarded spoons from cooked heroin on sidewalks, used diapers and other trash, wrappers from thin cigars used to smoke blunts, and tiny Ziploc drug bags of different colors signifying the products of local dealers. I shopped in local markets and supported local businesses, ate from local takeout, walked my dogs on local streets, and visited local parks. Attuning to the surrounding neighborhoods helped me understand and appreciate the women's frame of reference in many of our discussions.

For this project, I devoted much of my days and nights, weekends and holidays to the women at the house and outside the house. Rather than researching during "work hours," I was able to adjust my social, professional, and personal schedules so that my time at the house would be the focus of my every day. After a while I felt so much a part of the culture there, almost as if I had been pulled in, that I usually had to force myself to leave the house at night. I became psychologically immersed not just when I was at the reentry center doing ethnography but also when I was not physically there; the women were always on my mind.

Requiring more than physical presence, the psychological part of immersion requires focused listening and observing, asking questions, and connecting to the women under study. To understand "what life does to them," as Goffman writes, and to convey "how they react," an ethnographer must relinquish all history at the door and humbly open her heart to a new world. In an environment of women who, as a group, have endured so much struggle and hardship and whose reference points have come from a tough street life, extreme poverty, and battle against subjugation, I worked hard to shed the customs and rules of my comparatively privileged life, to discover their culture, and to make sense of their struggles. Shedding preconceptions and normative routines is sometimes the easy part. Ethnographic researchers must also work to be accepted, gain trust, and maintain rapport.

Being accepted by people under study is perhaps the greatest challenge in ethnographic research. An observation by one of the house residents about a volunteer treatment provider serves as an example of how important it is for an
outsider to fit in. Rosa said: "You get in where you fit in." The treatment provider
in this case "fit in" with the administrative staff, spending much of her time mingling with them rather than focusing on the women she was there to serve and
demonstrating to the women that her allegiance was with the staff—with those
who controlled and supervised the women. For this and other reasons, the residents rebelled against the volunteer, refusing to participate in her class. Whatever
good the volunteer hoped to achieve was lost. Fitting in requires being aware of
and controlling the impression one conveys through one's appearance and dress,
demeanor, habits, and speech (Hammersley and Atkinson, 1995). So I learned the
argot used by the women, dressed in a most casual style, and behaved as they did
when summoned by monitors; during chores, meals, and mandatory "classes";
and during activities outside of the house, including riding the bus and interacting with strangers. Though I could never really become one of them, I worked
hard to be perceived by others, including the residents themselves, as a woman
doing research who is "among" residents—that is, engaged in and comfortable
with their way of life and not an outsider or, worse yet, an "official" affiliated with
the criminal justice system. One interaction with a new resident indicated early
on in the research that my appearance and demeanor conveyed the impression I
desired. She looked at me from across the dinner table, and, making eye contact,
I said, "Hey, I'm Gail." "Polly," she said, as she tore into her fried chicken breast.
"That's Gail; she a professor," said another resident to Polly, who smiled at me as
she shook her head, saying, "Happens to da best of us. I don't even wanna know
what *you* did to get in here."

More than dressing the part, or "talking the talk," as the women say, a researcher must develop and maintain rapport. Rapport is a "harmonious relationship"(Spradley, 2003, p. 44) between researcher and subject and a signal that
the researcher has gained the trust of subjects. Rapport should not be confused
with "deep friendship or intimacy." Still, the "capacity to feel, relate, and become
involved" is key to ethnography, writes Liebing (2001) because "research is after
all, an act of human engagement" (p. 474). Caring about the women and their
experiences does not equate to bias. However, as Becker (1966, p. 241) argues,
acquiring some sympathy for those we study and their life circumstances can
"provoke the suspicion that we are biased in favor of the subordinate parties in an
apolitical arrangement when we tell the story from their point of view." And it is

true that ethnographers must resist a "hierarchy of credibility," the false idea that those with higher status and authority over a subordinated group have the right to define how things really are and the knowledge to do it accurately.

Trust is everything for ethnographic researchers. To the ethnographer, trust is like a treasure (Fetterman, 2010). The women at this reentry center did not give trust easily; just as they lived in tense mistrust on the streets and behind bars, they were naturally suspicious of strangers in this correctional environment. Yet, defenses against trust can be overcome. Candy put it this way: "I analyze you. I dissect you like you a goddamn frog. I sit back 'n I analyze you, 'n I go by your first impression, your demeanor, how ya carry yourself, how ya speak. I give you a little, 'n see what you do wit it. Tell you a little about me, 'n see what happens. See where you go wit it. You don't go to nobody wit it, we good. See in order to talk you got to relate, got to relate to trust."

Gaining trust involves more than making assurances of confidentiality or promising women that their stories will be told with integrity. It is more than minimizing interaction with administrative staff or adopting the women's particular argot and routines. Trust is earned through character and action. Two factors come to mind when I think about how I was able to "fit in" with the women and to gain their trust. On a personal level, I have always felt at ease among people of different lifestyles; I have lived in middle-class suburbs and in high-crime minority areas and never felt out of place. A second factor that worked in my favor was my previous work with women from this particular organization. The women residents said they thought it was "right" and "good" that I wrote a book giving voice to women's lives before and during their drug use and criminality. More importantly, the women knew that I cared about them and that I genuinely wanted to learn from them. I showed them I could be trusted by being with them at the house day after day, hour after hour, rather than being outside in the summer sun or at home on cold winter nights. I wanted the women to know that they were my primary focus during this time. Some of the women said they felt comfortable with me at the start. Rosa remembered feeling a connection almost immediately: "I felt comfortable wit you da day I met ya. The way ya carry yourself. I always had a good vibe wit ya." Others needed more time, as Candy's comments illustrate, to test me with knowledge and "see what happens. See where you go wit it." Candy would test me by giving me information—on one occasion that she had broken a rule and had sex with a woman during her last time outside of the house—and wait to see what I did with that. Once she realized that I would neither repeat anything nor act differently toward her, she began to open up steadily. Then, she told me, "You 'hood," one day when I entered the living room and shook her hand in a style she liked, followed by a "bump" or a quick shoulder-to-shoulder hug. This meant we were connected. Like Candy, Laurel was highly suspicious of me at the start. She said of her initial suspicions and ultimately her trust:

> When you came in, we didn't know who da fuck you was. You coulda been a cop like dese otha mothafuckers, but it's you, Gail; there's just sumthin' about you. You fuckin' give it up real. You 'hood. You don't perceive to be this muthafucker, you're a fuckin' criminologist like you got some shit wit ya, but you still wanna use your role to be teached for understandin' 'n for betterin' our situation 'n in the world. I loves dat shit. Don't you know we look for you? You see how crazy we are when ya come in da fuckin' door? 'Cause we love you, you been in my life, to me you're my friend now.

Gradually, the women said they felt comfortable with my presence, which naturally led to stronger connections and dependable routines. The women would reveal secretes about their lives, their fears, dreams, and troubles; I would look to them for support and encouragement at times. Laurel's comment "You still wanna use your role to be teached for understandin'" illustrates the importance of care in ethnographic research, as does Adeline's remark "Everything you do, talking to us 'n listenin'—you care 'n we need you." I share these comments to convey just how important it is for a researcher to listen and to truly care, not just to maintain trust and acceptance. I was privileged to have been "let in" to the women's world, and over the course of a couple of months, I transitioned from stranger to friend. Eventually I became "homey," "my nigga," and "family now," who was "locked up in here wit us."

Once I felt accepted by the women, the fieldwork was simpler. I spent many days and nights participating in routine activities with the women. Some days I would stay for thirteen hours or more. Other times I would come and go two and three times between morning and night. I would often rest at the house after a long run in the neighborhood, stop in for a talk with women before I left to teach a class, and spend hours in front of the television with the women on long weekend nights. This physical immersion and the corresponding psychological immersion entrenched me in the resident world. As I took part in groups and "class" for treatment, completed chores, ate meals, played games, broke rules, and passed time with the women, the monitors also began to see my presence as routine, even summoning me over the intercom, which is used to communicate only with residents of the house. In many ways, I did what the women did and felt what they felt, enabling me to "witness" their experiences during their phases of stay at the house and, in some cases, as Goffman writes, "taking the same crap they've been taking." In time, new staff and treatment providers, as well as new residents, often assumed I was a resident at this halfway house for reintegration, which was another indication of just how comfortable the women and I had become with one another. The work also led me outside of the house with the women as they ran errands, rode buses, participated in treatment programming, deviated from outside appointments, and used drugs. The research carried me to the women's neighborhoods and, in some cases, inside their homes and families.

Ethnographic data collection happens constantly—through listening, observing, asking questions, and interacting. It took place while at the house when I was "doing" the research, but also afterwards when I was reflecting on the experiences of the day. Most of the time, I carried a digital recorder and notebook, which I used to record information while I was in the house, then afterward when I detailed notes of my observations in the field. With the women's permission, I conducted many interviews and often recorded conversations at mealtime, when women played board games, at chore time, and in many instances of idleness in the living room. Scenes depicted in this book as well as the women's narratives are taken from these recordings, carefully kept field notes, reflections at the end of each day, and digital images. Some information was gleaned from publicly available records and house materials provided to residents.

An ethnographer must sometimes struggle with how to report findings, especially when results are critical of a system or organization. Ethnography, says Van Maanen (2011) carries both moral and intellectual responsibilities. The goal of the written ethnography is to tell a story of a culture without distorting it. It is through intensive and focused participant observation or fieldwork that this culture, argues Van Maanen, will be revealed. While I write with as little personal bias as possible, situate my findings within a broader body of literature, and keep the actual name and location of the study site, as well as the identities of the women, confidential, my research reveals harmful aspects of the reentry experience. Nevertheless, the right approach in my view is to be true to the data and, most importantly, to the women who are the best narrators of their own experiences. By virtue of the women's graciousness and open hearts, this book reveals life inside Alpha Omega House,[1] a home for the reintegration and reformation of criminally involved women.

ACKNOWLEDGMENTS

I WISH TO THANK those who assisted me in this research, including staff at the reentry center for providing me access to the women inside. I recognize the important work of scholars Walter DeKeseredy and Molly Dragiewicz, who reviewed an earlier version of this manuscript and gave me valuable insight, as well as Claire Renzetti at Northeastern University Press and Phyllis Deutsch at University Press of New England. I also want to acknowledge UPNE staff involved in the production of this book, including Lauren Seidman and Barbara Briggs. I thank Debbie Shadle Ross for her help editing an early version of the manuscript. I am most grateful to the women whose stories are told in this book for opening their lives to the world; their strength and perseverance, successes and failures demonstrate the power of a feminine will. The pages of this book represent real life and true emotion. I wrote this book in times of joyfulness (my marriage to Holly and birth of our daughter, Gia) as well as profound uncertainty (Holly's sudden sickness, our daughter's very premature birth, and my father's advanced cancer diagnosis). I thank Gia's primary nurse, Denise McCausland, for her devoted care of our sick Gia in the Neonatal Intensive Care Unit at Cooper University Hospital. Denise also cared for Holly and me over those forty-seven days, even setting up a bedside table in the NICU so that I could write next to my daughter's isolette. I thank my family—Anthony, Betty, Kathleen, Susan, Howie, Christopher, Sue, and Bob—for their ongoing support and encouragement. I never thought I could grow any closer to my father, but I have. Thank you, Dad, for every beautiful moment. By getting strong, little Gia helped me to write this book. So did Annie, Sara, Lucy, Lily, and Cicero by their companionship. My greatest appreciation is to Holly, not just for her insight and reassurance during the research and writing, but for her strength and care. She is the bravest woman I know. As I sit with my father who reflects on his life, I realize just how precious every moment really is. While the women in this book may continue to experience great challenges as they negotiate the next phases of their lives, I wish them many moments of peacefulness.

A HALFWAY HOUSE FOR WOMEN

INTRODUCTION

I was dealin' with facin' time, a life sentence, but the judge gave me a chance
... The van pulled up, I was handcuffed, and they walked me up the path.
It was a beautiful day outside. Even though it was cold, the sun was shinin'
'n it was just like, "I'm out!" The first thing I did was look up 'n just seen the
cross on top and I said, "Oh wow," 'n I looked back down 'n just seen the
handcuffs on my hands. It was just a real, kind of a religious or spiritual ...
it was a personal feeling I can't really put it into words. It is hard to explain.
It was more of a feeling, comin' into what was a convent, comin' in with
handcuffs. It was kind of embarrassing, but really powerful. Then when I
walked in, for them to take the handcuffs off it was just like, I'm finally free.
I felt like I came to the right place. It started the next chapter.—Adeline

THE NUMBER OF WOMEN incarcerated in prisons and jails has grown dramatically in the last several decades.[1] Most women are incarcerated for drug-related
crimes, and limited correctional resources for treatment mean that many women
return as they were to their communities and the troubles that contributed to
their involvement with the criminal justice system. When incarceration is complete, some women return to communities under community supervision, others
are released without surveillance, and a growing number are transferred to residential reentry centers before their final release from custody. Reentry centers
(traditionally known as halfway houses) were devised to meet the increasing demand for transitional housing and services for offenders returning to communities after incarceration. As is historically the case for correctional programming,
reentry centers were developed with the needs of male offenders in mind, and
most still focus heavily on the treatment needs of men.

Some programs, however, are geared to women's needs, and a developing body
of scholarship on gender-responsive strategies for female offenders makes the
case that women benefit from such services and programming. This approach is

not without criticism, however. Related literature explores the irony that gender-responsive correctional practices, such as reentry and community supervision, can function counter to the goals of rehabilitation, reproducing the various forms of oppression and domination that women have experienced throughout their lives. While the goal of reentry programs, which are designed to be reintegrative rather than punitive, is to provide a transitional setting with services to assist women as they move from prison to productive, free lives, the structure, supervision protocols, and programming may be so restrictive and punitive that they render the reentry programs counterproductive.

Scholarship on gender-responsive services as well as contributions on the effects of correctional interventions have brought necessary attention to these issues and to the women they affect. What is missing from this scholarship is an exploration of how women experience and manage gender-responsive reentry in the residential setting of a halfway house. This book aims to fill that gap. The argument I make is that, counter to what is promised by a reentry center called Alpha Omega House, women receive few services and little support for their transition to civic life, and they are damaged by experiences they have at the center. Rather than helping the women, the center reproduces in extreme form the patriarchal domination and oppression its residents have faced throughout their lives. Nonetheless, women at the house exert agency through resistance to manage and mitigate conditions they experience as harmful, though their efforts may also be destructive and subject them to further harm and penal control.

Incarceration and Reentry

More than 2.2 million offenders were incarcerated in state or federal prisons or local jails at the end of 2011 (Glaze and Parks, 2012). Although women represent a small proportion of the total jail and prison population (about 7 percent of prison inmates and 12 percent of jailed inmates), women's incarceration rates have far outpaced those of men over the last few decades (Guerino, Harrison, and Sabol, 2011; Minton, 2011). In prisons alone, the incarceration rate for women increased 740 percent between 1981 and 2011 compared to 371 percent for men (Carson and Sabol, 2012; Kalish, 1981). More recently, the rate of both jail and prison incarceration for women jumped from 110 for every 100,000 female residents to 131. This represents a 19 percent increase between 2000 and 2009, compared to a 7.7 percent increase for men (West, 2010). Even while the male imprisonment rate fell between 2009 and 2010, women's incarceration rate stood at 67 women imprisoned for every 100,000 female residents (Guerino, Harrison, and Sabol, 2011). Much of the growth of the female correctional population has been attributed to stiffer penalties for drug offenses (Chesney-Lind and Pasko, 2012; Covington and Bloom, 2007). Problems of incarceration are more troublesome for women of color; the incarceration rate for black women in 2009 was 333 for every 100,000 compared to 142 for Hispanic women and 91 for white women (West, 2010). One in every 300 black women was incarcerated in local jails or state and federal prisons in 2009, compared to 1 in every 1,099 white females and 1 in every 704 Hispanic females.

As more people are incarcerated, the number of jail and prison inmates returning to communities from incarceration also grows. In fact, nearly 95 percent of all prison inmates will leave prison at some point during their sentences (Hughes and Wilson, 2003). The majority of those released will be returning on post-release supervision (called parole in most states). In 2010 alone, more than 700,000 people were released back into communities from state and federal prisons (Guerino, Harrison, and Sabol, 2011). About 10 percent of these inmates are women (Hughes and Wilson, 2003). The number of inmates leaving jails is much higher, about 9 million annually (Carson and Sabol, 2012). Many of these men and women will reenter society under community supervision and, like inmates leaving prison, will be subject to behavioral requirements and restrictions for months and sometimes years. Nearly 975,000 women were on probation in 2010—about 24 percent of the total probation population (Glaze, 2011). Just as the prison and jail population has grown dramatically, so has the number of people supervised by probation and paroling authorities. Parole, for example, more than quadrupled from 196,786 adults in 1980 to 853,900 in 2011 (Hughes, Wilson, and Beck, 2001; Maruschak and Parks, 2012).

For many inmates, the strangeness of reentry into life on the other side of prison bars and corresponding reoffending risks pose significant challenges, not only for the offenders themselves, their families, and communities, but also for criminal justice systems. Invisible punishments that hinder participation in civic life, unmet treatment needs, and a lack of services and support for successful return to community make life after jail and prison difficult for many of the men and women who are released.[2] Statistics reveal the seriousness of the problem of inmate reentry. In 2000, just 41 percent of inmates completed parole successfully; 42 percent were returned to incarceration (Hughes, Wilson, and Beck, 2001). Nearly half of women released from prison will return to custody for new crimes or because they fail to successfully complete correctional programs, like probation and parole (Deschenes, Owen, and Crow, 2006). In a 2002 study of recidivism by the Bureau of Justice Statistics (Langan and Levin, 2002), almost seven in ten prisoners released in 1994 were rearrested within three years; more than half were returned to custody. In response to the growing demand for supportive services for inmates released from confinement, federal funding initiatives expand reentry services in various parts of the criminal justice system, including pre-release initiatives during incarceration and post-release supervision (see Lattimore et al., 2004; Seiter and Kadela, 2003).

Reentry is a broad term encompassing activities and services related to the release of inmates into communities and involving many actors and agencies. Successful reentry should begin during incarceration, with inmates participating in treatment programming geared to their needs, and be followed during the prison-to-community transition by community supervision that links released inmates to a variety of community agencies for support (Taxman et al., 2002). Some jurisdictions are putting to work the particular type of community residential program that places offenders in residential settings under supervision as they transition out of incarceration. Historically known as halfway houses and today popularized as residential reentry centers, these programs are designed in large part to reduce reliance on imprisonment and reduce the high cost of incarceration, while simultaneously providing necessary resources to men and women who are making the difficult transition from incarceration to independent community life.

Although the term reentry centers might sound new, halfway houses were actually developed in the 1950s. In fact, they were one of the first community-based programs used in the rehabilitation and management of offenders returning home after serving punishments inside of prisons (Caputo, 2004; Tonry, 1995). Following decades of burgeoning prison and jail populations and overloaded probation and parole caseloads, the 1980s saw a rapid increase in the use of the programs as an intermediate sanction and an early-prison-release option. Thus, in addition to their use as part of a transitional program for inmates, halfway houses themselves became an alternative to incarceration for offenders otherwise headed to jail and prison. Today, reentry centers provide a period of transitional housing and assistance for inmates nearing release, for released inmates who are having difficulties with community life and who risk reincarceration, and for offenders headed to jail and prison. Federal funding through the Second Chance Act of 2007 has expanded the use of reentry centers for federal inmates released from prison, and many states have expanded the use of reentry centers for prisoners nearing release. Reentry centers exist in every state and at the federal level, but the exact number of programs and participating persons is unknown. Despite the renewed interest in prisoner reentry, reentry centers appear to be underused (Austin, 2001).

Diverse in the populations they serve, the agencies that administer them, their size, and programming they provide, reentry centers are generally low-security residential facilities that offer housing and other services to help facilitate productive reentry for criminal offenders. Consistent with their goals of providing residential transitional services, they are normally located in or around residential neighborhoods, often with architecture styled to blend with existing neighborhood structures. Organizationally, reentry centers can be integrated into correctional agencies as components of probation, parole, or county jail and state prison systems. When used in this way, the centers are under the control and oversight of the criminal justice agency to which they are connected. More commonly, reentry centers are operated by private agencies that contract with correctional systems for the management of offenders in their care. Oversight and monitoring of private programs might be handled by government agencies that fund private programs—an arm of the criminal justice system devoted exclusively to monitoring private programs—or by other systems. The Bureau of Prisons contracts with more than two hundred privately run residential reentry centers for upward of 24,000 inmates each year. States might also offer a mixed private-public model. The state of Pennsylvania, for example, operates fourteen centers itself and contracts with fifty private centers for inmates returning from prisons and many more for inmates returning after shorter sentences in jails (Pennsylvania Department of Corrections, nd). In neighboring New Jersey, the New Jersey Department of Corrections operates and contracts with twenty-three centers for the release of state prisoners (Travis, Keegan, and Cadora, 2003).

The sizes of reentry centers range considerably from small facilities with limited staff to large facilities such as those in New Jersey that resemble prisons, with a thousand or more beds. The duration of stay at centers also varies, from about three and a half months in some programs to two years in others. Generally, terms are six months or less. In addition to being supervised by center staff, participants normally remain under the authority of county, state, or federal criminal justice systems during their stay. Furthermore, participants are subject to probation and parole (sometimes called post-release) supervision for a period of time after they successfully complete reentry programming, during which time they are required to abide by certain behavioral requirements and restrictions.

Like most community-based programs for criminal offenders, reentry centers structure programming and supervision according to levels or phases of stay. Participants progress from more tightly controlled levels with intensive services to levels with more freedoms and responsibilities on the assumption that transitioning from confinement to independent life necessitates a gradual change. What distinguishes reentry centers from all other correctional programs is their primary focus on prisoner reentry and reintegration rather than punishment and control. Reentry services almost always involve job readiness and training as well as services such as substance-abuse treatment (Austin, 2001). Yet even as prisoner reentry has become a priority for many agencies (Petersilia, 2001), we still have much to learn about what makes offender reintegration successful or unsuccessful.

The populations participating in reentry programs are as diverse as offenders themselves, ranging from violent felons who have served long prison terms to those accused of so-called "victimless crimes," such as drug possession and prostitution. Reentry centers may focus on subpopulations of offenders with special needs, such as sex offenders or women with histories of substance abuse. Today most centers serve men, some serve women, and some are coed facilities. Even in women's reentry centers, programming traditionally focuses on the reentry needs of all offenders, like transitional housing and employment services (Spjeldnes and Goodkind, 2009). However, women reentering society after incarceration face unique challenges. Many will leave with untreated substance-abuse addictions, mental illnesses, few job prospects, and disconnected relationships. The expanding correctional control of female offenders and the challenges women face before, during, and after incarceration suggest women would benefit from reentry programming geared to their needs (Chesney-Lind and Mauer, 2011; Dodge and Pogrebin, 2001).

Created in 1987, Alpha Omega House is privately run and contracts housing and services with its state and county criminal justice systems. The center, which the residents simply call the "house," is a small facility located in a former Catholic convent building in a troubled urban setting in a northeastern city. With an administrative staff of four women and a host of women monitors, many of whom are reformed offenders and substance abusers working on two-person shifts throughout the day and night, Alpha Omega House is a uniquely female-oriented program. It houses up to twenty-five women at a time, some of whom are drawn from the state prisons and others who are transferred from local jails. (Women incarcerated in state prisons are usually serving lengthier sentences for more serious offenses than women detained in jails. Jailed women are either serving sentences no longer than two years or are being detained during court proceedings.) Normally, women complete the program within nine to twelve months, although this time may be extended if needed. During residence at Alpha Omega House, women are supervised by house staff and remain under the jurisdiction of either county probation or state parole authorities. Women released from prison to Alpha Omega House are on parole supervision, and those coming from jails are on probation. The women meet regularly with their parole or probation officers—about once per month—while they reside at the house, just as they will continue to do following release from the house. During their stay and afterward, they live under behavioral requirements and restrictions that vary little from woman to woman. Examples of these include reporting to the supervision officer, remaining in the county, seeking and maintaining employment, refraining from drug and alcohol use, and participating in any treatment ordered by the court or paroling authorities.

In addition to serving as a reentry program, Alpha Omega advertises itself as a therapeutic community (TC). Originally developed to treat substance abusers, the TC model has expanded to treat a variety of populations both inside institutions and in the community, including people released from incarceration.[3] Research shows positive outcomes, particularly when participants remain in treatment.[4] Fundamentally, the TC model uses a self-help approach—geared in halfway houses toward reconstructing positive lifestyles and reentering mainstream society—that relies heavily on peer involvement and personal responsibility (Schram et al., 2006). Like reentry programs traditionally, activities associated with the TC model include treatment, functional and productive activities such as work and education, reentry activities such as social and interpersonal skills, financial planning, family involvement, and housing assistance (De Leon, 1999; Schram et al., 2006).

The gender-responsive strategies advertised by Alpha Omega House include individualized plans, family therapy, housing assistance, parenting classes, family reunification, self-esteem and interpersonal skill building, and financial planning. Drug and alcohol treatment, medications for chronic illnesses, and mental-health counseling are also available. Employment assistance is a key service provided by reentry centers (Caputo, 2004), as well as by therapeutic communities (Inciardi, Martin, and Surratt, 2001), and a fundamental need of both men and women returning from confinement. Thus Alpha Omega House promises literacy and GED programming as well as job-skills training and job placement to "help women overcome poverty and live independently." The stated mission for Alpha Omega House is geared toward reformation and reintegration: "to empower female ex-offenders to become independent and responsible law-abiding members of the community with the capacity and confidence to care for themselves and their families."

Gender-Responsive Strategies

Many scholars make the case for gender-specific strategies by demonstrating how women offenders are different from men in terms of the crimes that bring them into contact with the criminal justice system, their pathways to criminal behavior, and their treatment and supervision needs. Female offenders as a group engage in less serious and less violent crimes than men; their crimes tend overwhelmingly to be property offenses and drug related. Women offenders experience much more trauma and abuse than do men in their pathways to criminal behavior, and they face unique treatment needs such as unresolved childhood trauma and neglect, woman abuse, homelessness, drug addictions, medical and mental health problems, weak employment skills and experiences, and child-rearing responsibilities in addition to community exclusion and fractured relationships.[5] Furthermore, women offenders pose a lower risk for institutional security and therefore require less intrusive controls and supervision than do men (Hardyman and Van Voorhis, 2004; Steiner and Wooldredge, 2009).

In response to growing concern for female offenders, jurisdictions are moving toward a focus on the needs of women in correctional programming, including reentry through gender-responsive strategies that, in correctional practice, are guided by several concrete principles:

- Women take different pathways to criminality, have different treatment needs, and require different supervision than men.
- The correctional environment best suited to women's reformation and rehabilitation is not punitive, but rather based on safety, dignity, support, and respect. Given their lower public safety risk overall, women offenders should be supervised with the least restrictive controls.
- Relationships are essential to women's lives and should be fostered in correctional programming. Connections with significant others, children, family, and peers should be supported and strengthened whenever possible.
- Essential to women's treatment needs and successful reentry are services

for substance abuse, trauma, and mental health provided through comprehensive, integrated, and culturally relevant programming and with appropriate supervision.

• Women should be encouraged to be self-sufficient. This is best addressed by improving social and economic health and requires education and training so that women can move past public assistance and care for themselves and their children.

• A system of comprehensive and collaborative services is needed for community supervision and reentry to help women manage the stigma of the criminal label and navigate life after prison. According to this model, programming should include housing, employment, medical care, and education.[6]

These principles require training correctional agencies, including agency administrators and line staff, about the needs of female offenders. Ideally staff should reflect the gender, race, sexual orientation, spoken language, ex-offender, and recovery status of the female clients who are being served.

Many scholars argue that any programming geared to women first requires individual assessment of their particular needs. However, traditional gender-neutral assessment tools may leave out considerations for women offenders, namely those needs that bring them into contact with the criminal justice system.[7] Building upon the Canadian model of assessing and treating the particular needs of offenders,[8] researchers called for gender-responsive assessments geared to need areas like dysfunctional relationships, depression and mental health, self-esteem, childhood trauma, and abuse to guide the planning of both individualized programs and supervision.[9] Some of these need areas—such as education, housing, and employment—are shared by men and women, but many are thought to uniquely contribute to women's involvement with the law. The Women's Risk/Needs Assessment (WRNA) is one such instrument created specifically for female offenders (Van Voorhis et al., 2008). It incorporates the needs principle inherent in the Canadian model with the offending risks and treatment needs of women. Another assessment tool for creating programming geared to women is the Women Offender Case Management Model (Van Dieten, 2008).

Prison-based and community-supervision strategies based on the gender-responsive model are still emerging, and both positive and mixed outcomes are being reported.[10] One model is a prison-based substance-abuse treatment program that helps women address self-esteem, addiction, and mental-health issues; physical and sexual abuse; and parenting and relationships. The in-prison program is followed by a residential phase in which women continue to receive services while in the community. Research reports positive outcomes in prisoner reentry: comparatively, program participants who participated in both the in-prison and the community phase had lower rates of drug use one year later and were more likely to successfully complete parole supervision (Prendergast, Wellisch, and Wong, 1996). Evaluation of another in-prison substance-abuse treatment program designed around gender-responsive principles (in this case same-gender environments, nonconfrontational and nonhierarchical programming, and peer mentoring) also indicates positive results. Compared to women who took part in a traditional treatment program not geared specifically to women's needs, women in the gender-responsive program were less likely to return to drug use and prison after release (Messina, Grella, Cartier, and Torres, 2010). Likewise, an evaluation of a reentry program geared to women's parenting responsibilities as well as to substance-abuse treatment and employment reported lower reoffending among the mothers who participated (Grella, 1999), and a program with a cognitive-behavioral approach to build upon women's particular strengths and relationships was credited with reducing reoffending among women on probation (Gehring, Van Voorhis, and Bell, 2010). Finally, in her analysis of gender-responsive programming for women on probation and parole, Morash (2010) reports favorable results. Comparing traditional community supervision of male and female supervision officers with a model incorporating an all-female staff supervising only woman with services and resources that address parenting, addiction, and needs specific to the particular women on the caseload, Morash concludes that the gender-responsive services promote positive changes in the lives of women.

Still, the practice of gender responsiveness is not without debate. An emerging body of literature questions whether gender-responsive strategies are actually oppressive and overly coercive to the very populations they aim to empower. Some researchers argue that programs designed around women's needs fail to live up to their purpose, instead reinforcing gender stereotypes and limiting women's opportunities. Homelessness is a reality for many women in trouble with the law both before and after their incarceration. However, a focus on housing at the expense of other services for women can produce oppression in the lives of women. For example, in her ethnographic analysis of a hostel for homeless women, Harman (1989) notes that the hostel helps to reproduce patriarchy. Hostel women enter having lived dependently on men and, because of the comforts of the hostel, become dependent on social service rather than empowered to live independently.

Harman writes that "the hostel [had] come to replace home for them. Women who become dependent upon hostels learn that they may exist, in perpetuity, without money or resources of any kind" (p. 106). Moreover, through everyday routines—like domestic chores—they learn to value domesticity, and hostel rules and regulations train them to act powerless and obedient. Similarly, Hannah-Moffat (2010) criticizes a gendered-responsive approach that targets victimization, motherhood, self-esteem, and similar need areas without considering the causes of these needs. This approach reinforces stereotypes about women as emotionally fragile, insecure, and dependent. Furthermore, Hannah-Moffat (2001) argues that the assumption that women need an environment of empowerment, support, and care distinct from the male prison model that is based on control and discipline reinforces stereotypes about what all women need and normative standards of femininity. Gengler (2012) makes similar arguments about a battered women's shelter designed to empower women but that reinforces gender stereotypes.

McKim's (2008) study of drug treatment for women in the community reports on interventions that reflected harmful penal practices because they were based on psychological notions of women's deviance rather than on the important conditions that affected the women's lives. Pollack (2004) also argues that such correctional programming harms women while the real social issues contributing to women's involvement with the law are understated. Other research suggests that programming designed around needs identified as being unique to women can create further harm if the design limits programming for other needs shared by women and men alike—like training and placement for jobs with competitive pay and housing that can help offenders to live independently.[11]

Hannah-Moffat (2010) makes a good point that while focusing on relationships is important for the treatment of women offenders, this strategy is difficult to accomplish through correctional programming in a system that is inherently punitive and geared toward middle-class ideals. For example, the relationship choices of women offenders and their ideas of parenting might not live up to middle-class standards. Thus, efforts at reform serve to discipline and govern women by redefining ideals of mothering and "healthy" relationships—setting the women up for failure if they do not live up to the new ideals. Gender responsiveness in practice can thus become a strategy of "gendered governance" (p. 199). Similarly, McCorkel (2003, p. 58) describes how a therapeutic community treatment setting for female inmates advertised as gender neutral actually harms women through gendered surveillance that targets the "flawed" character of women. Strategies applied to the women were based on notions about women as weak in character and void of agency; thus expressions of, for example, emotion and female connectedness were punished.

Although it is reasonable to assume that gender-responsive programming would avoid defining women in patriarchal terms, patriarchal assumptions can and do remain, creating harm and interfering with successful outcomes. From historical analysis of women's imprisonment in Great Britain and interviews with incarcerated women about their daily lives, Dobash, Dobash, and Gutteridge (1986, pp. 60–61) argue that women's imprisonment, including supervision and women's therapeutic interventions, are shaped by patriarchal assumptions about women offenders, leading to oppressive conditions for female inmates. Assumptions that women are morally weak have led to closer forms of surveillance and control compared to men, a "tighter regime . . . created specifically for [women]," as well as increased penalty for infractions. Shaylor (2009) argues against gender responsiveness, citing California's use of elective sterilization for women inmates during labor and delivery as an abusive policy with racist roots promulgated under the guise of gender responsiveness. Though touted as gender responsive for women with special needs, the California policy results in sterilization of black women without consent—one example of a gender-responsive policy that obscures continued racial and sexist oppression.

Along the same lines, Lawston (2013) and Braz (2006) scrutinized California's plan to transfer nonviolent female offenders from state prisons to new community correctional facilities. On its face, the policy would appear to benefit women who would move from the punitive confines of state institutions to smaller community-based facilities where they would receive specialized treatment for trauma and vocational job training and be closer to family in order to strengthen ties with their children. However, the researchers concluded the strategy would work against women. As Lawston argues, the small size of the community correctional facilities would lead to much closer supervision and control over women's behavior than occurs in state prisons. Furthermore, the design of program rules means women would have fewer opportunities to visit with families. In addition, while the community corrections centers would be operated by private agencies, state prison guards would continue to supervise women. Thus, argues Braz, the promised rehabilitative residential setting would be undermined by continued supervision by state prison guards. The move would actually widen the net of correctional control, as well as free up state prison beds for female offenders. All of this would effectively transfer the punitive culture of prison to new community settings and work against women's needs.

Poorly conceptualized and implemented gender-responsive strategies, argues Hannah-Moffat (1999; 2010), may actually turn women's treatment needs into risks, particularly in a custodial setting. She argues that the use of actuarial risk assessments, which are based on statistical models rather than clinical assessment to predict risk of reoffending or institutional misbehavior, characterize women's programming needs in a way that redefines them as risks, resulting in more controlled correctional supervision. For instance, an incarcerated woman's concern for her children may be identified as a potential escape risk factor, effectively redefining her need for relational connection as a security risk. This may lead to greater institutional controls over her behavior through security classification, therefore disadvantaging her. Pollack (2007; 2013) makes a similar point that gender-responsive prison programming focused on the victimization of women and pathways to criminality creates a false notion that women in crime are abnormal and at risk, which tends to expand control over women and their decision making. Findings of other scholars indicate that focus on women's needs such as motherhood, substance abuse, and mental health that are also tied to risks like institutional maladjustment and misbehavior leads unfairly to more restrictive controls (Kilty, 2006; 2012; Salisbury, Van Voorhis, and Spiropoulos, 2009). Part of this problem is the inherently punitive and restrictive nature of the prison environment. However, even in community settings, gender-responsive strategies unnecessarily increase controls over women. When women's needs indicate risk, corresponding surveillance conditions increase chances of detection and punishment for violations that could send them to jail or prison (Morash, 2010; Turnbull and Hannah-Moffat, 2009).

Gender-responsive services and programming, including needs assessments, do reflect much-needed progress in the supervision of women in trouble with the law. Yet, like policy change in any context, new initiatives based on the gender-responsive model can become problematic in theory and practice. The most relevant of the concerns to the present research is that gender responsiveness in correctional programming may actually harm women, reproducing oppression in their lives rather than enhancing correctional services that can benefit them.

Oppression and Resistance

why does the pain show
in my brown eyes
can't you realize that I'm just a girl
trapped in this world feeling completely alone
I try to hide it, but I can't deny it
I'm terrified of me
—how evil I can be
if given the opportunity.

—Adeline

The theoretical argument I make in this book is that that women's experiences of oppression and resistance are linked over time and space. Even faced with repeated instances of victimization, subordination, and repression that harm the psyche, hinder social and economic growth, and affect personal relationships, women demonstrate a natural inclination to care for themselves and others. In their motivation and agency, they are able to direct their lives within their limitations, even if doing so means weathering domination through internal strength or resorting to violence used against them. Moreover, acts of resistance empower women in these circumstances, but the uncertain consequences of resistance often lead to further oppression and domination.

OPPRESSION AND DOMINATION

This study examines one reentry center as a gendered organization where familial patriarchy structures women's routines and everyday interactions. Alpha Omega House is an organization with a population of women under the control and supervision of other women. Its structure and programming, geared toward women's needs in a setting reminiscent of its past as a Catholic convent, are designed to prepare women for change and transformation. Yet in this gendered organization, as in all others, sexism and inequity are present in process, practices, and distributions of power (Acker, 1990; Britton, 2003). And like other gendered organizations, sexism and gender inequality are fostered and maintained in routines, hierarchies, and rules,[12] creating harm in women's lives and reinforcing female subordination, passivity, and dependence (Charvet, 1982; hooks, 1984; Pringle and MacDowell, 1992).

Women at Alpha Omega House are affected not only by patriarchy but also by other systems of oppression, including classism and racism, in what Collins

(2000) refers to as the "matrix of domination." This idea is referred to as intersectionality.[13] While I recognize that power and privilege as well as exclusion and subjugation move within intersecting systems of oppression, I situate patriarchy as the dominant theme in this book.

Patriarchy is sometimes difficult to operationalize (Ogle and Batton, 2009), and it has been variously defined. Delphy (1988) refers to patriarchy broadly as the subordination of women here and now. In a study of professions, Witz (2003) refers to patriarchy as a society-wide system of gender relations of male dominance and female subordination in which male power is institutionalized in different sites of social relations. Walby (1990, p. 20) defines it as "a system of social structures and practices in which men dominate, oppress and exploit women." Lerner (1986, p. 239) defines patriarchy as the manifestation and institutionalization of male dominance over women and children in the family and the extension of male dominance over women in society in general. Exhibited in normative expectations about femininity and girls' and women's place in society, as well as in the power and privilege afforded to males, societal patriarchy operates as a hierarchal social force in which boys and men occupy positions and influence that are superior to those occupied by girls and women (see Dobash and Dobash, 1979). Societal patriarchy is manifested in virtually every social institution—the economic system, political institutions, education, work, the criminal economy, and, of significance here, criminal justice organizations (DeKeseredy and Schwartz, 2009; Renzetti, 2013).

A broader conceptualization of oppression that moves beyond female subordination by males and acknowledges women's role in the subjugation of other females is also important to analysis in this book.[14] Kandiyoti's point (1988, p. 279) is especially relevant: women who are themselves oppressed and who inherit positions of authority over other women may participate in the oppression and domination of other women through an internalization of patriarchal values. Equally important to this research, argues Connell (1990, p. 517), patriarchy can also be "embedded in *procedure,* in the state's way of functioning." The "state" in this research is the criminal justice system and, in particular, Alpha Omega House. Its procedures include rules and regulations, phases of stay, and the various activities and processes of reintegrative programming. Female subordination through patriarchy involves everyday interactions repeated across time and location, or what feminist geographers refer to as "space" or "place" (Massey, 1994). For instance, Hunnicutt (2009, p. 557) defines patriarchy as "social arrangements that privilege males . . . across history and space." As Scott (1990) points out, domination does not persist on its own once established. Rather, the domination and oppression of women is reinforced and maintained through continuous action, moving from place to place.

Research locates the roots of patriarchy in many different areas, such as biological production, work and the division of labor, compulsory heterosexuality, mothering, sports, and religion.[15] Criminological research demonstrates patriarchal processes most notably in violence against women and girls in their homes and on the streets,[16] gender inequality and subjugation in the illicit economy of crime,[17] and the control and subordination of women in correctional settings.[18] What is missing from this literature is a study of women's subordination in the domestic setting of a reentry center for women.

DeKeseredy and Schwartz (2009) point out that familial patriarchy is a subset of social patriarchy, and because of this connection, the two cannot be pulled apart; one must be understood in reference to the other. Referring to the domestic site of patriarchy, familial patriarchy involves power, control, and economic privilege held by males in domestic or household contexts, and it includes decision making, roles, and behavior.[19] Walby (1997) calls patriarchy in domestic contexts private or domestic patriarchy that serves to exclude and subordinate women. Familial patriarchy produces and reproduces women's dependence, obedience, and sexual fidelity; reinforces domesticity; and supports violence against women as well as sexist stereotyping of women's presumed roles, their attitudes, and behaviors.[20] Furthermore, familial patriarchy encourages women to be content with occupying "their place" (Bartky, 1990, p. 23) in the domestic sphere. This "cult of domesticity" identifies women with home so much, argues Golden (1992, p. 116), that women who are not in traditional homes—such as women in hostels or homeless shelters and, in this case, residential reentry centers—are not truly women. As mentioned, patriarchal oppression and domination also involve females in positions of power. So too does familial patriarchy.

As a residential reentry center, Alpha Omega House is an institution of social control in a context that resembles a home. Moreover, it advertises "a homelike atmosphere" that makes familial patriarchy and its corresponding oppression and domination of women through sexism and reinforced gender inequality a fitting analytic approach in this book. Thus this book examines the reentry center as a domestic sphere or satellite (Comfort, 2002), both a home and a public place where individuals engage in everyday life public and private. Extending the model of familial patriarchy to the context of women's participation in a reentry center made up entirely of women also allows for examination of how women participate in the subordination of other women. In this study, the site of patriarchal female oppression and domination is within the Alpha Omega House and its corresponding structure and routines.

RESISTANCE

A large and diverse body of literature investigates the form and context of opposition to domination, oppression, and control in many contexts, including domestic and residential sites, and organizations and social service agencies.[21] A host of studies concentrate on women's resistance to violence, risk, domination, and inequity in other spheres.[22] The present study is informed by this diverse scholarship. What remains to be theorized is women's resistance in the context of transition from prison to community life (but see Werth, 2012).

Foucault (1990) famously reasoned that resistance is contained in all oppression; every form of power and domination brings about its own forms of power and resistance. Wade's (1997) conceptualization of resistance as more than physical action is helpful. He says: "Any mental or behavioural act through which a person attempts to expose, withstand, repel, stop, prevent, abstain from, strive against, impede, refuse to comply with, or oppose any form of violence or oppression (including any type of disrespect), or the conditions that make such acts possible, may be understood as a form of resistance" (p. 25).

By this definition, resistance to domination and inequity may vary widely. One of the women in this study says plainly: "There's all different types of control 'n there's different ways to deal wit it." Resistance efforts by individuals and groups, sometimes called survival skills and coping strategies (Wade, 1997), are said to fluctuate on a continuum from action that resembles compliance but is subversive in intent to unmistakable forms protest.[23] In their review of resistance literature, Hollander and Einwohner (2004) describe resistance as individual, collective, and institutional strategies that can range from physical and material to cognitive and verbal, including silence. These strategies include overt, covert, unwitting (i.e., unintentional), missed, and attempted resistance.

The idea that in addition to overt resistance subtle, private, and internal forms of dissenting behavior are common expressions among oppressed groups is important to my research. In his analysis of domination and resistance, Scott (1990) points out that resistance to oppression is not always overt but takes on subtle everyday forms that often involve elements of compliance. He says of the oppression-resistance relationship: "Those with power . . . are not in total control of the stage. They might write the basic script for the play, but, within its confines, truculent or disaffected actors find sufficient room for maneuver to suggest subtly their distain for the proceedings" (1985).

Resistance efforts and coping mechanisms used by the less powerful are what Scott refers to as "weapons of the weak." These "hidden transcripts" are commonly not practiced on the public stage but are alive in safe, private settings. Sometimes mistaken for compliance or false consciousness, hidden transcripts reveal private desire for resistance as well as efforts to control the desire publicly. Often, these hidden transcripts emerge in songs, euphemisms, jokes, gestures, and similar forms of dissent by subordinated groups, and they are similar to what Goffman (1961, p. 181) refers to as "small acts of living"—those everyday forms of communication used to express resistance like posture and tone of voice. Studies of women's imprisonment document such everyday acts in challenges to diet and dress. But resistance is more than action and talk; women's thoughts can manage resistance as well, and women's bodies can represent sites of resistance, as can women's personal identities.[24]

In an effort to define resistance, Hollander and Einwohner (2004) offer a typology of resistance that distinguishes actions of resistance by visibility, recognition of resistance, and the intent behind resistance. Even forms of resistance that are not visible or known to oppressors qualify as resistance, and these are more common in spaces where women can interact more freely among themselves (Hollander, 2002). This point is consistent with McCorkel's (1998) argument that "critical space" is needed if resistance efforts are to be shared among women in a total institution (a place where residents are under tight control and strict supervision). It also aligns with findings that everyday resistance of the less powerful in subtle and private behavior produces a collective awareness among the less powerful (Gilliom, 2001; 2005). Relatedly, the goals of resistance vary. While some resistance efforts are intended to produce material or social change, awareness, or action, other efforts seek no material outcome (Hollander and Einwohner, 2004).

Resistance is rarely isolated from compliance and often involves forms of accommodating behavior;[25] thus discerning between the two can be difficult. Kandiyoti (1988) points out that resistance and accommodation work together in the contest of "patriarchal bargains"; for example, women may tolerate a weaker position in exchange for whatever power they can glean. Through other bargains, women employ active and passive strategies to accommodate and resist oppression within the constraints of particular patriarchal systems. This perspective is important to the present research, as women at the reentry center accept certain constraints over their behavior while simultaneously resisting other inequities and controls.

Just as context shapes oppression and domination, so does resistance vary by situational, personal, and contextual forces, including the types of problems encountered.[26] Further, just as a host of social and structural forces interact with gender in the production of control, intersecting forces affect resistance efforts (Gengler, 2012; Gerami and Lehnerer, 2001). The space or place of resistance is also critical. As Hartmann (1981, p. 368) points out, the family or household is a "locus of struggle" where tension and conflict over interests interact. Jurik and colleagues (2009, p. 7) conceptualize resistance in a social service organization as "a multidimensional and contradictory continuum of responses that are shaped by organizational and societal contexts." Both ideas are helpful for appreciating how resistance might play out in a domestic-styled organization. In addition to conflict, pursuit of interests, and organizational factors, social support plays an important role in resistance in domestic contexts (Shorter-Gooden, 2004). For example, Agarwal (1997, p. 4) considers women's bargaining power for change within household contexts as a function of their "fall-back position," which includes a woman's ability to meet her needs outside the confines of the household and social-support networks. Sen (1999b) finds that women's ability to resist woman abuse changes depending on the options open to them, including employment and, especially, supportive social networks. Taking a similar approach in this book, I describe how women's resistance strategies are a function of options that include social resources that vary by phase of stay at the Alpha Omega House.

While resistance may or may not produce anticipated change or relief (Shorter-Gooden, 2004; Hollander, 2002), according to van Dijk (1993, p. 250), "bottom-up relations of resistance" to "top-down" relations of dominance can shift power relations. However, as Mumby (2005) points out, oppression and resistance are dialectical processes that continuously interact. When resistance is met with counter-resistance, a cyclical process of action and reaction may be created (Faith, 1994). This is what Collinson (2000, p. 182) calls "a vicious circle in which power is exercised through mutually reproducing strategies and counter strategies." Where resistance and domination coexist over time, it is often the case that the resistance will be met with efforts at retaliation for a woman's self-determination (Wade, 1997), because those who dominate and oppress are often aware of and act to suppress challenges to their authority. As Zoeller and Fairhurst (2007) note, the production and reproduction of resistance affect strategies of resistance, its collective and individual character, and its goals. Consequently, resistance that takes the form of open defiance is less common than subtler, everyday forms of resistance (Scott, 1990; 1985). This insight can be applied in this study to the lives of women who, through individual and collective action, both covert and sometimes overt take (and often return) power by their efforts of resistance.

Implicit in resistance studies is the idea of human agency or self-determination.[27] The individual's subjective assessment of oppression, her intent in acting against it, and her resistance behavior are said to be most important markers for qualifying action as resistance (Leblanc, 2000). My position in this book is that while women may accommodate or acquiesce to control, they are motivated to resist what they experience as domination and oppression. By acting as agents in their own lives, they develop a personal capital that strengthens their efforts to withstand oppression and domination—as is demonstrated in their primary reliance on individual resistance alternatives and their "dissent from within" (Last, 1970). The following statement about oppression and resistance by one of the women in this study illustrates these points: "I find that everything I go through makes me stronger. Us women, after everything we have to go through in life, we still take care of ourselves."

It is argued here that agency, understood as the motivation to act on one's own behalf under conditions of control, requires personal accountability and responsibility; to be a thoughtful agent, a woman needs to express a considerable degree of judgment about her personal choices. While human nature can be at times both passive and active, as Ryan and Deci (2000) explain, motivation can become constrained by social circumstance and setting. Women residents of Alpha Omega House talk about themselves as active agents in their own lives, sometimes even taking responsibility far beyond what we might expect. While their histories of victimization give them good reason to do otherwise, they blame nothing and no one for their confinement, criminality, drug addictions, destructive social relationships, or even their youthful homelessness. In addition, while they frame decisions they have made as reactions to oppression, they also take personal responsibility for the outcomes. Arguably, they do this because failing to act against oppression is to become a "weak" woman, a sexist stereotype they reject. One woman in the study puts it simply: "What's worse than oppression is when you have understanding and don't do anything with it." Another says of resisting the oppressive confines of prison: "If ya don't fuckin' find a way to deal wit dat shit, ya belong in a fuckin' cell." These comments suggest that women not only have an ability to resist, they have a responsibility to challenge oppression, and if they fail to act, they suffer in their own weakness.

The fierce agency displayed by the women who participated in this research is a testament to their strength. Despite the correctional officers who taunted her, watched her undress and called her "bitch," her "cellie" (cellmate) who hanged herself with a sheet, and mentally ill inmates she calls "the crazies" who tried to burn her with "the 190" (a prison term for hot water), Laurel survived the horrors of her jail time. Though she was victimized by these events, she rejects the victim label as she expresses a sense of agency and accountability for her incarceration and subsequent placement at Alpha Omega House:

> Jail is for a reason. 'Cause you weren't doin' somethin' right in society. Nobody opened up all the cells 'n say, "Come in here, you've been a great person in society. So come join us, we got shit goin' on in here." No, you break the fuckin' law, you do some shit, 'n you go to jail. Don't break the fuckin' law, you won't go to jail. You're not a victim. You brought your fuckin' self in here. I brought myself in here . . . I made a choice, absolutely. I had choices, but not many. But just 'cause I grew up in poverty, I used to say I was a victim. Oh, poor me. I was beat, poor, but that's bullshit. [Now she is loudly yelling] I made this fucking choice to be in dis place—me. Now I gotta find fucking ways to deal wit it.

Laurel now takes responsibility for her plight and to act on her own behalf, but she also knows her choices can be limited. Thus motivation to act is one thing; capacity to act can be quite another. In short, women have agency *within* their capabilities (Hollander, 2002; Sen, 1985), and these capabilities vary with lifetime experience and personal resources, as well as with such factors as mental and medical health, social position, and more. Immediate contextual situations affect our capacity to act too. What we can decide to do today is vastly different than what we could choose when we were children or what we might be capable of tomorrow or what we can accomplish under duress or in great pain. Once again, these ideas are articulated clearly by the women in this study. Although homeless, Clair was able to care for herself within the limits of her life:

> I was controlled but I was in control. Even bein' homeless out there, not knowin' what's gonna come next, I always made sure I had control of my own situation. I controlled how I got what I got. I controlled how to react to what's comin' the next minute. I was sleepin' behind a dumpster, but I still

ate, I still had a little bit in my head [telling myself] you need to do this, you need to do that. Even though I didn't have a place to sleep, I always made sure I had food in my mouth. Clothes, they weren't clean for weeks 'n weeks at a time, but I had control.

It is true that Clair controls her decisions. It is also the case that her ability to create the end she seeks—a stable income, a safe home life, and healthy relationship—was limited when she was a homeless drug addict because her capacity to carry through actions of resistance was affected by the context of her life.

Because of the dynamic nature of resistance and counter-resistance (Mumby, 2005), the consequences of various forms of attack may not be fully appreciated by the actors who resist or those who counter-resist. Furthermore, others might not interpret the actions a woman takes to meet her own needs as responsible or even healthy. Thus resistance can lead a woman to greater control and subjugation. What makes a woman's choice to act against domination and oppression so much more powerful is her willingness to act despite the inherent risk of resistance. Thus, consequences are sometimes less important than action. Another woman who participated in this research comments on this point. Says Mimi: "I am trying to figure out what to do. I have control over my own situation. I might not know the outcome, but I can handle it because I have control in what to do." Through their efforts at resisting oppression and domination, the women at Alpha Omega House demonstrate the powerful capital they took with them into the reentry center as they negotiated the next phase of their lives.

Purpose of the Book

Despite the fact that every year thousands of offenders pass through reentry centers for structure and support before tacking life completely on their own, little is known about how women actually experience reintegration in reentry centers or halfway houses. Though program evaluations show mixed results for completion rates and the effectiveness of reentry initiatives at improving women's lives and reducing recidivism, the practical application of a gender-responsive strategy for women in correctional programming is a source of debate. Many programs are built on or integrate such a strategy, but the day-to-day experiences of participants in reentry centers geared to women's needs has not thoroughly been explored. In fact, there has never been an ethnographic account of a reentry center or halfway house, for either men or women. Further, while scholars have successfully used the subset of social patriarchy called familial patriarchy to guide analysis of women's oppression in domestic contexts, and resistance studies have informed the ways in which subjects of oppression and domination interact with control, never has research considered the patriarchy of the reentry experience and corresponding resistance efforts.

This book fills these major gaps in the literature by bringing to public view women's lived experiences at the reentry center called Alpha Omega House geared to changing women's lives through gender-specific programming. With analysis focused on women's oppression and domination as well as their individual and collective efforts of resistance, this study contributes to the growing body of literature on prisoner reentry and to the feminist literature on gender-responsive services, with corresponding concerns about women's oppression, resistance, and agency. Chapter 1 profiles the women residents whose experiences at Alpha Omega House are explored in this book. It describes commonalities in their lives as well as their diversity. The four phases of stay at Alpha Omega House are described as they are encountered by the women—Blackout, Zero, C Level, and B and A Levels—as is the women's ultimate departure from the house. The book describes the women's routines and illustrates how they experience coercion and restriction, and it documents how they subvert, challenge, and otherwise manage oppression in this setting between confinement and the community.

Chapter 2 takes the reader into the first phase of stay and its isolation, status, and codes of dress. This Blackout phase is the most highly controlled and introduces women to the reentry center's organizational hierarchy, its rules and regulations, and the formal sisterhood promulgated by the house administration. Chapter 3 focuses on the second phase of stay, called Zero. It describes the center's physical setting, introduces everyday routines, and reveals how women are socialized into the informal sisterhood of residents. With advancement to Zero come new expectations and experiences, as well as new opportunities to resist what the women experience as coercive control.

Getting out of the house for treatment in the community and programming offered in-house is the focus of the C Level phase. Chapter 4 explores in narrated detail the varied forces at Alpha Omega House that act against women's treatment needs and how residents take charge, as well as the consequences their resistance sometimes produces. By the time women make it to B and A Levels, they are the most senior members of the house. Oppression, domination, and resistance at these levels are the subjects of chapter 5. Anticipating release to com-

munity supervision, women await services focused on reintegration like employment and housing. While the last few months at Alpha Omega House at B/A
Level represent the least restrictive controls over women's actions, their resistance
strategies at this stage tend to be among the most destructive.

The epilogue of the book invites the reader into this reentry center to experience graduation as it takes place for women. Departure from the house, con-
cluding remarks, and directions for policy and research are the subjects of che
final chapter.

ONE

||||||||||||||||||||||||||||||||||||||||||||||||||||||||||

RESIDENTS

MORE THAN TWENTY women appear in this book, with a smaller number of them taking center stage. Ranging in age from their early twenties to mid-sixties, the women's racial identities are about evenly split Caucasian and African American or Hispanic. As is the case with many women who come into contact with the criminal justice system, they have led difficult lives with much struggle and heartbreak. Sadly, their personal, economic, and social histories prior to coming to the reentry center are those that often characterize the backgrounds of women in trouble with the law. Even so, those whose lives are revealed in this book reflect a diversity of women in the criminal justice system.

The majority of the women in this study have suffered physical, emotional, and sexual abuse and victimization that started very early in life and typically in their own homes. Many of their childhoods were marked by parental drug abuse, parental violence in the home, urban poverty, and periods spent as runaways. As a group, the women also share adult experiences of victimization in their criminal activity and in their intimate relationships. They have medical problems, limited education, and weak employment histories. Almost every one reports mental illness, including depression, anxiety, and more serious psychiatric disorders. Substance abuse touches almost every one as well. The women report addictions to heroin, cocaine and crack, "wet" weed, prescription pills, and alcohol. Quite a number are mothers, and some have had little or no involvement in the lives of their children before incarceration. Their substance-abuse histories and pathways to crime and drugs are similar to profiles reported in the literature about female drug users and women in contact with the criminal justice system.[1]

Most of the women in this study are those who normally commit low-level economic crimes such as sex work (prostitution) and theft, including shoplifting; female offenders according to literature tend to engage in such crimes as a consequence of the gendered organization of labor in the criminal labor market (Maher, 1997; Steffensmeier and Terry, 1986). Other women in this study report histories of violent crime, namely robbery, and drug dealing as a means to earn money. In terms of their criminal justice involvement, only two of the women had never been in trouble with the law before their participation at Alpha Omega House. The rest report multiple contacts (some have lost count of the number) with the criminal justice system, including incarceration. Some have been homeless or lived in shelters, and about a quarter of the women have spent time in hospitals for psychiatric needs. While they have all lived in the same major city and very often in the very same neighborhoods, rarely did the women have personal connections before they become residents of this house.

The following profiles introduce some of the women who participated in this study more personally. To protect their privacy, the women's names have been changed, as have names of the reentry center staff, neighborhoods, and correctional institutions that are mentioned.

Adeline

"Angel eyes," Adeline reads from her journal. "We were in love. He was the love of my life. This is the man I loved. I need help. I grieve for him. I'm a murderer." Despite years of violence suffered at her lover's hands, she says, "I look at this poem and don't see the violence. I loved this man." Then she whispers, "I'm starting to get worse again. I need help. Everybody I look at looks like him. I need help."

Adeline killed the man she loved in self-defense when he hunted her down after being incarcerated for violating a restraining order. Held in jail without bail on a charge of first-degree murder, Adeline was facing the possibility of a lifetime behind bars when she was offered a chance at earlier freedom by way of a plea deal. By pleading to voluntary manslaughter—admitting she took the violence against her boyfriend too far—she would serve anywhere from twelve to twenty-four years in prison. Adeline took the deal, and during sentencing, luck or compassion was on her side because the judge agreed to a technical change to her plea that introduced the possibility of serving much less time. "It was some kind of lawyer crap, I dunno," Adeline explains; "anywhere up to twelve to twenty-four years in prison or as low as work release." After serving two years in prison,

Adeline was granted early release via the Alpha Omega House, followed by five years' probation.

Adeline's childhood had been disrupted when she moved across the country to live with her maternal aunt because her mother was in a physically and emotionally abusive relationship where drugs were present, Adeline says. However, she quickly settled into a new school and grew quite close to her aunt. She was a good student. She graduated high school and moved back to the East Coast eager to start her young adulthood. While living with her mother in a rough minority urban setting, she began tending bar not far Alpha Omega House and fell in love with a bar patron, a drug dealer who would become the father of her only child. The pair lived together in a simple low-income rental blocks from her job. However, the man quickly turned abusive, and she ended the relationship. Despite working extra hours to pay the rent and using food stamps to help offset expenses, Adeline was in over her head and made the tough decision to send her young daughter to live with her mother outside of the city. To cut expenses and save for herself and her little girl, Adeline rented a room above the bar and worked many extra hours late into the night. Her almost full-time presence at the bar led her directly into the path of Orlando, a local drug dealer who would win her heart but turn her life into a nightmare.

Adeline and Orlando quickly took up residence together in Adeline's boarding room above the bar. Soon Orlando's jealousy began to stress Adeline, who began to withdraw socially as a consequence, to no avail. A violent man, Orlando on one occasion threw Adeline from the second-story window in the middle of a winter night after punching her repeatedly and strangling her in a fit of jealous rage. In the cold and darkness, her naked body bloody from the fall, Adeline limped the city streets until she collapsed, waking in a hospital ward the next morning. She endured another year of abuse before she turned to the criminal justice system. Feeling somewhat protected by a restraining order, Adeline began to feel more confident about herself and hopeful that she could live on her own again. But Orlando violated that restraining order, beat Adeline on the street in front of the bar, and was subsequently arrested and incarcerated for the offense.

One night after he was released from jail, Orlando came back again for Adeline—and this time would be his last. He kicked her door down and destroyed her room, knocking a set of knives from the kitchen countertop onto the floor. Instinctually, Adeline grabbed a knife and hid it in her shorts pocket. It was just a "little dollar-store steak knife," she remembers. Orlando punched Adeline across the room and into the hallway, booted her down the stairs, and dragged her out the door to the street below while neighbors peeked through doors and windows. No one came to Adeline's aid. As Orlando strangled her from behind with an arm around her neck and punched her in her side, Adeline grabbed the knife and flung her left arm up and over her shoulder, directly piercing Orland's heart through his T-shirt. He fell limp before her and grinned to her as he said, "Ya finally got me." He died as she held his head in her arms.

Adeline feels a desperate need for counseling to help her overcome the guilt and grief of that night, as well as the damage to her esteem and personal identity caused by the abuse. She explains:

> I have to figure out who I am now. But then, well, you get told that's Orlando's girl, Orlando's wife. That's all I am. I was his wife, his girl. That's all you really are, that's it, you're somebody else's. Like people would say, She can't stay here 'n talk, she's gotta run home. Like people knew [about the abuse], and it was embarrassing. Like I would go to the store 'n see people but say, I gotta go, I gotta hurry up 'n I get home, 'n he'd be like, Who'd you bump into, who was talkin' to you, you seen anybody when you left? But you start to think that's normal. After a certain amount of time you just get used to it. You just suck it up. . . . There's no winnin' . . . until that final night, but I still feel like I lost 'cause look at me now. It's gonna follow me for the rest of my life. He still won. He's still controlling my life.

Although she needed—and deserved—it, Adeline says she received not a single moment of counseling or treatment when she was incarcerated. In fact, she feels that from her arrest to her confinement the system portrayed her as the villain. But with her transfer to the Alpha Omega House, Adeline is hopeful that she can get the intensive psychological treatment she desperately needs to help her heal and a job that can help her feel independent. She also hopes to reunite with her daughter, whom she has not seen since she was arrested, and eventually become her primary guardian. Having witnessed the struggles of women who are incarcerated, Adeline aspires to start her own reentry center geared to the needs of this population.

Grace

Grace calls the Alpha Omega House her home, announcing, "I'm ho-ome" every time she reenters from the outside. At forty-two, she has cycled through the criminal and mental-health systems of this city for many years. Her criminal charges are mostly petty in nature and include harassment, mischief, violation of restraining orders, and burglary. Most of these crimes, she asserts, result from visits she made to the rooming house where her boyfriend lived either to see him or to retrieve her belongings despite a court order for her to stay away. Grace also has arrests for shoplifting and possession of drugs. A meek woman, Grace is uneducated—she says she never attended school—and cannot read or write. She has difficulty speaking ordinary words and appears childlike.

Grace's childhood is a tragic case of abuse and neglect. The youngest of nine siblings, all with different fathers, Grace was beaten and sexually abused by her siblings as well as her mother, a drunk who was never around, says Grace. Grace never had a bed and was forced to sleep on the floor of her mother's bedroom. She remembers watching her mother and strange men having naked sex. On one occasion, a brother broke her jaw so badly that her face was cut from her lip to the middle of her cheek. After forcing intercourse upon her, he left her bound to a chair, naked and bloody, until someone responded to her cries for help from the basement of her dilapidated row home. She says of her childhood: "I was da baby one, an I know my ma no have ti [time], 'n I can't go schoo [school]. I alway get rape by my broths [brothers], 'n my sis hit on me, caw me tard [call me retarded.] I so skin [skinny], my clo [clothes] no fit. I go dirt lookin, my clo stink. Eh body look ah me, somethin's wrong her. My ma out on da street, lon ti [long time] no food in how [house]. I go daw ta daw, peep feed me. I hungry all ti [time] . . . Nobod love me."

Harmed in so many terrible ways, Grace has perhaps the greatest treatment challenges of any woman at Alpha Omega House. Sometimes I wonder if Grace really understands her circumstances of confinement at the house. She has already spent close to two years here, where stays are only intended to be nine to twelve months, and she has no idea when she will be released. But she calls Alpha Omega House home and feels safe from the dangers of the streets. This placement was, she says, an alternative to jail time because the judge and her public defender did not want her to serve out her sentence behind bars. She says fondly:

I lie he [like here]. I ha no pla [place] ta go. Dey puh me he. I wa pris bout sis mon [was in prison about six months], den dey sen me here, din wan me jail. Dey din wan me in pris fa eva. I like he. No lock in door. No chain roun me . . . I ga nowhere ta go. Dey done wan me on stree. Dey sen me he. I be he 2009. . . . I here feel ca [calm]. I lie [like] dis place. Eh thin I nee [everything I need]. I feel contbull [comfortable]. Na round peep owside, feel safe he. I glad I he.

Yes, yes. I come he, I feel betta. I come he, I slee [sleep] good. Dey help me, dey kee [keep] me biz [busy]. I come ho [home], I say, Honey, I ho-ome. Den I help clean, put da stuff in clos [closet], I lie [like] do wor [work].

Rosa

Rosa is a physically intimidating woman in her late thirties. She is obese, and her greased jet-black hair pulled tightly back in a ponytail accentuates her enormous hoop earrings and a thick neck. Her eyebrows are thin painted lines on a large brown face. Her eyes are like small black marbles. Her flat nose is dotted with piercings, and her large lips are covered in purple lipstick traced with a black outline. Various other piercings dot her chin and lips. On her very wide upper arm is a large tattoo of bloody fists with blood dripping from the fingers and the initials: ROLA. "It my street name," she says. "It mean roll a muthafucka, roll on a nigga, roll a bitch." In Rosa's neighborhood and surrounding area, roll is a synonym for fight. When I ask her to explain the reason for blood on the fists, she replies, "I never stop fightin' till there's blood." Throughout her life, Rosa has fought men and women. During her days as a drug "caseworker" (the drug dealer responsible for managing a block or corner and its individual dealers who handle the transactions) when she was dealing, sometimes she even faced men who were armed. Rosa is not afraid to roll. In fact, she is inclined toward violence, so she says—and demonstrates. Her most recent criminal charge sent her to prison for up to twenty-two months for aggravated assault and terroristic threats on a bus. She is always ready to get physical, to roll, if she feels "dissed."

Rosa cannot seem to stay out of trouble. She lost count of the number of arrests she has accumulated over her lifetime. Raised in an environment of urban poverty and violence in a home with a drug-abusing mother, Rosa was a homeless runaway stealing underwear from clotheslines to keep herself clothed and clean. In and out of foster care for years, she had at least five arrests before age eighteen. Since then she has wracked up charges for robbery, assault, drug sales, possession of drugs, weapons violations, shoplifting, and theft. "I'm always catchin' a case for sumthin,'" she laments, as if getting arrested is like catching a cold. Her primary "job" has been as a drug caseworker. Dealing drugs corresponded to her own drug use, which led her to commit economic crimes to feed her addiction to "wet," which is the street name for marijuana laced with PCP that gives users an intense but unpredictable high. I asked her what wet is made of, and she answered, "Fuck if I know, I'm told suntin' like horse tranquilizer, embalmin' fluid, 'n some other shit. All I know is da shit's good." But the drug, she tells me, also exacerbates Rosa's quickness to use violence.

Aside from her criminal history and drug use, Rosa lives a rather simple life. Residing primarily with her mother since her late twenties, who is now a recovering drug abuser, Rosa is content to collect Supplemental Security Income (SSI) for mental illnesses including schizophrenia, which she says keeps her from work. Like other women in this study, Rosa was recruited from prison by house staff who, she says, touted educational programming, substance abuse treatment, and reentry rehabilitation as primary goals. She could have served out the remainder of her sentence behind bars, but, she reasons, this placement at Alpha Omega House will enable her to get out of prison early and might even help her get herself together. At the very least, Rosa hopes, participating in Alpha Omega House offers her some protection: "Least here I can't get in no trouble," she says. She seems a woman conflicted: in one sense she makes many excuses for her inability to stay straight or get clean, but with comments like "I am the judge of my own destination" and "Nobody control me," she knows she is partly responsible for her own misfortune.

Laurel

"Yo, wassup, my nigga?" Laurel yells as she gives me a gigantic breast-filled hug. Her smile is as broad as her chest is large. It is a beautiful smile, even without two upper front teeth, gone years before from smoking drugs. Laurel brings energy and liveliness wherever she goes. Sadly, her story is much the same as others': raised in urban poverty and a culture of violence and drug abuse, she turned to drugs as a coping mechanism and then to crime to maintain her habit. But unlike many women in crime, Laurel took up a primarily male street crime as a drug dealer.

Laurel identifies foremost as a dealer and secondarily as a victim who turned to drugs to dull the pain of childhood abuse and neglect, woman abuse, and a poor self-concept. As a young child, she was fed drugs and sexually abused by her alcoholic, drug-addicted mother and violated by many of her mother's one-night stands. Laurel hit the streets at age fourteen. Running away from home and moving from pillow to pillow quickly taught her that her most precious capital— her body—could earn her money, food, and shelter. Laurel's formal education ended at seventh grade, but she is street smart. By sixteen, she had given birth to her first child; over the following years there would be nine more, all by separate men. The oldest and youngest share the same name, Treyvon, for different fathers. Like Rosa, Laurel is a caseworker by trade. She prefers to deal heroin but will sell whatever is hot on the streets. She learned to hustle at a very early age, having been brought "in the game" of drug selling by family members.

Like most of the women in this study, Laurel's children are being raised in foster care or by members of her family because, she says, she would not give up her destructive lifestyle. In addition to drug selling, her criminal history includes burglary, shoplifting, selling stolen goods, assault, weapons possession, child endangerment, and motor vehicle theft. She served time in the local jails as well as in prison and on probation. Over a period just shy of two years, Laurel accumulated more than eight charges of violating probation. Her most recent crime landed her behind bars for two years before she was offered placement at Alpha Omega House as an early release from prison. A five-year term of probation runs concurrent with her reentry-center placement. Of her status as resident, Laurel says, "Nobody but me put me in dis mothafucka." Laurel wants nothing from the offerings of treatment and reintegration, she says, even though she identifies as an alcoholic and addict. In fact, she is determined to return to her prior occupation as drug dealer. For now, she plans to do her time until she can again "hit da block."

Mimi

Mimi is a forty-two-year-old single mother raised in a working-class neighborhood on the outskirts of this major city. A sex worker and bartender by trade at this point in her life, Mimi has long, dark hair parted in the middle and combed tightly to her head. Her blackened and broken front teeth show signs of drug smoking, and her complexion reveals the trademark weathering of a regular drug and alcohol user. According to her recollection, her childhood in the trailer park with four sisters and both parents was ordinary and comfortable, like a "*Leave It to Beaver* family." But after entering high school, Mimi became involved in drugs and alcohol, and by the time she was sixteen she had given birth to a daughter.

Mimi dropped out of school and worked at a strip club as a dancer and bartender. For two years, she lived with constant physical violence at the hands of the man who impregnated her. She says that "he used to hit me with this big stick that had 'nigger beater' written on one side and 'mother beater' on the other." Once free of his control, Mimi worked many hours at the strip club to care for herself and her daughter, and selling sex became a routine part of her work, both inside and outside of the club. She was eventually promoted to a supervisor of the dancers, responsible for scheduling and maintaining an even flow on and off the club's various stages. Occasionally, Mimi would also work at massage parlors giving topless rubdowns to men, as well as the routine fellatio that was an expected part of the massage package at a parlor called "Happy Endings."

Over the next two decades, Mimi was arrested for prostitution and drug possession time and again, as well as for the occasional possession of drugs with the intent to distribute. She spent time inside jail and on probation. After years in strip clubs and sex work, Mimi began to work with a madam who operated a local prostitution business set up as an escort service. She soon realized that she could put her management experience to work and earn more profit if she took control of a business herself. She hired some of the dancers from the club, including her daughter, and brought her clients from the escort service to the basement of a row home where she lived with her unemployed boyfriend and her daughter—now a young adult in her early twenties with her own three young children.

With her "Dynamite Mother and Daughter" business under way, Mimi advertised for more customers on local websites, including Craigslist. The response was both strong and immediate. Mimi says, "People started callin' left and right. We would start early in the morning, real early. Guys would want to come before work. We worked all day and night and had set prices for different things, like $250 for one hour, $150 for a half hour. Anything goes during that time. We had about five girls in the house, 'n I made the deals." After several profitable months, police raided the house and arrested Mimi, her boyfriend and daughter, and several other women. Mimi was convicted for possession with the intent to distribute illicit drugs, for promoting the business of prostitution in a home, and for using the Internet to facilitate the transactions. In all, she was charged with five felony crimes. Mimi's daughter, who had been on probation at the time, was sent to prison and lost her children to foster care, in part because they were present much of the time in the home. Mimi's boyfriend was also incarcerated for his role in the crimes.

Mimi spent a year incarcerated while her case moved through the courts and was subsequently sentenced to two years' probation with mandatory participation in Alpha Omega House. She brings treatment needs for education, mainstream employment, and drug and alcohol abuse. Yet Mimi denies the need for drug and alcohol treatment and sees no need to earn a GED because her careers require no formal education. Mimi simply wants to get the system off her back and return to her previous life. But she knows she has to control herself while at the reentry center because she has prison sentence hanging over her head. She says, "I have to try not to plot revenge on these people for bein' here 'cause if I walk out I'm headed to Copley [a state prison for women]."

Phoebe

"I'm a junkie 'n whatnot." Phoebe's voice sounds like that of a child learning to put words together or a person about to fall asleep under general anesthesia, with one word slurring into the next. While this might just be her way of speaking, it could also be the effect of years of heroin and cocaine abuse and heavy alcohol use. At least three times in any conversation she typically repeats the phrase "and whatnot," using it to fill in for words she cannot articulate.

A twenty-something woman who grew up privileged in a single-family home outside of the city, Phoebe is, as she puts it, the "rich white girl" to the criminal justice system. But her life is not that much different from that of many of the women who enter Alpha Omega House after being raised in urban poverty. Phoebe's mother, stepfather, brothers, and two of her sisters are addicted to drugs or alcohol. Her father sells marijuana part-time. She was physically abused by her father when she was a youth and feels she was emotionally harmed by her mother, who drowned her own sadness in bottles of vodka and pills. Phoebe lived in constant fear for her safety and tried to wash her own troubles away with liquor and drugs. Phoebe is not a new "junkie" as she calls herself; she has been getting high since her teenage years. But unlike other women at Alpha Omega House, Phoebe was long able to pay for her drug addiction with her own cash or money she was able to steal from her family. It was not very recently that Phoebe tried selling sex for money.

Never really in trouble with the law before being sent to Alpha Omega House, Phoebe is nevertheless no stranger to residential treatment. She was sent by family to a number of inpatient and outpatient drug-treatment programs, but she says "it was a waste and whatnot" because she never wanted to quit getting high. Unlike most other women, who come to Alpha Omega House after their criminal history finally catches up with them, Phoebe came to the center as a result of a car accident and the criminal liability thereof. She had crashed her mother's Mercedes into the back of another car and woke up in the hospital handcuffed to the bed. Her sister, who was her passenger, spent months in the hospital, as did the driver she harmed. Phoebe was charged with seven crimes for her actions that night, including aggravated assault by vehicle while driving under the influence. She was sent to jail and subsequently chose to attend Alpha Omega House followed by two years' probation instead of a six-year term of incarceration. In addition to her needs for intensive drug and alcohol treatment, counseling for unresolved trauma, education, and work training, Phoebe brings a host of mental and emotional issues to Alpha Omega House, including depression and severe anxiety. Her greatest challenge will be, in her words, "to stay clean 'n whatnot."

Candy

Candy, forty-six, is participating in Alpha Omega House after spending most of her life in prison. She is one of few women released to Alpha Omega House from state prison rather than county jail. Often repeating the words "I'm State Parole," Candy makes it a point to remind other women at the halfway that she has a different status, one that can only come with experience in, as she calls it, the "hen house."

Her voice is strong, deep, and raspy and is matched by an equally tough physique. Candy is tall and extremely masculine in appearance and has exceptionally dark skin that shows off her lean musculature. Both her body and attitude depict street and prison violence. Looking past the crisp collar of the men's long-sleeved button-down shirt she wears, I can see a long scar across her neck, which she explains is the consequence of a box-cutter and a jealous girlfriend in prison. She has badly scarred puncture wounds on her upper chest from prison shanks. Her shaved head reveals ears scarred from earrings having been ripped out, and part of her left ear seems to still dangle away from the long-healed cuts. Her visible forearms resemble part of a tic-tac-toe board with blistered crisscrossing scars from "getting cut" in fights. These scars do not obscure the prison-made tattoos on both of her forearms, one of which is the name of her wife in the unmistakable color and form of prison ink. Candy is battle-scarred inside and out.

About her pathway to crime, Candy says simply, "I grew up angry." She spent much of her teen years incarcerated for "beatin' on my girls." But her adult case was the most significant in terms of how it removed her from regular society. To her, the key event was all about respect. As Candy explains it, she was protecting the father of her son (whom she carried to labor to be raised by her mother) from being pushed around by a much younger drug-using relative who stole money to finance his drug addiction. Candy wanted to get even. She says:

I wanted ta hurt him. I kissed my son father, got in my car. I drove down there ta Eastville; I had a propane tank in da car. I had my gun. I kicked da back door in. He was on da stairs wit a machete, smoking crack. I turn around 'n that's when he swung—see the scar across my back? 'N then he had a knife. 'N we start fightin,' 'n all I remember is dat I was stabbin' him 'n that was it. When he stop movin,' I went outside to my car, 'n walked back up to da step. Pulled da top of da propane off, lit it, 'n threw it, 'n I went 'n sat in my car. The whole place exploded. Cops come up in front of da apartment —dey pointin' guns thinkin' I'm a dude cause I had a hot fade [hair cut] then, a bomber jacket on, just sittin' there. I got fifteen to life for dat 'cause it involved a body.

Candy was sentenced to fifteen years to life on charges that involved arson, bombing, and murder, but she was just as defiant and violent inside prison as she had been outside. She says, "I goes up for parole [after having served fifteen years], dey give me an eighteen-month hit. I goes up before dem again, dey give me a two-year hit. Why you hittin' me? Dey say cause I don't feel remorse." The "hit" she refers to is the parole-board decision to defer her case until she can return before the board for early-release consideration. But the board was correct; Candy admits she never did feel remorse for killing the man. He had it coming and knew it. At Alpha Omega House, Candy continues to exude an unpredictable and volatile manner. She says, "I can snap da fuck out fa nuthin.'"

Yet Candy says she is done with the fast life of drugs, women, and crime. She knows the road ahead is not going to be easy. She brings with her significant reentry needs. Her wife, whom she has been in a relationship with for a decade, will remain in prison for many years, and Candy has no immediate family left alive on the outside. She would benefit from mental-health treatment not only for the multiple abuses she suffered in her childhood but also for her inclination toward violence. She also requires substance-abuse counseling for an addiction to angel dust. Having developed seizures as a result of beatings she sustained in childhood, Candy is on a variety of medications. She has worked many occupations behind bars—mason, cook, seamstress, janitor—and hopes to bring these skills into the workplace as she settles into a new life. But her biggest challenge will be the strangeness of reentering the social world outside of prison, which has become foreign to her. She says, "I want to learn to live outside da box." Candy knows the transition will be tough, because she failed to "reintegrate" the first time she was released from the hen house. She committed a new crime involving drugs and a weapon just three months after exiting the prison gates. Candy knows that community life does not mirror the prison world and simple things most people take for granted—riding a bus, shopping for clothing, paying a bill, going for a walk, or interacting with men—can seem foreign and frightening. "This time," Candy promises emphatically, "I'ma make it."

Billie

I ask Billie where she is from. She replies, "I'm from HSC," which is an acronym for a local jail for women. "No," I reply, "where are you from on the outside?" "Da street," she says. And she means it. Billie is a homeless sex worker, although she claims she has a husband with whom she sometimes stays. Billie exemplifies the revolving-door problem for women offenders in the criminal justice system. She has too many arrests to count and has spent nearly all of her life cycling through the juvenile and adult courts, detention facilities, jails, and treatment programs. Her early life illustrates the tragic realities for many women who turn to drugs and crime. She was born into a violent home in urban poverty and lived with a drug- and alcohol-addicted mother. She started smoking crack at age ten, because, she says of her family, "Dey all seem so happy when dey come out da basement all hollerin' 'n ha ha. I wanted ta know what was in dat basement. One day I went in dat basement 'n I seen all da paraphernalia, da pipes, da lighters, bowls, da cookers. I tried it 'cause I seen how my mother was doin' it, 'n ever since den I been on a race for crack."

For the next twenty-eight years, that race took Billie on a wild ride. Of school, she says, "I never went ta school. I walked in one door 'n out da other." At age twelve she was found as a homeless runaway, trading her body for a warm bed and money for drugs. The child-welfare system was supposed to help her, she says, but just as she ran from her mother's home, she ran from abusive and neglectful foster care to the streets she now calls home. Billie was "raised by da streets," she says. Although she had sex-work customers who would sometimes help her with personal needs, such as temporary housing or food, she basically lived as a homeless prostitute fending for herself. Her lifestyle has led to serious medical problems. Among other ailments, she is cross-eyed, has severe asthma, and is HIV-positive; she twitches constantly; and her severe underbite shows off four crooked and rotting lower teeth, the only teeth she still has.

Billie is tired of the hard life she has endured in drugs, poverty, and crime; she wants a different life. Offered placement at Alpha Omega House for one year

followed by probation in place of serving the remaining six months of her incarceration, Billie was at the "end of her rope," she says. "I ain't never accomplished
nuthin.' I wanna accomplish somethin.' I wanna learn how ta live wit society. I
wanna learn how ta live life. I never had a childhood, so sometime da little girl
come outa me, you know what I mean? But I gotta learn how ta live life. I think
about it every day. Damn, I gotta learn how ta live life in society."

Victoria

Victoria is an African American woman about sixty years old with short graying
hair. She lived alone in a simple apartment in the surrounding high-crime urban
area for many years, riding the bus to the same unrewarding nine-to-five clerical
job day after routine day. Her only son is an adult, living on his own. Her life is
ordinary, she says, even "dull." She seems organized and has a quiet way about
her. Victoria is the sort of woman who wants "no drama" and likes to keep to
herself. But do not let the outside fool you; Victoria harbors a tense coldness in
her eyes, and she can quickly turn cruel when she "snaps."

Like many women in the system, Victoria has significant health problems
requiring medication and monitoring—she has fibromyalgia, an inflammatory
disease called Sarcoidosis, high blood pressure, and acid reflux. She also has educational and mental-health needs. What differentiates Victoria from most others is her short, albeit violent, criminal history and lack of any substance abuse.
But her actions on one spring day resulted in seven felony charges, most notably
possession of a firearm without a license, intent to terrorize another person, and
aggravated assault. That day started like any other, she says, but then a young
woman riding the bus hit a nerve. She explains:

> It was the last straw. I had years of sittin' on the bus wit these punks 'n
> teenagers wit no manners, cursin,' pushin' past people on the bus. And *she*
> just hit a nerve. She yelled at me stone-cold ghetto, something like, Bitch,
> I'll kick you fuckin' nigga ass . . . I had enough. I zoned out. The next thing
> I knew she took off her jacket, so that means this girl was gonna try to hurt
> me. She was real bigger than me—she was gonna hurt me. Protective mode
> kicked in. I stood up and got the gun out my pocketbook. All I could see 'n
> hear was her mouth goin.' I heard somebody sayin,' She got a gun, she got
> a gun. I got my gun in my hand by my side, and I confronted her. I stood

in front of her, 'n when she realized I had the gun then she started cryin.' I
said to her, Say one more word, say one more word. I was standing in front
of her 'n lookin' up at her 'cause she was bigger than me. And I said, You
need to respect your elders. And I heard this guy who had two kids wit him.
He stood up beside me 'n [was] sayin,' Miss, please don't hurt my kids. The
bus had stopped, 'n some guy getting on the bus was sayin,' Miss, you don't
wanna do this. I was in a daze. And I quietly and slowly walked off the bus. I
got a block away, and next thing I know I turned around 'n it looked like all
the cops in the city was there, every cop in the world. It was the beginning
of a nightmare. That was the beginning of horror.

Victoria's life was turned upside down. The attack landed her in jail for six
months. Fortunately, she had no prior criminal history, which helped her avoid
a longer term behind bars even though she had committed a violent crime. But
that half year was still especially hard on Victoria. In addition to experiencing
anxieties and hardships as a prisoner that nearly drove her to suicide, she lost her
job and apartment while she was incarcerated, and thus the quiet and simple life
she had led. As she begins Alpha Omega House, Victoria also starts a two-year
term of probation, during which she must abide by conditions such as avoid-
ing physical confrontation, not possessing a firearm, gaining employment, and
maintaining a crime-free lifestyle. Victoria is grateful for her placement at Alpha
Omega House and plans to take every advantage of the services and get back on
her feet with a job and apartment.

Clair

Court-ordered to Alpha Omega House in place of a jail term, twenty-seven-year-
old Clair has tried all: prescription pills like Oxycontin, Percocet, Xanax, as well
as hard drugs like cocaine, crack, heroin, and wet weed. She is especially thin,
but for what looks like a distended belly. Her teeth are dark brown and yellow,
undoubtedly from her drug use. Her hair appears to be greasy, as if she has not
showered in days. Blackened circles frame her crystal blue eyes. Clair looks tired
and worn out. But she also has an obvious toughness about her that contrasts
sharply with her strawberry-blonde hair and soft, pale skin.

Raised in a tough, working-class Irish-American neighborhood by an alcoholic mother, sexually abused by a family friend, and routinely physically abused

as a child by her father, Clair suffers from lingering harms of violence. To deal with years of childhood sexual abuse and woman abuse, she turned to self-medicating with various drugs and alcohol, which has left her in poor health and with a bleak outlook on her personal recovery. Drugs, she says, have been her "number-one priority, not my kids, not any job, just drugs." Clair did anything to get high, and she specialized in sex work to finance her addiction. She sold her body for as little as five dollars and suffered violent victimization as a prostitute. She says, "I was out there sleepin' with these dirty, nasty men, jeopardizing my life."

Clair reached a low in her addiction that shocks her still today. While on a drug binge living and selling her body on the streets of a nearby neighborhood, she found her best friend dead from an apparent heroin overdose in an abandoned home they often used for rest. Rather than mourn, run to recovery, or even call for help, Clair searched her friend's lifeless body for drugs and then shot the heroin she found as she sat there. She said, "You would think that would wake me up and realize this could be you layin' there. No. I sat right over her, my best friend's body, and I got high." In a way, Clair was saved that night from her own self-destruction or perhaps from something more sinister. When Clair stepped outside the building, she was arrested and held in detention by police who were closing in on a local serial killer who was targeting prostitutes.

Clair was arrested several times for prostitution, shoplifting, theft, forgery, and possession of drugs. Unable or unwilling to quit drugs and crime, she lost custody of her children to her ex-husband and then to the foster-care system. Like many of the women indicted for lower-level crimes, Clair tended to abscond from court appearances when she was arrested and then released to her own custody. But this tactic caught up with her when she "caught a new case" for prostitution and possession of drugs while on probation. She was not released on bail and sat in jail for weeks before being sentenced to eleven-and-a-half to twenty-three months in jail followed by one-year probation. Her jail sentence was eventually suspended in favor of this placement to Alpha Omega House for reintegration into community life. So in fact, Clair's move is not for reentry after imprisonment; it is a court-stipulated diversion for rehabilitation in place of continued confinement for a violation of probation and new crime. Clair's biggest challenge for the year ahead is to stay put and complete the program. She hopes to reunite with her children and return to suburban living with her new husband.

Kelly

Kelly enters Alpha Omega House after a year incarcerated, as she has been many times before, for prostitution and "back charges" for crimes from which she fled after arrest and before prosecution. She also has a long arrest history for drug possession, with the occasional shoplifting charge. Kelly has been sent to jail eight times in her adulthood—spending the last ten years in and out of jails and prisons for income-generating crimes such as prostitution—as well as to treatment centers for her addiction to "crack cocaine, marijuana, heroin, meth [methamphetamine], anything under the sun." Just before her last incarceration over the previous winter, she lost the nails on her left foot to frostbite while she was living between two places she called home: an abandoned jeep at the end of an alley and a boarded-up row home with no utilities (known locally as an "abandominium" that drug users use for housing) in a drug-infested high-crime urban area.

At forty-six, Kelly is a frail, sickly looking woman. Her long stringy hair accentuates her skeletal body. She has only four lower teeth. Her upper teeth rotted away from bad hygiene and years of crack smoking; some were knocked out of her mouth by her last boyfriend. There is something wrong with her neck—it is permanently bent to one side. At the age of sixteen, Kelly gave birth to the first of her six children, all of whom were raised by her mother and sisters. Her voice is that of a husky smoker; she speaks very fast, in rapid spurts. She seems unable to sit for very long, jumping from one action to the next. Always laughing and joking, Kelly is, in her own words, "a fun-going, outgoing addict. I'm Crazy-Ass Kell."

In addition to needing counseling for woman abuse, years of sexual abuse by each of her five brothers, and the broken relationships with her children, Kelly needs medical treatment for HIV and damage to her heart from years of drug use, mental-health treatment, monitoring for depression, and, most importantly, substance-abuse intervention. She says of this placement: "Times runnin' out. I wanna get this done. I got a lotta provin' to do. I like gettin' high, but I have to stop . . . I need to love myself."

|||||||||||||||

THE RESEARCH collected in this book includes the stories of other women as well. Amelia, Ginny, Keira, and Charisse are heroin, cocaine, and/or crack addicts who support their addictions by selling sex along with occasional shoplifting and other theft. Like so many of the others, these women are mothers, and they report a variety of abuse experiences throughout their lives. Polly represents an older generation of revolving-door drug addicts who have cycled in and out jails and treatment centers. Shayla is a young offender incarcerated for robbery and a sex crime. She joins the women from the local prison's Z unit—a place for violent offenders who are escape risks. Her knuckles are marked with prison-made tattoos, with the word "God's" on one hand and "Grace" on the other; the last two letters are merely outlines and not yet completed. Violet joined the women at Alpha Omega House after a yearlong drug binge and the correspond-ing violent victimization associated with a life of street prostitution. She could resemble a college student in any classroom—that is, until she reveals the drug effects on her teeth or rolls up her sleeves.

Raquel, Freya, and Henrietta suffer more seriously than most others from mental and emotional troubles. Raquel talks into the television, and her paranoid outbursts and accusations frighten some women. Her official record pins her as a pedophile charged with eleven crimes involving sexual exploitation of children before she was sent to Alpha Omega House from a twenty-three-month prison term. Henrietta is a middle-aged grandmother who is self-reportedly schizo-phrenic and depressed, and who has never learned to read or write. She is apa-thetic and ready to be directed by the experiences and expectations of the women around her. She is at Alpha Omega House for "cuttin,' stickin,' slicin' people, 'n bein' violent" and sees her placement as a brief interruption in an otherwise sad life of welfare dependency, alcoholism, and urban lethargy. Freya has been in jail before and tried unsuccessfully to get clean many times. In addition to her heavy crack habit, she is bipolar and "hears voices." She sees her placement at Alpha Omega House as a cruel experiment, with the powerful controlling the weak.

These are the women of Alpha Omega House. Most enter the house at the back-end of their sentenced terms of confinement as a mechanism of early release and reintegration to community life, and for most of them, Alpha Omega House is an alternative to incarceration after a period of confinement has been served. Other women are sentenced directly by the criminal courts in lieu of confine-ment on the assumption that rehabilitation, employment, and housing assistance will best benefit both the criminal justice system and the women themselves. While they have been jailed between their arrest and criminal sentencing (a pe-riod of a few weeks to many months), these women are technically being released from serving the remainder of their sentences in confinement and are therefore being "diverted" from incarceration at the front-end. A few of the women were at advanced phases of stay when I started this research, others were just beginning, and more had yet to arrive. Thus, the women's experiences through the phases at the house are told both in the present and retrospectively.

The women's assumptions about the reentry center when they arrive at Alpha Omega House turn on their past experiences with the criminal justice system and undoubtedly their drug use, age, relationships, and other factors. Shared by all of the women is an expectation that this experience will be different from incarceration because the center is, after all, a place that promises them guidance toward productive and independent social living.

TWO

BLACKOUT

AS SHE IS LED handcuffed past the iron gates, across the narrow cement walk, up the steep steps under the rooftop cross of this former Catholic convent, every woman who enters the reentry center called Alpha Omega House begins a new journey. And while she might be well accustomed to different types of confinement cultures, like those in prisons or drug-treatment facilities, the experience that is about to unfold is unique. Once she steps through the front door, her handcuffs are removed, and she becomes a new resident assigned to the Blackout phase. Aptly called "Blackout girl" or simply "new girl" by other residents, she is searched by a staff member known as a monitor for contraband such as drugs or weapons. She must give all of her personal belongings, including identification, winter coat and other outerwear, money, medication, and cigarettes to the monitor who will lock up whatever meager possessions she arrives with. The "Blackout girl" is given a thirty-eight-page packet of rules and regulations in a manila folder, a legal pad that becomes her "Blackout journal," and a colorful water bottle depicting characters from the teen adaptation of *Romeo and Juliet, High School Musical.* She is then led down the narrow hallway past the living room and the inquisitive eyes of other residents to the last room in the back of the building. This room is also called "Blackout." As if in a late-nineteenth-century home with kept domestic servants where the use of space reinforced class distinctions (Sutherland, 1981), "Blackout girls" are physically positioned in the back of the house, out of the way of everyday activity and a floor below women at advanced phases of stay. This is how every new girl begins her journey of reformation at the reentry center, from criminal offending woman toward a reintegrated member of society.

More than a half century ago a community of Catholic nuns lived in the structure that now houses Alpha Omega House. While the nuns have long since departed, elements of the convent culture and monastic model persist.[1] Physically, both the convent of the past and the reentry center today occupy a space with an architecture designed for the isolation and seclusion of women and their particular form of communal living (De Paermentier, 2008). This design creates an "enclosure" for discipline and identity transformation (Foucault, 1977, p. 141). Set back from the busy urban street behind brick columns and rusted iron gates and surrounded by tall trees choked with ivy, its thick walls and small windows offer only the slightest view inside or out. A single narrow door atop a steep entryway emphasizes the sense of enclosure.

Both the convent and the reentry center resemble domestic sites of transformation and what Goffman (1961) calls a "total institution," a place removed from mainstream society at which participants undergo a change process under the tight control of a higher authority. Socially, the women of Alpha Omega House, like the nuns before them, are separated from their familiar social worlds, including relationships with men, for a period of time as they undergo resocialization toward new identities. By the authority of the church and in cloister, the convent was a space for spiritual change from secular to devotional life. It was a "household" within society (De Paermentier, 2008, p. 55), and "just like a family" (Baernstein, 1994, p. 787), the convent imposed limits on women's autonomy. In this space of the past, personal transformation necessitated obedience and sacrifice—just as it does today—as well as a denial of women's agency (Brock, 2010). Within the community but still outside regular civic life, Alpha Omega House retains its character as a household space organized to transform women, now from criminal offenders to productive community participants.

Also like the nuns of the past, the women residents today participate in a socialization process broken into phases or stages. For nuns, a ceremonious socialization through stages, especially in the cloister experience, was meant to dramatize the gradual transformation from secular life to a new identity (Eisikovits, 1983), for which the novitiate willingly relinquished her private life, her social status, and her sexuality (De Paermentier, 2008). Women of Alpha Omega House go through a similar process, as they are encouraged to discard criminogenic thinking and personal vices in favor of a new status as responsible women ready for personal transformation. Cloaked in the rhetoric of empowerment, this change process serves as a degradation ceremony, complete with physical and social isolation, ceremonious ritual, and distinctive dress (Garfinkel, 1956;

Goffman, 1961). It is designed to "break" the women and to transform their identities for their own good, and as such it is an expression of domination, just like the process was for the nuns of the past who were brought to their knees by the patriarchy of the church and forced to accept "humiliation as benevolence, as a blessing" (Daly, 1985, p. xx). Only such degradation ceremonies can "shield women from their own power," argues Daly, and enable the patriarchy to maintain power over women.

"Smooth and purposeful reentry" is Alpha Omega House's central aim, and Blackout is designed to prepare women for the change. During this first phase of stay, women begin a reconditioning process through which they are encouraged to relinquish criminal and antisocial identities and to acquire specific attitudes and behaviors within a highly controlled environment. It is on Blackout where "new girls" begin their socialization into the formal culture of Alpha Omega House, a culture that is presented to the women as an empowering sisterhood built around three main elements: shared identity as women in change, personal responsibility toward that end, and mutual support among residents.

Isolation

It is an ordinary summer afternoon in this busy city, but inside the dark room of Blackout, three women lie asleep in cots under thin cotton covers. On the floor next to each lie a water bottle, flip-flops, and the thirty-eight-page packet of re-entry center rules and regulations in a legal-sized manila folder. At first the image evokes memories of naptime at a child's daycare, but it is missing the softness and peace that naptime conveys.

The dreary, institutional green walls of the three-hundred-square-foot room are interrupted by four large windows, two of which are iron-barred on the outside, and framed by heavy, dark blue drapes that block the outside light. Stretched thinly over the concrete-slab floor is a long, worn, gray- and blue-spotted industrial carpet torn at the entranceway. Four mismatched wooden dressers line one wall. Six cots with white sheets and thin blankets line the two windowed walls. The room has no chairs, no tables, no lamps, and no clocks. It is not designed for comfort or for socialization.

Historically, the room that confines "Blackout girls" was meant for women's sequestration and silence. It still retains symbolic and physical boundaries that separate women from outsiders, as was intended by convent rules and architecture (De Paermentier, 2008). It was, in its convent days, a space for prayer and confession. Its adjoining sacristy, still adorned with vestments from the past, is visible only through the confessional screens in the dresser-lined wall between these rooms. In convent years, visiting priests seated in the sacristy would take confessions through these screens.

Replacing the cross as a centerpiece of all activity, a television rests atop a tall utility cart on the stage that was once the altar. In the loudest of volumes, the television maintains a constant presence in this otherwise quiet room, showing movie after outdated VHS movie from morning until the nightly routine of lights out at 10 p.m.

Just outside the Blackout door sits a monitor dressed in medical scrubs at a small, wooden, desk-and-chair combination that one might see in an elementary school. She is there as a guard—not so much to stop "Blackout girls" from leaving, but more likely to prevent contact between the seasoned members of the house and the fresh "new girls" inside.

Unlike the traditional reentry-center model whereby residents are set to work in jobs or other routines that take them outside in the community soon after their arrival, Alpha Omega House isolates women for their first thirty days. Without exception "Blackout girls" must remain in this room for that period, unless the term is extended to sixty for exhibition of "marginal behavior patterns." This strict confinement, according to program documents, is necessary before women can be truly ready for the transformational process. An administrative staff member explains the rationale: "We don't let you out in the first thirty days 'cause there's no stayin' power."

In addition to being cut off physically, "Blackout girls" are socially isolated; they may have no visits from family or friends, may not use telephones, may have no smoke breaks, and should not speak with the other residents. Furthermore, "Blackout girls" may not participate in therapy or treatment intervention, educational programming, or vocational training. Their only break from the Blackout room comes in the form of restroom use when permitted by the monitor, exercise and morning meditation in another room of the house, meals in the dining room, and cleaning duties at chore time.

The daily routine of Blackout begins at 5:30 a.m. with the sound of a monitor's voice crackling over the intercom, calling the women to morning exercise in the living room in front of a television. Exercise is followed by breakfast at 6 a.m. After a quick restroom break, the women return to the Blackout room and normally to bed for a nap until they are again summoned by the monitor's voice over the intercom. At 9 a.m., "Blackout girls" report to the living room for a half hour of meditation. "Blackout class" starts at 10 a.m. Lunch is at noon and, like breakfast, is spent in silent separation from the other residents. The cloistered silence is especially dramatic during dinnertime, when "Blackout girls" can be seen facing a wall at a table away from the other residents. "Blackout girls" normally eat quickly and in silence, then discard their dishes, cups, and dinnerware, and stack their chairs against a wall before returning to the Blackout room. After a short rest, chores begin at 7 p.m., and evening medications are distributed about an hour later. "Blackout girls" have their greatest freedom on weekends, when they are allowed to use the living room with the other residents, who are further along in phases of stay.

Though isolation is not part of the traditional reentry model (the process of reintegration normally commences when a participant joins a program), restriction from full social involvement is sometimes part of the therapeutic community (TC) model. Even in community settings TCs have traditionally involved a period of separation from the outside world and its negative influences to jumpstart personal transformation (Schram et al., 2006). Sometimes referred to as "Blackout" in TCs, this adjustment period may restrict telephone use and personal visitation but normally involves screening, assessment, and treatment, though group therapy is often limited (De Leon and Wexler, 2009; Inciardi, Martin, and Surratt, 2001; Ottenberg, 1982). New residents typically also live and work with other residents to discourage isolation and "withdrawal into the self" (Schram et al., 2006, p. 114). Thus the near-total isolation of new residents during Blackout at Alpha Omega House and the lack of treatment intervention provided to the women seem to run counter to the spirit of a therapeutic community. And as a reentry center designed as a therapeutic community, Alpha Omega House's use of Blackout complicates matters structurally and conceptually.

"Blackout girls" are certainly surprised to begin their reentry experience with isolation. Take the case of Victoria. It is her first day of Blackout, and Victoria is sitting on her bed reading through the rules and regulations and writing a makeshift calendar for her plans over the year ahead. Victoria agreed to spend the remainder of her jail term at Alpha Omega House, hoping that she would be given help to find a job and an apartment. "It was a great opportunity," she remembers thinking when she read the advertisement for the house, highlighting its focus on reintegration and helping women. She says, "I'ma get hooked up wit a job 'n housin.' Before long, I'll be on my own again soon." She turns the calendar toward me, smiling. But two days later, Victoria's mood is dramatically different.

It is noon, but she lies in her bed under a cover. Now anticipating a tough road ahead, she renames Blackout "the pit" and likens it to a "closet," her term for the small jail cell she occupied the week before. Victoria says, "I'm quite sure I had a positive feelin' on the first day 'cause I had just gotten out of a closet. I remember thinking, I'm so thankful that God sent me to this place. It's only been two days. The depression is worse. I feel like I'm deterioratin.' I'm not eating. I don't feel like bein' involved, period."

Victoria's surprise quickly turns to anger and feelings of depression. Freya sees the isolation as illogical, saying: "They lockin' us in this room so we don't leave. It don't make no sense. This ain't supposta be jail. Lockin' us in just makin' us wanna leave in the first place." For Victoria, Freya, and other new residents, Blackout is experienced as a shock and the period at Alpha Omega House when they feel the most alone and vulnerable. The overwhelming impression of Blackout isolation is that it is punitive, designed to "break you down." After just three days into her Blackout phase, Violet says, "I remember thinking what did I do so bad that I couldn't stay in jail." In fact, many women prefer jail and prison incarceration to Blackout, because in those institutions they are normally able to leave their cells, interact with others, smoke when they want to, and attend classes or work. Here, women are simply locked up. Laurel has not been on Blackout for months, but remembers it as "hell" for good reason. She spent almost her entire thirty days alone because she was the only "new girl" at the time. As she and I read through her "Blackout journal," a mandatory log of emotions women are required to keep while in Blackout, the change in her attitude is almost immediate— from hopeful upon arrival to defiant and angry after just the first few days. She wrote: "I'm not a fuckin' animal. I don't belong in a cage. You can't go outside, nuthin.' You have to sit here, just sit. I just came from prison. This place is supposta be for rehabilitation."

Candy also experienced the shocking realization that Blackout was not the beginning of reintegration as she had expected. Like Laurel, Candy was the only "new girl" during her Blackout time and spent all thirty days in what was basically solitary confinement. Candy, who has spent half her life in prison (the "jawn" as she calls it), knows what she needs to become part of the community again: a treatment-focused experience in a program that does not replicate jail. She says: "I need a halfway house. I need a job. I want outa here. I want outa here. I been up in da jawn a long time. This is not a fuckin' halfway house, it's another jail." Just three days after Candy advanced from Blackout, Adeline began her Blackout stay. By the end of her second week alone, Adeline began to return emotionally to the first few days after her arrest when she was left to suffer alone in a locked room. She draws a parallel between her emotional state in Blackout today and that night of her arrest: "They stripped me naked 'n threw me in this cold room in a paper gown. Nobody came in for three days. They just left hard sandwiches on the cold metal tray at the door. I was goin' crazy alone, tryin' to figure out how to kill myself. I was planning on drownin' myself in the toilet. This place is just like that. I got nobody. I need to talk to somebody. I need help."

Unable to speak to friends or family, to feel the warmth of the sun, or begin treatment they need, women on Blackout suffer in seclusion. Amelia, who shares Blackout with Violet, is lonely and worries about her family, especially the son she gave birth to in prison and whom she has not seen since that day more than a year ago. She expected to reunite with him when she arrived at this house, but she quickly learned that there would be no visits during Blackout. During her first week, she finds that the separation creates a constant worry: "On Blackout you can't see ya family 'n ya spend a lot of time doin' nuthin,' so that gives you a lot ta think about, like a lot be on your mind. You constantly be in ya head, ya know, worryin' is your family okay 'cause you can't call. Like I haven't seen my baby since he born."

Shayla is also having a hard time her first day at Alpha Omega House. She has been told about the rule preventing non-family visitors for the duration of her stay, and she is wrecked. She is terrified she will lose her new girlfriend to another lover. She says as she closes her tattooed fingers to her face, "I miss my girl. I need ta be out dere wit 'er . . . I can't leave 'er out dere alone. I gots to take care of 'er." Shayla has an estimated 364 more days of separation if she wants to successfully complete this program and have the system "off her back."

The stillness of Blackout is anxiety provoking, say the women, and psychologically troubling. With no leisure activities beyond watching the television, women are "in their head" or "in their bag," as some say. This "being weighted down in your mind" is what Bartky (1990, p. 23) calls psychological oppression. When institutionalized in routines and structure, psychological oppression enables agencies and to exert authority and domination more easily by breaking the will of those who are dominated.

When Ginny enters Blackout she feels so troubled by the inactivity and idleness that she questions her staying power. Even on her first day, she says, "I don't know how I'm gonna do this, I wanna leave this lockup now . . . I wanna be out." Clair is also feeling negative effects. With twenty-nine more days to go of the thirty-day isolation, she is starting out terribly shaky. She notes that for an addict like herself, the isolation is torture: "The devil is playin' with my mind. Here, you're in your own head, you're locked inside, and you have no freedom from your head." Clair came to Alpha Omega House assuming she would be walking a new road toward freedom, but she quickly realized that her new home is much like lockdown in jail. She continues:

> If you leave an addict to her thoughts for thirty days, it's a bad idea. You are your worst enemy. It is torture because here you are in this room, you don't have no bars, you are not locked in, but you can't freely be. I'm lookin' at that window, lookin' down 'n I'm thinkin' it's really not that far. I'm thinkin' in my mind, Clair, you won't even have to jump, you just climb out and just go. What's runnin' through my mind—ok you're out, your neighborhood's not that far from here, ya know, go get high. And it's about self-control . . . here, you're on your own, but I feel like I can't do it alone right now, I'm not ready. I need outpatient.

Clair has not seen her husband in months, and her children have been in foster care during her incarceration. With nothing but time, she can do little more than worry and think about how to escape her negative thoughts. The window to freedom tempts her every moment, just as it does Kelly, who likens the room to the prison's solitary confinement but with the company of other suffering women. For Kelly the only way to survive her first week is to sleep through it, and the thought of jumping out the window is always on her mind. She has fled from treatment programs many times before, but this experience is much harder on her because she is physically and socially isolated. She says: "I gotta sleep just to get through the day, to get through another day. You have temptations to jump out the window. I left a program last time, but there I could smoke on the porch, have a cigarette as soon as I got there. I could go outside 'n get fresh air. I wasn't locked up like this. Here, it's so much worse."

Jumping through the window to the relief just steps away is constantly on the minds of the women. In a way, Adeline admires the actions of a woman who jumped the night before. Still, she is working hard to stay focused and positive, holding out for better days ahead. She notes: "Some girl jumped out the window yesterday. She is my hero. I got a week left till Blackout's over, so gotta hang this out 'n then see what the next stage is poppin' for. Right now I'm in my bag."

It takes a strong-willed woman to endure the isolation of Blackout, the heightened worry and negative thoughts it causes, the disconnection from loved ones, and the seeming relief and normalcy of the outside that is just steps away. But seclusion, say the women of Alpha Omega House, is not the only troubling aspect of Blackout.

Dress

Adeline is alone in Blackout. She is sitting cross-legged on the floor in the middle of the room with her head tilted up as she stares at the television high above her like a child in her playroom. Shayla and Polly, her "roomies" who joined her two nights previously, fled together in the darkness of night, leaving only the manila folder of rules and regulations, water bottles, and flip-flops by their beds.

Behind Adeline is a ratty wooden dresser that holds her belongings: one pair of black sweatpants, one short-sleeved black T-shirt, one palm-sized transistor radio she bought from the prison commissary and managed to keep here, one bra, two pairs of underwear, and two pairs of mismatched, balled-up black socks. Her "personals" line the top of the dresser: body wash, laundry soap, toothbrush, comb, body powder, and deodorant. A rosary and a large wooden cross hang from the knob of the first drawer. Beside her bed, which she made neatly with hospital corners, lies her *High School Musical* plastic water bottle, a pair of black flip-flops, and her folder of rules. Adeline is dressed very neatly, entirely in black. Even the tiny cross that is tattooed below her right eye is black. Two rosaries hang around her neck. She was given one by a chaplain who often visited her in prison and one by her prison cellmate before she was sent away for a term of life without parole. The plastic rosaries are also black.

Throughout Blackout, all residents must wear a "uniform" of black. Every visible piece of clothing must be black, including socks and shoes. When women do not own "blacks," the staff recycles donated clothing out of a basement closet and belongings left behind by women who have escaped. Most of the time, the clothing does not fit: it is too large or too small, too long or too short, and almost always visibly worn out.

The required dress code is symbolic for residents, just as it was for the nuns. Through requirements of dress and restrictions on appearance, "new girls" are encouraged to relinquish their past, minimize their individuality, and obscure their femininity (Ebaugh, 1977; Griffin, 1975). Unadorned black clothing— the sweat pant and T-shirt uniforms of Alpha Omega House residents and the monastic habit of the nuns—signifies a shared status as women in transition to new, theoretically more desirable identities. But like nuns who often viewed the habit negatively (Michelman, 1997), "Blackout girls" unanimously view this dress code as oppressive and counterintuitive. Rather than being transformational, the Blackout uniform is an instrumental part of the degradation ceremony imposed on "Blackout girls" at Alpha Omega House.

Prison uniforms of varying colors are common throughout correctional systems for men and women. Uniforms vary in color depending on the type of institution: some federal inmates wear white, local jail detainees might be dressed in orange jumpsuits, and state prisoners could be in brown, blue, or other colors. Uniforms may also be used to distinguish inmates within institutions, for example by levels of security classification. Additionally, they can distinguish inmates from guards or correctional officers. The purpose of the Blackout uniform at Alpha Omega House, it seems, is to distinguish new residents from women who are past the Blackout phase. It is also, according to house rules and regulations, to foster the process of "change in lifestyle," consistent with the idea that rejecting fashion may foster self-improvement (Thompson and Haytko, 1997). But Arkles (2012) makes a case that prison-uniform regulations justified on a variety of grounds such as rehabilitation and inmate control actually enforce race-based gender norms by repressing self-determination, enforcing dominant social norms on marginalized populations, and using dress as a means of humiliation. In a historical analysis of prison dress, Ash (2009) similarly points out that prison uniforms are designed to strip autonomy and impose humiliation as part of a degradation ceremony. The striped prison uniform, for example, reflects a criminal status with its symbolism to prison bars. What makes the Blackout uniform at Alpha Omega House more troubling is that uniforms are not used with reentry centers generally or any other community-based program designed to reintegrate and rehabilitate offenders, and the small resident population of the house does not necessitate the use of uniforms to distinguish newly admitted women. In short, the uniform requirement does not seem to serve a legitimate penal or therapeutic purpose.

Combined with the isolation of Blackout, the requirement to wear a uniform of black makes it difficult for the "new girls" to interpret their stay as anything but punitive and prisonlike. To Clair, the uniform requirement and status it conveys makes this reentry center just like "state row," a term women use for the local jails and prisons. She says, "I realize it's just another uniform we have to wear to show we're different from everybody else; it's just like state row." Victoria also interprets the Blackout uniform as conveying a diminished status, noting its incompatibility with reform and rehabilitation: "We shouldn't be wearin' a uniform in a place that's a'posta help you. It's a label. This is a uniform to them signifying to me that this is like a prison. You're an inmate. That's how it feels."

Taking into account the realities that dress is a symbol that conveys credibility and status and that uniforms may be used for social control and discipline,[2] the women's feelings of subjugation and punishment in response to the Blackout uniform are quite reasonable. Furthermore, the color of the uniform carries negative connotations (Dovidio et al., 1996), considering the use of the term black in such phrases as "black plague," "black market," "black Monday" and its cultural associations—black is worn at funerals and by outlaws (Smith-McLallen et al., 2006). Black may also be tied to perceptions about criminal offenders and race biases.[3] Finally, the color fosters negative emotions, say the women, conveying a sense of darkness. Freya explains how the rule of black harms her emotionally: "Just like you dress how you feel, you feel how you dress. We gotta wear black, it's more you feel how you dress. Well then, how do I feel? I feel dark. That's how I feel. They want us to feel how we dress. They do make it as miserable as possible."

Violet agrees. Through years of depression and active drug addiction, she used her appearance to make herself look and feel better. Being forced to wear a uniform of black brings to the fore dark feelings that she has tried so long to trap inside. She explains: "I used to get dressed and be pretty to feel good on the outside even though I hurt on the inside. It's like dressing up would move the outside in. But now 'cause I have to wear black it's like my inside is out, like the dark on the inside is out for us to see everyday."

Uniforms and dress codes can also be understood as being sexist technologies that preserve patriarchy (Bartlett, 1994; Whisner, 1982). Correspondingly, in addition to interpreting the uniform as a social status symbol and a means of discipline, Billie comprehends the requirement to wear the black uniform as control over her feminine identity:

> The uniforms is like a hold, like dey got a hold on me. They watch every move I make. I'm havin' to wear another uniform. It's like blues in jail. I go out, dey know I'm in jail 'cause the uniform tells it. This is another jail 'cause I have to wear all black. I can't wear my own clothes. And when we go out those doors, we still have ta wear black on. I don't think that's fair. I wanna identify myself as a woman for society; I wanna dress the way I wanna dress 'n feel good. You should be able to dress as a woman. It's still a uniform, 'n dey still have the upper hand.

Beyond Blackout, the reentry center continues to exercise control over dress. Some jewelry is prohibited, and clothing the staff deems to be provocative or that reveals the shape of a woman's breasts, hips, or buttock is tightly controlled. Like nuns of the convent whose dress covered their breasts and masked their femininity (Sullivan, 2005), women of Alpha Omega House are faced with rules that constrain individuality, femininity, and sexuality. Given arguments made by some scholars that dress regulations reproduce gendered views about appearance, the house's attempts enforce a dress code is not terribly surprising. Expectations about everyday dress and appearance and about how women should present themselves amount to gendered evaluations of women, their worth, sexuality, and status (Crockett and Wallendorf, 1998; Davis, 1994; Klare, 1991). What is surprising is the reductiveness of the house's expectations. In its mention of "hair weaves," Rule K of Alpha Omega House, which applies to the entire length of stay, even hints at racial bias. It reads: "Clothing is to be neat, clean, and conservative attire which exemplifies your change in lifestyle. Jewelry is to be simple. No large earrings or expensive jewelry is permitted. Hair is to be combed in an orderly fashion at all times. No extravagant hairdos, no hair weaves or hair coloring." Laurel interprets Rule K as a mechanism to strip away all female identity and, in her case, replace it with a prison identification number. She puts it this way, "You're no longer a woman, a mother, a daughter. You are 748666. You're a fuckin number." To be a woman, a mother, and a daughter—and to dress how one chooses—is a freedom that should not be controlled, say the women.

As the residents see it, restrictions on how they wear their hair, how they dress, and how they want to display their faces are intended to punish and weaken. Take Adeline, who is dressed in large black sweatpants and a loose-fitting black shirt. She wears no makeup and her once short hair now hangs in her eyes. The weekend before, Adeline's mother dropped off a care package at the monitors' office. It wasn't much, Adeline explains, just "a handful of makeup 'n things to make me feel good about myself, to feel better 'n pretty." But monitors would not allow Adeline to keep any of the makeup. When she asked why, a monitor told her that it violated the rules of Blackout. The monitor then noticed a small plastic barrette holding back a lock of hair from Adeline's face. The monitor demanded that Adeline remove it and hand it over. "'It's jewelry,' she said, and she took it," Adeline recalls. She was also fined two dollars for the violation. For a woman locked alone in a dark room with nothing but worry on her mind, a little makeup and hairpin could have done wonders for her mood. Months later, Victoria had a similar experience. She said:

The other day I was called in the monitors' office. I had been wearin' my earrings—you already know what I'm gonna say—called to the monitors' office where Miss Wendy, she looks at me she said, You know what I want, I want you not to wear your earring 'n I fine you two dollars. What? I can't wear my earrings? You can't makes yourself feel good. They talkin' to somebody whose been wearin' earrings since she been a teenager. Did'ja eva hear of such ridicilis rules? What does this have to do with me gettin' a place to live or a job back?

Victoria knows Rule K, but she chose to resist by wearing earrings because doing so is part of her personal identity. Violet likes to wear short shorts to "feel and look sexy." Mimi wears halter-tops in the summer because she likes to show the shape of her breasts, shoulders, and midsection. Billie and Grace wear dresses whenever they can because it takes them away from the drabness of the everyday sweatpants and T-shirts normally worn at the center. The jewelry Rosa wears, large hoop earrings (which are prohibited) and facial piercings, make her feel womanly. Lots of lipstick and low-cut shirts are fashionable. These are not women who shed traditional expressions of sexuality for any sort of inner or other demonstrations of femininity. In fact, quite the opposite: they embrace outward displays of femininity. Sitting on her bed in Blackout wearing her oversized black sweatpants and a large, black, crewneck T-shirt, black socks, and black flip flops, Violet picks up on this idea: "I can't feel like a lady here. I used to dress up my outsides to make myself feel better even though the inside was still messed up. It made me feel better." Being able to display an outward appearance of having it together helped Violet manage chaos in her life. Similarly, being prevented from the clothing, makeup, and hair styles that make her feel good prevents Amelia from feeling feminine and harms her emotionally. She says, "You spend a lot of time wonderin,' ya know, when can ya get your hair done, when can ya get dressed 'n start feelin' like ya used to feel? I guess, feelin' like a lady. We should be allowed to get dressed 'n get our hair done so we can feel better about ourself."

There is one resident, however, who is not told to look less feminine, to cut her hair, take off her earrings, button up her shirt, or wear looser clothing. This is Candy. From how she talks about herself to how she dresses and interacts, Candy demonstrates her gender in highly masculine ways. She will grab her genitals over her jeans, gesturing to make a point as she speaks, spit on the sidewalk when she is outside running errands for the staff, ogle and catcall other women residents, even refer to herself as a man who wants to "fuck" and her genitals as a "dick." At first meeting, many people mistakenly think Candy is a man.

On this day, Candy wears crisp denim jeans with immaculate men's construction workboots worn with laces open. The hem of her jeans falls inside and wrinkle at the top of the open boots. She wears a deep purple men's dress shirt, buttoned to the collar and neatly tucked in her jeans, behind a thick black leather belt with a large gold-colored buckle. She has on a very large gold-plated watch with fake diamond studs on the bezel and a similarly large fake diamond stud earring in one ear. She wears a thick gold-plated necklace that sits outside of her shirt on her flat chest, just as a nun would wear her cross outside of her habit. Candy's hair is longer than it was when she arrived, but still short enough for her to be mistaken as male.

Beginning in childhood when her father dressed her as a boy and called her son, taught her how to fist fight and make bombs, and kept her away from girls and everything female, Candy has struggled to express her feminine self. The problem she poses to Alpha Omega House staff is that she does not fit their desired image of woman. So just as other women are stripped of their typical expressions of femininity and sexuality in dress and makeup, Candy is prevented from displaying her sexuality and forced to adopt more stereotypical feminine ways and routines. Candy says, "They tellin' me not to cut my hair 'cause it look like a man. I wanna cut my hair. I'm cuttin my fuckin' hair. Dey don't like da boots. Fuck 'em. Dey sayin' I should dress more like a woman. I don't know *how* ta be a woman."

Telling Candy to dress more like a woman and let her hair grow, dress in women's clothing, and put away the workboots is just another way to control her gender expression. The rule applying to Candy might be unwritten, but it clearly exists—not only are women prohibited from expressing overt femininity, they cannot express themselves as masculine either. They cannot express their gender at all. But Candy interprets the dress rules more broadly. She is, in her words an "aggressive" lesbian and believes the staff wants to change her because they are "worried I'll wanna fuck da other women." Her very masculinized way is a threat, and so is her homosexuality, she says. To Candy, Alpha Omega House rules are not just sexist, they are also homophobic.

According to Bartlett (1994), mandatory dress regulations inhibit women's choices and self-expression, creating what Klare (1991, p. 1428) calls "appearance autonomy," and they subordinate women to judgments about appearance made by others. Dress and appearance restrictions at Alpha Omega House seem to correspond to traditional stereotypes about femininity—inhibiting dress that is too sexual or, in the case of Candy, too unfeminine. Such normalizing of dress, says McNamara (1994), demeans women as objects and enforces dominant views about proper behavior (Klare, 1991).

Victoria raised an important point when she questioned the correspondence between restrictions on dress and women's reintegration. That is, why should women's dress have anything to do with the criminal justice system or any efforts to help women move into crime-free, independent living? Enforcing gendered dress codes and forcing women to wear a uniform of black while isolated from the world outside fosters an oppositional culture and erases any real potential for the women to buy in to the formal sisterhood of change offered by Alpha Omega House.

Class

Every morning in Blackout, "new girls" participate in "Blackout class," held in a basement room led by a staff member accompanied by a flip pad on a standing easel and the thirty-eight-page rules and regulations. The class is held daily regardless of the number of "Blackout girls" in attendance: Adeline sat for three weeks of Blackout class by herself, and Candy took it alone for her entire Blackout phase. But Clair takes the class with Billie and Freya. Victoria also had company, as do most "Blackout girls."

Blackout class teaches newly admitted women the rules and regulation of the house as well as its chain of command. Like the nuns in the monastic culture of this building's past, Alpha Omega residents participate in daily ceremonies and rituals. They begin with a daily recital of prayer and pledges designed, it seems, to produce solidarity among the women as a sisterhood and a common goal of recovery and hope. Prayers and pledges include the serenity prayer, the house's own "We Can" prayer, and its "Alpha Omega Pledge" for the house's sorority. After thirty days of Blackout class, the women take a written quiz in which they must recall the rules and regulations and the pledges and prayers before they can proceed to the next phase of stay and move into the main residential quarters. On the very rare occasion a woman fails to pass the quiz, she will remain in Blackout for up to sixty days and be retested weekly until she completes successfully.

Having just returned from the basement and Blackout class, Billie sits on her bed, holding her now dog-eared manila folder. She flips through the rules and regulations, reading aloud: "Stay in Blackout for thirty days, wear nuttin' but black. Can't have no phone, no money, no smokes, no visits. No minglin' wit others 'cept for weekends. Do exercise at five o'clock every mornin.' Do chores ever day; we gotta clean da bathroom. Say goin' up when you're goin' up da stairs, goin' down when you're goin' down. Know da chain of command. Never go to da monitors or staff wit no permission. Just basically sit in here 'n do what you're told."

Billie had hoped to spend her first month learning skills to live more productively once she is released. She is frustrated. From a theoretical standpoint, Blackout class reproduces patriarchy. From their social positions outside of the reentry center to their Blackout status in this domestic sphere, the women are reminded of their subordinated position. This is similar to notes made by Harman (1989, p. 106) on the reproduction of familial patriarchy in a hostel for women. She finds that the hostel reproduces domesticity by forcing upon women "rules and regulations of a larger structure that makes the decisions and has disciplinary power." And, in this domestic structure of the reentry center, not only are women's behaviors controlled and their needs dismissed, Alpha Omega House monitors their thoughts and feelings. Of her second day in Blackout class Kelly says:

> I go down there and learn about the rules 'n regulations. That's the class. That's it. We only can talk about the rules 'n regulations and it's it. I talked about self-respect 'n gettin' self-love, 'n she gave me a write-up, 'cause the class is not about that. It's about the rules 'n regulations. Why do we have a class on rules 'n regulations? That pisses me off. I was mad. I can't talk about my feelins? So, today I was just like, you tell me what you want me to say, and I'll say it. Fuck it. I can think and feel, but don't say it.

Kelly has a variety of treatment needs, and along with wanting to learn useful skills for a new way of life, she expected to start intensive mental-health and substance-abuse treatment as soon as she entered the house. She says: "I have HIV 'n dual diagnosis addiction 'n mental health, depression. I've been fighting depression for twenty-four years. I'm an addict—crack cocaine, marijuana . . . heroin, did meth. I been around the block quite a few times. I got picked up for prostitution 'n a couple of old warrants, that's why I got locked up. I can't wait to go to IOP [intensive outpatient]. When I was in jail, I was told that I was gonna be here for a couple days 'n then to IOP. I need help, I need rehab."

Adeline's thoughts sum up all of the women's views about Blackout class. She says:

I came in here for help. I need therapy for abuse stuff. I thought I was comin' here for help and housing. They said they'll help with everything, with counselin,' with housin'; they'll give me clothing. I don't see that happenin.' How is this helpin' me havin' me in a room watchin' movies all day long or makin' me repeat the chain of command? I'm not lookin' forward to this place. It's not helpin' me. If I was out there, I'd have a job already … I need counseling. Even though he [her boyfriend] beat me 'n did what he did, I still feel horrible guilt. I loved him. I don't know if God's gonna forgive me, I don't know if anyone's gonna forgive me. I don't forgive myself … but here, I can't get no help. Nobody will help me. I just need someone to talk to. It's hard for me to say it; normally I say I'm cool, I'm fine, but I need domestic-abuse help. I still feel like I'm getting beat down and abused. I'm still not gettin' help.

The purpose and meaning of rules and regulations are discussed later in this chapter, but it is important to account for the women's experience of Blackout class. They are frustrated that the review of rules and regulations and daily rehearsal of pledges and prayers occurs at the expense of treatment assessment and programming they all anxiously need.

Ideally, this period at the outset of transitioning from prison to community life would be devoted to assessment and treatment planning, as it generally is in halfway houses and similar programs (Caputo, 2004; Listwan, Cullen, and Latessa, 2006; Taxman, 2004). Typically, needs assessment and treatment/supervision planning takes place during the early period of any correctional experience, and researchers have made great strides in developing assessment tools that are geared to the complex needs of women in crime.[4] During this period staff would gather information about medical and mental-health needs; employment histories; family, child, and marital status; life skills; trauma and victimization; substance abuse; educational and vocational training; social circumstances; leisure activities; and other relevant information that could help them to better know the range of each woman's treatment and supervision needs. Based on the idea of "responsivity" in treatment planning (Andrews, 1994), individualized treatment interventions would then be devised for every woman (Gendreau and Goggin, 1996). But according to program documents, Alpha Omega House does not implement assessment or treatment in the early part of the reentry experience and offers no treatment during Blackout. It does advertise individualized service plans for its residents, carried out in subsequent phases, but the women say these plans have little form or substance.

Assessment for eligibility for participation at Alpha Omega House takes place at court or where women are incarcerated before they are admitted. Explains Mimi, "When you're doin' your interview they ask you a few questions like do you have any health issues 'n stuff like that." It will become clear in subsequent chapters of this book that women at the center suffer not only from a failure to thoroughly assess their needs at the beginning of their stay but from a lack of continuous and comprehensive programming to meet their needs.

Chain of Command and Communication

Structured hierarchically, Alpha Omega House is an organization of women under the control and authority of other women. The organization employs four administrative staff members at various positions of authority who work normal daytime hours and who dress in business attire. At least two of these employees are present on any given day. At lower levels in the organization are the monitor supervisor and a host of monitors distinguished from administrative staff by their medical uniforms. Monitors work round the clock in two-woman shifts.

Alpha Omega House is a patriarchal-styled organization not unlike the structure of an ecclesiastical chain of command. It also exists within a larger patriarchal structure—the county and state criminal justice system. Again the comparison to the convent is telling: the house's female authority structure compares to the convent's, including the mother superior who managed day-to-day operations under the delegated authority of the male church figure (Woshinsky, 2010). The organization can also be compared to the patriarchal family (see, for example, Fromm, 2012). It involves a dominant decision-making authority responsible for directing the organization, including lower-ranking members and clients. Its hierarchies, particularly the rigid chain of command and wide span of control, processes and rules, even codes of dress among workers and residents serve to restrict program participants to domestic work, reinforcing power arrangements that maintain patriarchy and subordinate women.

Feminist critiques of organizational structure, including of bureaucratic models and power arrangements,[5] explore how women, particularly workers, are subjugated by patriarchal organizations. Within this field, it is understood that patriarchy cannot function without the cooperation of women (Dinnerstein, 1976; Lerner, 1986). And as Hunnicutt (2009, p. 558) points out, while patriarchy has often been understood as "a fixed and timeless structure that obscured differences in context and . . . did not permit variation," women's oppression is possible in an organization of women because other systems of status and privilege—in this case reformed offender and addict status, class, and social capital—mediate the gender structure and power arrangements. While women workers at the house are no doubt themselves subjugated by the organizational structure, the concern here is how the structure and processes, particularly the rigid chain of command and communication, disadvantages women residents. On the whole, the organizational style of Alpha Omega House appears to residents, in the words of Amelia, as "jail, just shrunk."

Women residents are particularly troubled by how the administration's impersonal top-down decision making combines with tightly controlled formal communication and interaction between residents and staff. Mimi, who has been at Alpha Omega House for months, offers an illustration of this problem in communication and information flow:

> It gets lost with the monitors. Like the first shift, they should tell the second shift what they told everybody, what happened. Like Miss Lula told Raquel she could do her laundry 'n then when Miss Kerry came in, she told Freya and Billie they could do their laundry. So now they're all tryin' to do it, 'n them three are fightin,' 'n it's because the monitors didn't tell each other what is going on. That's just an example. The fix is simple. It should run differently. If I were to run this place, I would make sure the people were trained right. Like I said, I would make sure each shift talk to the next shift. Even just write everything down so the next shift can come in 'n read what happened all day, what you're letting somebody do, what you're not letting somebody do. There's one set of rules 'n that's it. Every monitor follows them, not make 'em up as they go along.

In this chain of command, residents must communicate only with monitors. They cannot ever bypass a monitor to speak directly to an administrative staff member without permission. "It's forbidden. You're not allowed," says Phoebe, who is on C Level. Instead, the women must make a formal written request to speak to administrative staff by "putting in a ticket." Phoebe put in a ticket to speak to Miss Ada in the downstairs office about her treatment (which means she wrote a note and handed it to the monitor called Miss Wendy) but is pessimistic that her request will be heard. She says, "Miss Wendy said they'll call me down. Let's see if that fuckin' happens." She continues: "I put three of them in in the past week and a half to see her [Miss Ada], and I haven't gotten called. I'm a'posed to see her every Tuesday at three-thirty for an hour, talkin' about what I wanna do and whatnot. She told me that a month ago 'n still hasn't called me down for that. Goin' on six months I've been here. I been down there once in six months. It makes me pissed off. I can feel myself ready to go berserk."

Phoebe waited two more weeks to be seen by staff so that she could discuss her treatment plan and future goals. By that time she was so upset by the delay that she walked away feeling the meeting was entirely unproductive.

Phoebe's case is an example of how the chain of command and corresponding information flow is understood by many of the women as a mechanism to control them and to separate them and their needs from staff responsible for their care. Structurally, such a model fosters a passive audience "uncapable of responding, interpreting, arguing, or counteracting this subtle but pervasive form of control" (Eisenberg, Goodall Jr., and Trethwey, 2010, p. 62). With a vertical communication structure that strictly prohibits lateral communication, critical decisions about residents' care and treatment are often made away from them and without their participation. Poor communication is further aggravated by architectural layout, with administrative staff located one floor below the main floor of Alpha Omega House, and by staff routines that limit direct interaction with program participants. Research on communication supports the view that so-called chain of command distance and office distance constrain communication (Zahn, 1991), and physical location communicates authority and power—in this case sending the clear message that residents of Alpha Omega House are to be quiet, powerless, and out of the way (Steele, 1973). In addition, the residents interpret these barriers to communication and noncollaborative care as ineffective and inconsistent with their relational and interactive communication styles (see Brown and Gilligan, 1993; Gilligan, Rogers, and Tolman, 1991). As such, they seek more democratic and informational communication in which they can be participants in the organization, not just clients of it. Consistent with feminist scholarship (Helgesen, 1990; Natalle, 1996; Rosener, 1990), such a system would include participative, collaborative, and personalized interactions.

Further supporting a patriarchal organizational structure, the disconnect in communication between staff and residents, and an oppressive environment is the intercom system, which monitors use for virtually all communication with residents. An example of hegemonic communication, the intercom is perfectly fitted for this bureaucratic structure: it is a rigid, indirect, and impersonal method of to communicate information, and as Steele (1973) would argue, it also wields power. Mediating communication through the intercom reduces the need for personal interaction, which among other things fosters relationships (Nardi and Whittaker, 2002). Even though the monitors' office is just steps from the women's living room, Adeline says, "They don't come over to ya, they just call ya to come over to them. They are about ten feet away. That is just like jail." As Adeline sees it, the intercom is a technology that reduces the need for personal interaction and limits confrontational resistance by the women. Others interpret the use of the intercom as a tool for dominance because it is routinely used to reprimand women. The commands "be quiet," "get your feet off the chair," "open your eyes," or "stop whisperin'" are often heard over the intercom. It also reduces the already minimal amount of privacy women have because it makes all communication public. When a woman is called or reprimanded, everyone knows it.

These points are further illustrated in the following example. Even while she was in Blackout, Victoria had some ideas about what she would like to focus on for her reintegration. As she entered the hallway outside of the dining room after a meal, she noticed an administrative staff member responsible for treatment programming entering the building. Frustrated by the staff's failure to meet with her about her ideas despite having used the required "ticket system," she walked to the threshold separating the hallway from the foyer near the monitors' office and front door. Rather than ringing the bell on the wall and waiting to be called, as residents are required to do, Victoria leaned into the hallway and asked to speak to the staff member as she was taking off her coat. A monitor who observed this from just feet away calls out over the intercom: "Victoria, come to the monitors' office." Victoria turned her head and said to the monitor who was still holding the intercom microphone, "Are you kiddin' me?" The staff member whom Victoria approached for help turned away and disappeared down the stairway without saying a word.

Victoria was imposed a monetary fine for four violations—not returning directly to Blackout after lunch, failing to ring the hallway bell, entering the hallway, and speaking directly to an administrative staff member without putting in a ticket. She was instructed to return to her quarters and later, when she was "better behaved," to put in a ticket to see the staff member. As Victoria later said, the intercom was used as a tool to humiliate, to publicize her misbehavior, to disconnect her from staff, and to abuse her. Furthermore, the rigid organizational structure preventing her from direct access to staff and the staff's reluctance to deal with Victoria outside of the official ticket channel made her feel insignificant.

Supervision

The first statement of a document provided to women titled "Client Bill of Rights" reads: "Clients have the right to be treated with dignity and respect." Nevertheless, the women of Alpha Omega House have much to say about how they feel mistreated by the supervision styles of staff. Some of the treatment they consider abusive may be unreasonable complaints given their legal status, but they are indeed mistreated, and this point is worthy of discussion.

Residents demonstrate deference to the authority of the house's top-level administrators, called "white shirts" by the women (a reference to prison administrators who are distinguished from correctional guards by their white shirts). This behavior seems to reflect genuine respect by some women at some times, but it is sometimes a front. Scott (1990) describe changes in demeanor, posture, and behavior when authority is present as "command performances" that puts at ease those shown deference even while they may themselves be oppressed. This deference by performance serves to maintain the unequal power relations between the administrators and women, especially when it takes place in the confines of the basement administrative offices, away from the women's "space" in the living room or dining room. On the rare occasion these administrators interact with the women outside of administrative offices, administrators are friendly and show concern for the women, rarely engaging in any behavior women interpret as confrontational.

The residents and monitors interact differently and with underlying tension. This may be due, in part, to the proximity of their positions in the patriarchal order inside and outside of the house; monitors are women who live in and around the same disadvantaged urban neighborhoods as residents and are former drug abusers and criminal offenders who have been incarcerated. Further, like residents, monitors are subject to supervision and to organizational restrictions, such as the dress requirement that they wear medical scrub uniforms. As the lowest level of workers in the organization, they, like the women clients, are also subjects of control. Their role, however, is to supervise residents, and they do this primarily from the confines of the monitors' office, although they complete "counts" of the women throughout their shifts. In addition, monitors prepare meals, dispense medications, search residents when they return from outside of the building, log visitors, provide residents with cleaning materials during chore time, and dispense cigarettes at smoke breaks. Monitors do have a certain level of authority over residents. As "street-level bureaucrats" (Lipsky, 1980) working on the front line of this organization, monitors exercise wide discretion in their supervisory roles, including how they interact with women and how they respond to rule violations. When routinized, such discretion can alter the practice of an organization. Sometimes, it can also lead to abuse (Evans and Harris, 2004), which at Alpha Omega House, the women argue, takes the form of verbal intimidation.

Rosa describes one example of mistreatment by a monitor with whom she was previously incarcerated this way: "Dey put pressure on us every day 'cause dey so quick to threaten us wit a write-up or ta threaten us wit restriction or ta threaten us period, or ta threaten us wit goin' back to jail. Like dat new monitor was locked up wit me up state row, the woman wit da tattoo 'round her neck. She fuckin' wit me, so I snap, 'n dey say I'm doin' somethin' negative."

While it is likely that monitors who have experienced punishing incarceration themselves may equate effective supervision with coercive supervision focused on rule enforcement, authority by coercion and domination runs counter to effective treatment intervention (Andrews and Kiessling, 1980). Often confused as a leadership style (Northouse, 2012), coercion involves the use of threats and punishments to gain compliance or bring about change in subordinates for the sake of the individual—in this case, the monitor (French and Raven, 1959). The sort of behavior is similar to what Ashforth (1994) calls the "petty tyranny" of organizational and personal power arrangements that humiliates and stresses subordinates. Monitors may also equate effective supervision with masculinity. As many organizational social scientists have noted, effective leadership—even by women managers—is often associated with masculine traits like aggressiveness and abrasiveness.[6]

Freya, however, sees the supervision by staff as more than a style of leadership. Her concern is that the supervision is designed to control and dominate. She points out that monitors call women by their first name but themselves are called "Miss." This is similar to the practice Rollins (1987) describes of women in patriarchal households who are able to hire domestic workers routinely referring to workers by first name while expecting to be addressed with a title themselves. As Hunnicutt (2009) points out, patriarchal hierarchies easily take shape in hierarchal institutions. Like the patriarchal family where male domination over females in the household structures everyday life,[7] familial patriarchy is fostered and maintained in homelike institutions when supervisors use status and power to subordinate residents. Another example from Freya illustrates exactly this sort of supervision by monitors: "I think they enjoy bossin' us around. They enjoy tellin' us stupid little things, like don't say Lula, say Miss Lula. These little things that are meant to upset you so that ya feel like a failure. The control is outrageous. It's controlling in every way here, in every way. It's sad to see someone that enjoys dominatin' and controllin' you. I do believe that they enjoy their power or control over you, but too I think maybe they were in this situation before, so maybe they transitioned from where we are."

Freya's point that monitors are reproducing oppression is especially troubling. All monitors at Alpha Omega House have themselves experienced correctional control and, no doubt, oppression and domination in many other spheres of life. Victoria gives a thoughtful analysis of how oppression can be reproduced even by women who are victims of gender inequality and domination:

> It made me see just how bad it is with womens in authority. It made me see how far they go. 'Cause they don't have authority on the outside, so they come 'n take it out on us. They have no authority on the outside, so they come 'n take out their frustrations on us. I listen how they talk ta people. That's what's goin' on with them. I bet you they have no authority even wit their kids, their men in their lives, I bet you they don't. They have no control, not at home, not with their man, not with their kids, not in the world, but they have it here. They know if we snap, we go back to jail. It goes to their head . . . I had women bosses in the world out there for so long, 'n they don't act like them because there's men there 'n most of them are white. I've observed them a long time, 'n the black women are the worse to work for. The black ones have a problem 'cause when they get a little authority, they worse. 'Cause it's like they been oppressed so long that now that they got this power, instead of treatin' everybody the same, they get worse on their own kind. They treat you like dirt. These women here, they have complete power that they will never have anywhere else.

As Victoria sees it, reentry center staff, both monitors and administrative staff, have significant responsibilities outside of their organizational roles, but because of social and familial patriarchy (and no doubt racism, as all are African American) they hold little or no power in those roles. With near-complete control in the isolated environment of Alpha Omega House, staff members might consequently and perhaps unknowingly use their unfettered authority to degrade just as they are themselves degraded. Indeed, some scholars make a case that gendered hierarchies of power influence women's individual use of power (Chesler and Goodman, 1976; Wells, 1973), and hooks (1984, p. 48) even argues that sexist socialization trains women (and children) to think and act negatively toward other women, effectively teaching them "woman-hating." Through this socialization, argues hooks, women accept hegemonic, patriarchal values of control and domination and, in their drive for their own power, use authority to oppress others, effectively buying into the stereotypically masculine ideal of effective leadership, "might makes right" (p. 88).

Rules

The rules and regulations taught to women in Blackout cover a range of topics titled Cardinal Rules, House Rules, Absolute Don'ts, Personal Living Space, General Conduct and Behavior, Urine Screen, Escort Rules, Medication Regulations, Physical Examination, Gossiping and Snitching Rules, Financial Plan, Visitation Rules, Pull-Up Regulations, Association with a Walk Off or Escapee, Community Meeting Group, Disciplinary Measures, Service Plan, and After Care. These rules dictate what is required and prohibited, structuring every aspect of the transition experience, from appropriate food consumption to money allowances. Since Alpha Omega House is a place for women to take on the rights and responsibilities of everyday civil life, the rules vary by phase of stay.

The women of Alpha Omega House understand the need for rules, and some even welcome the structured guidance because they need it. Laurel says: "It's a controlled environment. What are you gonna do? The rules are in place for a reason. This is an alternative to incarceration. Most of us have never lived a normal life so we do need rules to teach us how to do things accordingly." She accepts rules that can help her to live a normal life. Formal rules and other, unwritten rules outline the expectations of residents as well as staff and govern everyday interactions. They also reveal how staff perceives and values residents. Reed (1992) points out that social practices sustained by formal and informal rules become, over time, built into an institution and convey its culture. If rules interpreted as harmful become formalized, they may create a culture of oppression for those who are affected. As the women of Alpha Omega House tell it, the rules and regulations are often so restrictive that they run counter to the goal of reintegration. They are inconsistently applied, creating uncertainty and stress, and sometimes overly punitive.

Freya adds a caveat to Laurel's statement about rules: "We need rules, but the rules don't make sense. It defeats the purpose." She notes rules at Alpha Omega House that run counter to the correctional ideal of the reentry-center model, like the requirement to remain inside at all times except for approved outings to treatment, court, medical offices, and other official business. For Freya, the tight control does not help her improve personal responsibility or prepare for life on the outside. She says, "You only give me a little bit of leash? Come on, I'm not a dog. Yeah, walk me on a leash. It's crazy. I think they intentionally set you up for failure." Freya appreciates that the rationale for limitations on activities outside the house is well intended and that unrestricted freedom would likely lead to failure, but she sees a middle ground. Structure is important, she reasons, but flexibility is also essential—flexibility that allows the women to venture out into the world and be trusted with the everyday social interactions that make up life's challenges. This view is consistent with the philosophy of the reentry center as a criminal justice program.

Rules are so restrictive, says Victoria, that they reproduce the environment of prison. She adds:

> The nonsense, the simple things they gettin' write-ups for is takin' me out. It's just really unbelievable. You gotta throw food away before you can give it to anyone who might still be hungry. Here, we can't laugh too loud, don't sing in the shower, don't give any food away. I mean they not suppose to be guards, this is not supposed to be a prison, but its more rules here than in jail or prison. I don't understand that at all. Here, you're a resident, but you're treated like a prisona. You're a prisona. I am so serious. It's the same thing as jail. It's supposed to help you.

At the very least, the women argue, reentry-center rules governing what the women can and cannot do should coincide with the transitional nature of the program and assist them at developing autonomy, self-control, and self-reliance. Candy vents about the restrictive rules in this place she also likens to prison: "You're not gonna tell me when to wash my ass 'n when I can go to bathroom, what time to get dressed 'n all dat shit. I'll do that when I want to. I ain't gonna take it."

According to Lipton (1998), rules must be clear and unambiguous for therapeutic programs to be effective. But on top of the restrictive nature of rules at Alpha Omega House is an atmosphere of confusion and anxiety. The problem seems to be that because of monitors' wide discretion (and probably inadequate training), rules are differently applied and residents are often unclear about expected, required, and prohibited behavior. For instance, Adeline was ordered by a monitor to attend a mandatory class (not Blackout class) for all residents even though she was in Blackout. Adeline and I were sitting on the floor of Blackout talking when the monitor swung open the door and shouted to Adeline, "Ain't you hear the intercom? All residents to mandatory class. You gots to go." Adeline and I looked at one another, confused, and she followed the monitor to the stairway, where she descended into the basement. The next day, she recalls, Adeline got up to leave Blackout for the living room when she heard the intercom sound: "All residents report to the living room for class." But she was stopped at the doorway of Blackout by a different monitor who reprimanded her for stepping across the threshold into the "house" and scolded her because she should have known better that "Blackout girls" do not participate in treatment. This left her worried that she might "catch a fine" for doing the wrong thing. Victoria is also confused during her second weekend at Alpha Omega House. She says, "We don't know the rules, 'cause they never stay the same. You always doing somethin' wrong, 'cause you neva know what the rules are today, whose gonna tell you this, whose gonna tell you that. Life's uncertain, but rules shouldn't be."

To help women negotiate rules, Mimi takes charge to teach "new girls" the ropes in hopes of minimizing women's worry. She says:

> Cardinal rules are all the rules that are in the Blackout book, which none always apply. So I don't know why they call 'em cardinal rules. Like in the TV room, there's supposed to be no talkin' when the TV is on—that's a cardinal rule. Okay, so if we are loud and Miss Monica is there, she'll come in and tell us to be quiet, but have you ever heard of Miss Kerry caring about that? Another one is do not tell on people. Like don't go to the monitor 'n tell that someone's bother you, but the monitor's will be the first ones ta tell ya, You better come tell us if they're botherin' you. So I say to the new girls, you gotta learn the rules day by day. I tell the "Blackout girls": all right, learn everything in that book, learn all them rules, pass that test 'n then forget everything you just learned. And they're like, What? I'm like, You wanna get through this program, do what I'm tellin' you. None of those rules apply. And then take it day by day because each monitor has their own rules too, nobody does anything alike, and the rules change every day. And they might have rules for everyone 'n then rules just for you . . . We feel like we have to start all over here when new girls come. 'Cause they don't know the rules, they're gonna break them, 'n once they break them, we all get in trouble.

Discipline

It is two-thirty on a Saturday afternoon. The television is blaring. Rosa is slouched in a living room chair, snoring. Moments later the intercom calls out, "Rosa, report to the monitors' office." Rosa does not move. Again the intercom sounds: "Rosa, report to the monitors' office." "Shit," Rosa curses as she opens her eyes and hoists her frame from the chair with much effort. She heads to the monitors' office shaking her head, then returns saying, "I got a two-dolla fine for shuttin' my eyes, ya believe dat shit?" Two dollars might not seem like much, but it is a steep fine when her biweekly cash allowance is fifty dollars.

Like the traditional patriarchal family, women residents of Alpha Omega House are subject not only to control and supervision but also to disciplinary measures. In the domestic context of Alpha Omega House, monitors and administrative staff hold the power to maintain discipline over the female residents who occupy a subordinated status. In the main, this discipline is enforced through a punishment-based system of upholding rules and status. Hidden from public view, discipline at Alpha Omega House serves also to reinforce patriarchal authority. Tellingly, Kann (2005, p. 215) notes in a historical study of prison reform and the politics of punishment inherent in prison discipline that "patriarchal power could thrive where it was largely unnoticed and unknown."

Punitive discipline is demonstrated in various forms. Any rule infraction is a violation. Failure to rehearse the pledges and prayers in "Blackout class" is a violation. Sharing food is a violation, as is dozing off in the living room. Lateness to exercise or morning meditation is a violation. If a woman contests staff orders, borrows money from another resident, plays cards, turns the television when she is not past Zero, or stands in the hallway, she is in violation of the rules. When women at further phases of stay do not return from treatment on time, if they bring anything back they did not leave with, if they skip treatment, or if they stop into a store on their way to treatment, they have broken the rules.

Punishment for a violation of rules might involve verbal reprimands, while formal reprimands are write-ups kept on file and shared with a woman's probation or parole officer, judge, or other agent of the criminal justice system. Write-ups are the most common punishment. Henrietta gets a write-up for wearing slippers outside of her room, and Grace gets a write-up for going into the kitchen. Rosa explains how the write-up system works: "When you get a write-up, if it's a petty write-up dey might just not say nuthin' about it 'n just put it in your record, but if it's a write-up dat needs to be addressed, dey'll call ya downstairs to the office 'n dey'll ask ya why it happened, 'n dey'll confront ya about it 'n dey decide what to do. Usually, dey pinch ya wit a fine wit it."

Normally, monetary fines accompany formal write-ups, although fines are commonly used also as a sole sanction. Monitors have extraordinary discretion in both the application of fines and fine amounts, say the women. Monetary penalties are charged for things such as leaving a bed messy, taking too long in the shower, not showering at all, putting feet up in the living room, and using the vending machine before nighttime. Mimi was recently tagged with a two-dollar fine when her half of the bedroom closet was in "disarray" and another two dollars when a monitor observed her flip-flops crooked in the closet. Grace was hit with a two-dollar fine, she said, when a nighttime monitor observed "fuzzes on da flo [floor]" of her room. Phoebe was penalized the same amount for talking during morning meditation. Candy was fined six dollars for missing meditation one day and five dollars for being late on another. Alpha Omega House collects fines directly from women's income sources, which are held by the organization and distributed according to strict rules. The fines amounts are high in proportion to their women's income. Take Henrietta, who is handed seventy-five dollars of her income each month but who averages about ten dollars in fines per week: more than half of her income goes to paying fines for her punishment.

In a one-week period, Laurel accumulated more than ten dollars in fines for keeping her bedroom door too near shut, being late to dinner, speaking too loudly, lounging in the living room, and not saying "going up" when her foot hits the first step of the stairs. It is true that Laurel could have monitored her behavior more closely to comply with rules even if she did not agree with them. But to Laurel, the imposition of fines is often petty. She says of the monitors who were not too long ago offenders in her shoes: "You got the power so your gonna fuck wit me. It's the way they demoralize me. Yes, I went to jail. Yes, I did some things to get there. But enough is enough. That's not doin' any good." Victoria and many other women say they agree that fines are oppressive and overused:

They charge you for everything. Clair's bed wasn't made right, and they charged her a two-dollar fee for that. They fined Candy for singin' in the shower the other day, do you hear me? This is worser than jail. We had rules, but nuthin' compared to the rules here. You cannot pass your food. If you don't want to eat something, if you give it to somebody else, you will be fined. They caught Henrietta givin' food to Grace and fined her four dollars for that. They prefer to throw the food away instead of giving it to somebody else who would want to eat it. What kind of sense does that make? They just want to control.

Victoria's last comment articulates the principle argument made by the women —punitive method of discipline are felt as oppressive control. The monetary fine is key to the house's disciplinary structure; it is a sanction, the women argue, that is foremost retributive in nature. The fine is also a tool used to subordinate women residents economically. As Hartmann (1981) argues, women's historically subordinate economic position within the family is a product of the family's patriarchal (and capitalist) organization. At this reentry house, the heavy economic toll of the fines combined with the very limited amounts of money women can access or manage (and the lack of paid employment, discussed later) subordinates the residents and perpetuates the dominance by monitors and administrative staff.

In addition to reprimands, write-ups, and fines are other sanctions. A resident can be forced to eat alone, held back from treatment appointments, kept from visits with family, and even be forced to undertake "major writing projects." Additional punishments include physical labor as "corrective measures" according to the rules and regulations handbook. These measures may require residents to "scrub and wax all floors," do "outside yard work," and "clean the boiler room." In cases of very serious violations, women may be returned to incarceration or required to drop down a phase of stay, thereby adding more time to her required term at Alpha Omega Houses.

Yet another common disciplinary measure is the so-called restriction. Like a "time-out" used with children, restriction means a woman is sent to her room for a period of time. There, except during chore time, she is isolated from the other women and all activities of the house. Her meals are taken in her room, and she uses the shower and bathroom only when other women are absent. Any privileges she may have, such as an upcoming visit or treatment at an outside agency, are revoked for the period of restriction, which can last days. Henrietta often gets restrictions for "cussin' up" and "talking back" to monitors. Even mild-mannered Grace and quiet Clair get restrictions. In fact, all of the women in this study served time on restriction multiple times during the course of this study. But Phoebe, who is quick to challenge the staff, has logged more than anyone else. On the first day of a five-day restriction for a major violation, she said, "It's not just that I have to stay in here, but being here means I'm just in my head more, I'm going crazy."

agency in action. A form of snakeskin, it is helpful not just as a tactic the women use to manage pressure and domination, but in some cases to change staff behavior. It can be compared to "clandestine retribution" (Adas, 1986). Mimi agrees, saying, "Ignore them 'n it pisses them off even more." Freya likes to "let them sit with it" because "women are naturally aware of what they do; we recognize when we are hurtful." She says, "Leave them where they're at, 'n let them feel and process the guilt 'n shame of their actions." In her mind, silence and snakeskin can produce positive change. Candy sometimes uses silence rather than confrontation or other strategies when she feels pushed around by staff or subjugated by rules. She says: "Silence kills 'em; fuck 'em, they ain't worth it. It shows 'em we better than they are. You got to learn to control your emotions. Be silent. Be in control. Don't cry 'n be a pussy. Let them sit with it. Ignoring them makes them crazy."

Snakeskin is a form of covert resistance that is intentionally oppositional and is recognized by others similarly situated. As a covert strategy, resistance may go unnoticed by the oppressors (Hollander and Einwohner, 2004), making it common among repressed groups and a key strategy for women at the reentry center. Similar findings are reported among African American women who use courage or "armoring" as a means of self-protection and psychological resistance against racism and sexism (Edmondson Bell and Nkomo, 1998). Snakeskin is comparable to the strategies Shorter-Gooden (2004) reports that women use to deal with racism and sexism: sustaining a positive self-image and "role flexing," that is, altering one's outward presentation and behavior through psychological means. In line with Scott's ideas (1985, p. xvi), the snakeskin strategy used by women beginning in Blackout brings attention to the subtle power plays in force as soon as the women enter Alpha Omega House, the "constant, grinding conflict over work, food, autonomy, and ritual—at everyday forms of resistance." Like other covert forms of resistance, snakeskin is persistent resistant behavior, involves a measure of self-help, avoids direct conflict with authority, requires little or no planning and tends to be more effective than confrontation in the end. Still, as Edmondson and colleges (1998) caution, psychological protective strategies can also work against women in their focus on persistent personal strength and fortitude often at the expense of a woman's needs and outward expression of frustration. Despite putting on snakeskin, the women are not free of their subjugated status during Blackout. They are constantly reminded that they are dominated and that the outside is just steps away from the window. Even knowing they will suffer by their actions, sometimes a woman must express herself outwardly.

JUMPING

The Blackout room is quiet and still. Two unmade beds are empty. At the foot of one lies a pair of black sweatpants next to two manila folders of rules and regulations. A window curtain above one of the beds dangles from its now bent curtain rod, letting sunlight into the room. Alone in the room, Adeline looks up from her bed and smiles as she points to the window, "They jumped out *that* window." Polly was the first to leave, skipping out just before dinner the night before. From the looks of it, she swung open a poorly secured wrought-iron window bar on the outside of the window and jumped six feet to the ground below into the night. Shayla followed an hour later.

Earlier that evening during chore time, Shayla asked Mimi and other women: "What happens when a person leaves? When do the cops start lookin'?" "She thinks this place is like the movies," Mimi recalls. "I told her the police got better things to do than hunt down a drug addict from a halfway house." She had re-assured Shayla: "The cops ain't gonna be out lookin' for ya." Mimi is correct. The criminal justice system in this city does not actively hunt down women who escape from Alpha Omega House. Upon discovery that a resident has escaped, staff notifies the woman's probation or parole officer, and an arrest warrant is issued for the woman's return to custody. But "Blackout girls" do not top the list of most wanted. The system usually catches up with women when they are rearrested for new crimes. Mimi continues, "I told her, You'll get picked up when you catch a new case. They'll just check the usual places you go, like home or at your girl's house, but they won't look for ya. If ya want to work, just get a job under the table. She said thanks, did her chores, and took off out the window." Adeline adds: "I come back from doin' the toilets an see the curtain blowin' in the wind. The bar's danglin' down. I told Mimi, 'n we didn't say nuthin.' Shayla didn't go when they called her for meds 'n that's when they found out they both jumped."

Two weeks later, different women share Blackout. Ginny writes the following narrative in her "Blackout journal":

> I looked out the window to the fresh air. My mind drifts to those nice moments before my life turned to darkness. The days when nothing seemed to bother me and the days were easy. Best of all, motherhood and waking up with my son. Playing and going to the park. Getting dirty playing in the dirt or splashing in puddles. Going fishing, seeing my son getting excited when his dad caught a fish and seeing my son even more thrilled when he

mastered catching a fish on his own. These are the times I really miss. Those days were so peaceful and joyous. Today I want to be on Dunkin Lake fishing with my son. I'm missing him growing up. I need to be there with him and I will, soon! That's what's most important to me. He's my life.

The next morning the journal lies on her unmade bed, open to this last entry. The life Ginny writes about is now almost certainly farther from her grasp, as she too is on the run after jumping from the same window as the women before her. And, just as the others left behind the reminders of Alpha Omega House, Ginny's black converse sneakers and the manila folder of rules sit on the floor below. Ginny's dresser still holds black T-shirts and socks, as well as her personals. With just the clothes on her back, she took with her one item—the single tattered, pocket-sized photo of her young son. But Ginny had company. On the floor beside Kelly's bed are her folder of rules, a black sweatshirt, and a religious card of support and encouragement she received from her mother while in prison. A Bible rests atop her dresser, and a prison-issued rosary dangles from its drawer pull. Kelly jumped with Ginny under the cover of night. Adeline saw this coming. She attributes the escape to a lack of needed treatment intervention: "She was cryin' out for help. I heard it; how come they didn't hear? She was crying out, saying, I need treatment, I'm a drug addict. I need to talk to someone, please get me help. I need help. They didn't care. That's why she left."

Jumping normally happens in pairs and is encouraged in conversation between the "Blackout girls." As is the case in other settings, the smallest hint of social and mutual support fosters acts of resistance (Murphy, 1998; Scott, 1990). Just as Shayla and Polly entered Alpha Omega House handcuffed together, they experienced the shock of Blackout together, and they jumped one after the next. As well, Ginny and Kelly shared the experience of entering the convent structure handcuffed to one another, they felt the shock of its isolation together, and they too would jump as one. The pair discussed strategy the night before, says Violet: "I heard 'em and pretended to be sleepin,' and then they heard me move so knew I was awake. They said they was leaving, going to Northville to get high, that they would rather be in Copley [women's prison] than here." It was hard for Violet to resist joining them, she remembered, as they quietly left out the window and fled in the cold of a winter night toward the drugs they craved.

Kelly and Ginny never hid their discontent about Alpha Omega House; Blackout isolation without treatment intervention was too much for them to take. Ginny was twenty years younger than Kelly and early in her drug use but advanced enough to "speedball," which means mixing cocaine and heroin for a dangerous high. As an untreated and active drug addict, Kelly was tempted to jump and run, to use drugs, and to live on the lam as she had for so many years. She said days before she jumped, "I don't like people takin' control of me, so I'll do anything I can and do anything in my power to stop it. I want my independence back." At the same time, Kelly was tired of the hard life as a drug addict and felon dodging the system. She hoped she could find the will to decide differently. She said, "You have temptations to jump out the window. I wanna leave, but I wanna walk out the doors and not the window. I wanna not look behind my back no more, not have warrants on me. I'm tired of something holdin' over my head, always somethin' controllin' me." Had Kelly been without Ginny's support, perhaps she would have endured the hard Blackout days. It took only the slightest nudge from a friend to flee back to the streets.

Jumping from the Blackout room to escape the oppressive conditions of Blackout is overt resistance, according to one typology of resistance behavior (Hollander and Einwohner, 2004). Like women fighting back against sexual assault, nuns escaping from the abusive patriarchy of the church, seniors citizens attempting to flee the confines of nursing homes, and workers quitting in response to workplace bullying, it is a most visible and recognized form of resistance.[10] Jumping from the windows is opportunistic and, like other overt forms of resistance, often spontaneous insofar as it happens after a rather short period of deliberation (Wade, 1997) and when other strategies, such as snakeskin, fail to produce intended results.

A strategy of exit or flight, often called an avoidance protest, is said to be the most frequent and often effective response to oppression by subjugated individuals (Adas, 1986; Scott, 1985). By the numbers of women who select it, jumping is the most frequently used overt method of resisting Blackout isolation, dress, rituals, and lack of treatment intervention. It is a simple option accessible to women in this most restrictive phase of their stay. In fact, only Blackout women escape and most "Blackout girls" jump from the windows rather than complete the thirty days. Over the course of my focus on Blackout, eight women made it through Blackout and more than nine did not. But women jump when other methods fail, and this overt act was less common than other, more subtle forms or resistance when considering the overall reentry experience.

Jumping does risk many negative consequence, but so do other resistance acts, and many of these directly bring on counter-resistance. For example, Victoria showed her discontent during Blackout class by challenging its purpose and keeping silent during the rehearsal of rules and regulations because, she said, "We go over dees rules every day for thirty days. I says I'm tired of recitin' this. I says I'm not doin' it no more. Why we not gettin' no housin' 'n counselin'?" Victoria was fined for her defiance that day and the next, then reluctantly acquiesced because of the mounting fines. Mimi also learned directly the consequence for noncompliance. When she sat for her Blackout quiz, she remembers: "I took that Blackout test 'n wrote 'fuck you' across the front of it." It made her feel good momentarily, but it also earned her another week in Blackout until she would become compliant. Overt resistance was also demonstrated when women refused to dress entirely in black. Before she jumped, Kelly said of her resistance to the dress code:

> We still have a little bit of our own control, self-control, 'n I resist a little sometimes. Like them tellin' me I can't wear jeans. I'll wear jeans if I wanna wear jeans. I tell 'em I'm doin' wash even though my darks aren't even in yet, but they don't know it. I tell 'em, you're gonna write me up 'cause I'm washin' my blacks? Well, do you want yellow paper or white paper? Blue pen or black pen? What do you want to write me up? I don't care, go ahead. What are they gonna say? I'm finin' you. Whadda want, five dollas or ten dollas? Twenty-five dollas? Whataya gonna take? Gaw head, take it.

A "Blackout girl" may feel momentary freedom when she wears a color other than black and she may get away with it temporarily. But resistance can be resisted or neutralized (Kärreman and Alvesson, 2009), and as counter-resistance mounts at Alpha Omega House in verbal reprimands, fines, and restriction, compliance often outweighs the benefits of temporary relief. As a cyclical process, however, just as resistance breeds counter-resistance, counter-resistance fosters resistance (Mumby, 2005).

Jumping is understood at the house as a problematic solution. Compared to other methods of resistance, say the women, it is "the easy way out" because it seems like giving up or failing in the face of oppression and domination. But jumping, like quitting a job, can be more than that. It may be an expression of how strongly a woman rejects constraints over her autonomy and reflects desire for automony (Paules, 1991). It removes a woman from a particular location and form of oppression, at least temporarily. Still, the risk in jumping is the same as in other forms of overt resistance: that oppression will be reproduced (Lutgen-Sandvik, 2006), perhaps intensified (Mumby, 2005). Women who strike back at batterers only to suffer increased battering provides an obvious example of how oppression can be reproduced by resistance. While striking back might express a woman's autonomy and perhaps free her of abuse, it is likely to foster strong counter-resistance, including backlash at the societal level (Dragiewicz, 2011). At Alpha Omega House, women who refrain from jumping suffer consequences because of those who do. They are assigned the domestic chores left by those who escaped, subjected to more frequent headcounts throughout the day and night, and even punitive sanctions like group restriction from weekends in the living room. Meanwhile, the women who do jump might find immediate relief, but they will owe the criminal justice system the remainder of their original prison sentence that was suspended by placement at Alpha Omega House, and they may be sanctioned anew for failure to complete the reentry program as a violation of probation or parole supervision. Two months after her escape, Kelly was returned to custody for possession of drugs, prostitution, and violation of probation. Ginny's whereabouts is not known. Shayla might not have taken Mimi's advice to stay away from her girlfriend's residence and, if so, she might have been the first to feel these consequences of jumping. But Polly, having spent many years in the system, "will be all right" says Candy, at least for some time, because "she know how to be ghost" on the street—that is, until she "catches another case."

Consistent with the ideas of Scott (1985; 1990), Crewe (2007), and Werth (2012) that overt acts of resistance are often avoided in favor of alternative strategies because of strong counter-resistance, my research shows that women refrain from jumping to avoid negative consequences of further criminal justice control, especially when they feel they have alternatives that can better meet their needs. My findings are consistent with Crewe's view (p. 266) that the correctional environment minimizes overt acts such as escape because of their inherent counter-productivity and with Werth's finding that parolees are reluctant to resist by absconding because doing so is unlikely to produce positive change. Clair wants out, but the months of "back time" she would have to serve in prison is too much for her to chance. So she decides to wait out the remainder of her Blackout. She says: "Even though they're fuckin' with me so bad, if I leave, I'll do my back time in jail, eleven months. I won't get my kids back. I need treatment. Everything runs through my mind. I am bipolar. I have an addiction. I can't be locked up alone. I gotta hold out. I know there's light at the end of the tunnel. I'm always controllin' my situation, like leaving might be good, but in the long term, it is not takin' care of myself."

Still, knowing women have jumped tempts those who remain behind, even when they have a strong reason to avoid this strategy. Adeline says: "Them leavin' makes it harder on us to stay. I say to myself a lot, bye, I'm leavin,' this place sucks.

But the consequences make me stay. You can't do anything government. I won't be able to go to school or work, anything that involves your name in the system. You can't live a life. So I'm tryin' to think logically. I'll figure out a way."

Adeline did figure out a way; she stood firm through Blackout. Clair made it through too, and so did Victoria, Violet, and Amelia. These women did not necessarily feel the weight of Blackout any less than did those who jumped, yet their confidence and capacity to manage their emotions through other strategies helped them. Furthermore, social support links those who jumped as well as those who did not. As we know from resistance studies, reactions to oppression and domination are fostered in places where subjects can freely interact among themselves (McCorkel, 1998; Scott, 1985). Ginny and Kelly shared a desire to seek drugs, and being in Blackout together, they supported one another in that quest. But while Clair was vulnerable to jumping, she had Adeline, who had managed to weather the hardest first few days of Blackout and who supported Clair's resistance in other ways. Clair also was able to channel her anxieties to support Victoria when she first arrived in Blackout. The women's social support for each other and for each other's resistance strategies, fostered in the confines of Blackout, helps to explain how the women at the house manage isolation and control in that phase of stay. Although those who remained behind complied with organizational rules and regulations by not jumping, they did not accept the subjugating environment they found themselves in; they simply determined it was better to try to improve their lives within the constraints of the system. As Crewe (2007, p. 266) describes resistance among prisoners, compliance is not "acquiescence to the regime," but a means of individual growth and renewal. Violet was able to stay that night Ginny and Kelly left because, she says, "I held on to the sheet, tellin' myself over an over I don't wanna keep runnin,' I don't wanna keep runnin.'" Violet knows that if she leaves, she will never really be free.

||||||||||||||||||||||||||||||||||||||||||||||||||||||||

THREE

ZERO

TODAY IS MOVING DAY for Victoria. She completed the mandatory thirty days of Blackout and just this morning passed her written Blackout quiz. She was able to answer the chain-of-command questions, including the one that asked her to identify "who I can go to and can't go to" for information, complaints, or assistance. Victoria appropriately repeated the prayers and pledges of Alpha Omega House sisterhood and correctly identified the cardinal rules. Despite having been reprimanded, written-up, and fined for violations such as talking back to monitors, wearing earrings, and being late for her shower, Victoria still may be considered the "new girl," but she can leave Blackout behind for a room upstairs and officially settle in as a second-floor resident.

Like other so-called "new girls" fresh out of Blackout, Victoria is no longer subjected to wearing black or being isolated from other women, and she will never have to attend another Blackout class. Before she leaves the Blackout bedroom for her quarters upstairs, Victoria rushes out of her blacks into a comfortable pair of cream-colored slacks and a soft blue sweater. She relinquishes the label of "Blackout girl" (though remains a "new girl") and steps into O Level or, as the women call it, Zero. During this second phase of stay, which lasts at least thirty days but can be as long as three months, women have more freedom than they had in Blackout but are under tighter surveillance and control than women further along in the program. The physical and social scene has changed for Victoria and other "Zero girls," including Adeline, Violet, Amelia, Billie, Freya, Candy, and Clair, who now have a broader experience within this old convent structure.

Layout

Stepping out of Blackout into the narrow cinderblock hallway, Victoria carries a bundle of personals and clothing. She passes a stairway descending to the basement, a laundry room, a conference room used for Blackout class, and the administrative offices. Just steps outside the Blackout door she reaches the ascending stairway, grips the wood handrail, and sighs heavily. She announces, "Going up!" as she slowly climbs, pulling herself by the handrail to the halfway-point landing, where she takes a rest. Candy turns the ninety-degree corner in midair, announcing, "Comin' down!" as she disappears into the hallway below. This phrase is heard many times each day because residents must announce their travels each time they ascend or descend the stairway.

At the top of the stairs, the second level is laid out like a hospital ward with bedrooms along a long narrow cinderblock corridor. The doorways on one side of the hall do not face the doorways on the opposite wall. Rather, the view out the doorway of any room is always of cinderblock. Each of the eight bedrooms is marked with a simple black plastic number, similar to those typically found on home mailboxes. Numbered from two to nine, the rooms are roughly identical, distinguished only by residents' personal touches. They are small, with two cots, a dresser, a closet, and a small window. Sometimes a woman has her own room, especially when the house is not so full, but women usually share rooms. Mimi and Phoebe share a room and so do Violet and Amelia, who advanced to Zero the same day. Adeline rooms with Raquel and hates it. Candy has her own room and so does Freya. Henrietta has her own room too.

Video surveillance stops at the hallway; personal spaces such as bedrooms and the bathroom area are off-limits to cameras. In this building constructed specifically for women's communal living, it is only inside her bedroom that a woman might maintain a separate personal identity—if she can carve a private life at all in a public space. Women may go to their rooms any time after noon unless they are required elsewhere, such as meetings with staff, meals, or occasional classes. The upstairs rules are simple: no shutting the bedroom doors, no entering another residents' room, no mingling in the hallway, no congregating in the bathroom, and lights out when instructed. The women must always observe the "no naked" rule, as the women call it. In addition to the obvious prohibition against being naked, this rule prohibits women from exposing their breasts or undergarments at all times, even in the privacy of their beds. Like the nuns who lived at the house before, women must cover themselves and their sexuality.

Using fabric given to her by staff, dried roses she collected outside, magazine pages, and her own crayon and pencil drawings, Grace has put together something close to a French Provincial style in her room. Roughly hand-sewn floral curtains hang from the broken window that cannot open, and two matching pillows sit atop an old, matted, lace bedspread. Oscar the housecat can usually be found lying on her bedspread, nestled into Grace's collection of teddy bears. Grace has photos of her ex-husband and the youngest two of her ten children taped to the wall by her bed and on her dresser. She complains that her ex-husband prevents her sons from communicating with her. She says, "He tell dem dey have no mo [mother], but I dere mo. It raw [wrong]." She says, "I jus ga da divor papa [got the divorce papers] in mail." Still, Grace tends what resembles a shrine made of a wedding photo of herself and her ex-husband, a rosary, dried flowers, and one of her crayon drawings. Littered with pieces of long-discarded paper posters, her water-stained and paint-chipped blue walls are a gallery of more crayon drawings of herself, her new boyfriend, and teddy bears as well as black plastic prison-issued rosaries. She has created a refuge, a home where she escapes whenever she can. She often rearranges the room to relieve anxiety and stress and spends her time alone with the cat, listening to easy-listening love songs always slightly out-of-tune, much like the sounds from an old AM radio.

In sharp contrast to Grace's space is Henrietta's room across the hall. The room has two cots. One holds a naked and worn mattress cut at the corners, a sure sign of bed-bug examination. The other is made up with a single white pillowcase and a white sheet hanging to the floor, where Henrietta's shoes frame the bed. The paint peels from the walls, and steel pipes—what looks like the remains of plumbing for a sink—stick out into the room from one wall. A single light bulb hangs from the chipped plaster ceiling. Ripped paper shades sag in the small, cloudy window that is cracked and stuck in its track. A filthy gray screen blocks any view of the overgrown lot of trees below. The linoleum floor peeks through thinned, dim, brown carpet. Near the door is a dresser that holds Henrietta's personals and clothing. The dresser drawers are ajar from wear and age. Two of the drawers can only be opened by pulling on string tied through the holes that once secured drawer pulls, and the other has no string or drawer pull at all, so it always remains slightly open. Atop the dresser are Henrietta's personals, including toiletries like deodorant and the strongly scented body wash the women prefer, stacked two and three deep in neat rows. The ever-present black-plastic prison-issued rosaries hang from rusted nails adorning every wall. Henrietta is illiterate, but she displays a Bible and a serenity prayer card on one side of her dresser. She may not use the entire top of the dresser even though she has lived alone in this room for months; the other half is reserved for her room-mate, even when she does not have one. Residents are also strictly limited to half of the closet for hanging clothing, half of the closet floor for storing shoes, and half of the dresser drawers.

Hidden from view of occasional visitors or treatment providers, the bedrooms are cold and demonstrate years of neglect. Bugs are commonplace. Rosa's room is no better than Henrietta's. Rosa sits against the dirty blue wall on her side of the room on a bare mattress stained by a previous occupant. One foot is wrapped in a medical boot as treatment for fractures she suffered when she tripped on the building's broken front steps. The other foot wears a sneaker because Rosa never goes barefooted or shoeless even in her own room. She complains of the physical condition of her living space:

> I been to plenty of rehabs 'n plenty of mental hospitals 'n this has been da far worse place I ever been to. This is da most ghettoist hole in da wall I ever been to. Da building literally looks like it wants ta fall apart. My window's broken shut. Da carpet's filthy. Da place infested wit thousand-leggers, stinkbugs, ants, mice. I pay fuckin' rent in dis shithole? It makin' it seem like we're not worth it. Everything's disgusting. It's terrible up in here. It's like we don't matter. I don't even have handles on my dresser. It's just a shoelace tied goin' through it.

The bedrooms resemble the inside of an abandoned drug house. The rent Rosa refers to amounts to 20 percent of her income. Every woman pays rent, which comes from either her own bank account or her welfare or SSI payments, to offset the cost of her confinement.

A large bathroom is at the end of the hallway in the rear of the second floor. It is the only bathroom residents may ever use. Inside, a single light bulb is suspended from exposed wires in the ceiling above. The floor is made up of one-inch blue and white tiles that ever so slightly slope to a metal drain in the center. To the right are six toilets behind peeling and rusty blue metal stalls with doors that never seem to close. Directly across the room along the blue-tiled wall are three open alcoves, two containing bathtubs and one with a shower. Across the room from a small window an undersized sink with rusted cold- and hot-water taps hangs from another blue-tiled wall. Above the sink is a small rectangular mirror clouded at the edges; it is the only mirror residents have available to them. On occasion, women can be seen leaning into the mirror plucking their eyebrows or applying makeup.

Directly outside of the bathroom is the stairway leading down. In the hallway below and to the right of the steps is the backside of the house, where the small school desk sits outside of Blackout. Dead ahead is a utility closet that is always locked to the women, but where they gather to receive supplies during chore time. The small room that was once the convent's sacristy is now called the salon and used by staff. In the other direction, toward the front of the house up the narrow hallway on the right, is an industrial-sized kitchen of sparkling stainless steel, which only staff may enter unless a woman's daily chores take her there. Just five steps up the hall past the kitchen is an adjoining dining room, where the nuns would gather for meals. It is now just as bleak as the hallway, with the linoleum floor worn to the concrete below and the dimly painted walls long in need of paint. Just as in Blackout, heavy dark drapes block any glimpse of outside. It is a dining room only inasmuch as women eat meals here. Three times each day women gather at the two long plastic tables in blue plastic chairs that are stacked against a wall when not in use. A staff refrigerator, chained and locked when administrative staff leave for the day, sits against a wall near a water cooler. Across the room is the vending machine, stocked with candy and chips that are available to the women in the evening. Near the entrance to the room is a bulletin board advertising just one program—a bicycle riding on Monday and Thursdays afternoons. Sometimes, women come here to play a board game at a table away from the living-room television. They might also sneak short conversations away from others, but always under the watchful eye of the security camera perched high on the wall above the refrigerator. Henrietta and Rosa are playing the board game Sorry. They curse one another and talk loudly as they play game after game, dealing the tattered game cards over and over. Henrietta tries to cheat and laughs when she is angry because she is "a bomb inside" ready to "cut loose" at any moment.

Across the hall from the dining room is a living room. Also the nuns' living space, this large, open room is the central meeting place for residents today and the primary space where they pass time. Women on Zero are allowed to spend all day, midmorning through late evening, in this room. This space is truly the heart of the house, yet it resembles a waiting room more than a central living space. From the always shining florescent lighting, the pale green cinderblock walls, the rusted and cloudy windows, and the thin green industrial carpet with duct tape repairs on its seams, everything about the room is cold and impersonal. Direct access to bookcases, which are mostly filled with Bibles and romance or crime novels, is blocked by mismatched, sagging sofas draped with filthy, oversized slipcovers that gather in lumps at the floor. Two doors, which always remain open to the hallway, stand across from dorm-style wooden chairs with stained seat cushions below drafty windows covered with badly fitting, faded curtains. All seats have an unobstructed view of the small television that sits atop a table full of outdated movies on DVD and VHS tapes (for a VCR that no longer works) and exercise videos that the women despise. Two inspirational posters, one on motivation and the other on responsibility, frame the television. The room has no tables and no lamps. A security camera hanging from the ceiling by the television offers unobstructed views of every space in the room.

The rules for this room are simple: no lying down, no dozing off, no feet up, no food, lights remain on, no yelling or loud talking, no talking in front of the television at all, no turning the television off. In addition, women learn the informal rules that apply to things such as seating, choice of television program, shower time, and laundry use. For example, only the most senior girls can occupy the single settee between two doors out of view of hallway traffic. "Blackout girls" and "Zero girls" cannot take any seat or place on a couch that a senior girl has taken for her own when the senior girl is in the room. "Zero girls" learn as they go, showing deference to the senior girls because they realize they will one day have earned the privilege of being a senior resident.

Sometimes, especially early on, the "new girls" need to be reminded of the informal rules that govern life at the house. In the following example, Mimi explains a situation in which Billie was told to give up a seat Laurel had claimed. Billie resisted at first, but after a quick shouting match, Billie moved to a different seat. Mimi narrates Billie's resistance: "She said there ain't no assigned seating, I'm gonna sit here. She said I'm gonna sit here all the time. We all tell her no. She doesn't understand that there's an unwritten law that came way before me. I didn't make it up. It was made up before I even got here. You don't earn nuthin' yet. You're on Blackout or Zero. You have to be here for months and months before you have any right to anything, like pickin' TV shows, pickin' a seat. You have to earn that."

Having completed moving into her new room, Victoria takes a rest on one of the wooden chairs close to the television in the living room. She does not sit on the settee because she knows better, having observed Billie's mistake. She holds her usual belongings to her chest—the packets of rules, two dog-eared notebooks, one of which she uses as a journal, and a woman-in-distress novel. Appearing to organize the paperwork, Victoria is keeping a close eye on the others and appears, literally, to be on the edge of her seat. This is the first time she has ever been inside the living room on a weekday, and she too has to learn the routine. With two of the ubiquitous black-plastic rosaries resting on her large breasts, Laurel is lounging on the settee with her legs stretched forward, defying the no lounging rule. She is staring at the television but not really following the storyline. She appears lost in herself. Phoebe and Mimi are seated beside Laurel on the settee, also staring at the television. Dressed in an oversized white T-shirt, sweatpants, and white socks inside flip-flops, Phoebe squints to see because her glasses were broken in the car accident the night of her arrest almost two years before. Mimi's hair is in a tight ponytail, and she lounges with her two-sizes-too-big cotton sweatpants, extra-large white T-shirt, white tube socks, and flip-flops. Sitting in a wooden chair across from the trio is Raquel, who is staring into the television, mumbling to herself. Like Grace, she appears as an outcast and roams in and out of the living room. Keira is daydreaming, and Freya is sitting with her lover, Billie, staring toward the deafening television. The women are quiet and still as if "lost up in our heads." This could be a snapshot of any day as women do time in Alpha Omega House. Time moves slowly here, eerily similar to Blackout.

Moving from the living room left up the hall toward the front door is a tight foyer of cinderblock walls with the monitors' office directly right, the front door straight ahead, and a narrow hall to the left. Residents may never enter the foyer without first ringing a small desk bell, similar to those seen on counters of hardware stores, and hearing the monitor call, "Come!" Residents may never walk to the left where the short hallway leads to the basement offices. In the foyer between the hallway and the front door is a small, desk-sized table with two binders, used to log entry and exit dates, times, and trip purposes for women, treatment providers, or visitors. The monitors' office is a small room with worn carpet, two desks, a fan in the undersized dirty window, and dusty paperwork piled high on shelves. A whiteboard hangs on one wall listing names of women currently residing at the house along with their corresponding phase of stay in various colors. The women call it The Board and sneak a peek at it whenever they get a chance because it often indicates their official phase of stay and source of income before they are told. On one of the desks is a telephone, a computer, and a buzzer that unlocks the entrance. Two monitors, dressed in colorful medical scrubs as if the house were a health-care facility, occupy this office on each of three work shifts.

The monitors' office contains three notable objects. The first is the intercom, which is the staff's primary method of communicating with the women. The second is a security monitor with multiple screens showing resident movement from cameras positioned throughout the public areas of the house. The video surveillance is constant and captures almost every space in the building. "It's like being in a big fish tank," Phoebe says, adding, "the eyes are constant." The third notable item is a locked cabinet with drawers labeled with the name of each resident. Accessible only to monitors, some of the women's most import-ant possessions are kept there—identification cards, medications, money, and cigarettes—and distributed according to strict rules. In addition to functioning as a surveillance center, communication hub, and pseudo pharmacy, the moni-tors' office also serves as the commissary where women can buy soap powder for laundry, personals like tampons and razors, prepaid phone cards for the pay-phones, and bus tokens for transportation.

Routine

Having moved into room 8, Victoria digs out small gold-stud earrings from a plastic bag. Even before she arranges her personals on her half of the dresser, be-fore she puts a sheet on the bare cot against the dingy wall, or decides where to lay her shoes on the half-empty closet floor, she puts the earrings in her ears. Finally, she is on Zero. Zero, Victoria says, "means we get put on welfare and start getting our checks 'n food stamps. We can smoke twice a day, make payphone calls 'n get visits on Sunday. I can finally put my earrings in. I ain't had these earrings off in years till I got here. But still can't do nuthin' more than that."

This second phase of stay is named "O" for "orientation." The women call it Zero. The routine of the "Zero girl" now includes getting financial support and reestablishing some connection with the outside world. Yet as Victoria's last comment suggests, Zero still limits women's activities. In fact, the "Zero girl" maintains a routine much like she did in Blackout isolation.

IT'S TIME TO EXERCISE

One of the perks of Zero is an extra half hour of sleep. But like the routine of Blackout, every morning at Zero Level and beyond begins with exercise. Now Victoria is simply among a larger group of weary-eyed women assembled in the living room for the morning routine. Dressed in jeans or sweat pants of vary-ing colors, flip-flops or sneakers, and the ever-present large, boxy, white T-shirt or dull sweatshirt, the women hurry down the stairs, calling out one after the next, "Comin' down!" as they rush only to avoid being fined by monitors for lateness. Clair is late today and will pay for it. She heard the intercom—"Good morning, ladies; it's time to exercise. Report to the living room for mandatory exercise"—but she briefly closed her eyes instead of swinging her legs to the floor. She says later, "I got written up 'n got hit with a five-dollar fine for bein' five minutes late."

The routine of morning exercise for "Zero girls" and women at advanced phases is always the same; only the scene playing out before them on the television changes. With obvious reluctance, women silently and slowly position themselves in rows in front of a monitor in bright yellow medical scrubs by the television set. She is prepped with a DVD of an aerobics class. Yesterday's class was performed before a Bollywood exercise video, a "sexy, saucy, calorie-burning, full-body workout . . . that will tone you head to toe while unleashing waves of energy and joy . . . while having a blast and learning moves you'll love to flaunt on the dance floor." Today's class is set on a summer beach. With music blaring, the women half-heartedly mirror the movements of the overweight monitor, who appears equally disinterested. The scene playing out in the living room is in stark contrast to that on the television, where toned Spandex-clad women on a sunny resort beach enthusiastically dance to rhythms of tropical music. The women incarcerated at Alpha Omega House are, as a group, not health conscious. Nor do they enjoy keeping their bodies fit through regimes of exercise. They loathe morning exercise and complain that the routine is nothing short of punishment. Mimi says, "We roll out of bed and come down her and exercise in the morning. Not even juice or coffee, it seems like punishment. We can't stand it."

BREAKFAST

Following exercise, the women quickly cross the hallway to the dining room, where they line up to grab a plate of food at the threshold to a nook between the dining room and the kitchen. A monitor makes her final trip out of the kitchen with already plated food—usually cereal or eggs, grits, and bacon—that she places on a table. With a plate in one hand, women grab a chair from one of the stacks against the dining room wall and take a seat. They return to the table in the nook area for a paper cup of milk or watered-down coffee and a cheap child-sized tin utensil. Unless a woman wants to spend the little money she has on an overpriced snack from the vending machine in the dining room after dinner or take a small package of processed cheese and crackers or candy during "snack time" after chores, breakfast is the first opportunity for women to eat following dinner the night before. And with fourteen hours between dinner and breakfast, the women are hungry and consume breakfast quickly.

For women who spent all or most of their time alone in Blackout and ate alone in the dining room, graduation to Zero makes breakfast an entirely new social experience. Even as the meals are taken quickly and often in quiet solitude, the company of others similarly situated can be a welcome break from the darkness of Blackout meals. Some mornings, women talk of everyday life, like their ongoing court cases, a new nail polish, or the letters they received from their children or lovers who are incarcerated. They usually stay away from conversations that remind them of trouble, like the fate of women who have absconded from Blackout or of their own futures, because tomorrow seems so far away.

With breakfast over, women rise from the table to restack the chairs, toss their paper cups in the fifty-gallon outdoor garbage container next to the chairs, and return the dishes and utensils to the plastic table in the nook area. Women never fully enter the nook area unless chores take them inside to hand-wash dishes, utensils, pots, and pans. Laurel pushes up the sleeves to her gray Westville housing projects sweatshirt and moves the pile of plastic plates to the deep stainless steel sink. She collects utensils, fills the sink, and waits for the monitor to drop a blue dishwashing tablet into the steamy water before she begins her chore. The other women scatter either to the living room, their bedrooms for a quick change, the restroom upstairs, or to outside appointments if their phase of stay permits.

SMOKE BREAKS

"It's smoke time. Ladies, it's time to smoke." Alpha Omega House is an environment of tobacco users. How other reentry centers compare is not known, but research indicates that tobacco use is common among correctional populations. One study estimates that 74 percent of inmates smoke (Cropsey, Eldridge, and Ladner, 2004), and another reports a similar proportion of smokers in the female inmate population (Conklin, Lincoln, and Tuthill, 2000).

Cigarette smoking is tightly regulated when the women are in the house, but the practice of smoke breaks is one routine that pleases the women. The breaks occur only after breakfast and dinner. After the intercom announcement, women quickly line up single-file outside the monitors' office, the first in line ringing the monitors' bell. Each woman is handed two cigarettes from her own pack, which is purchased with money from her inmate account and which is kept locked away in the monitors' office. Like a mob, the women move deliberately through the hallway toward the stairs. They sing, "Going up!" sounding like an a cappella group as they reach the stairway and march to the end of the upstairs hallway, stopping before a locked door at the end of the hall. Momentarily, an out-of-breath monitor squeezes between the women to the door, unlocks it, and the crowd spills to a second-floor balcony overlooking the overgrown lot. The balcony looks like something out of a medieval damsel-in-distress story and appears inescapable with its dark rooftop overhang, twisted roots of ivy, and large gray stones draped in moss, high upon the convent wall. With no seating, women lean against the building's facade or balcony ledge, or sit on the floor where they anxiously await a light from the monitor, who spins the metal spark wheel of the lighter for one light, and then another and another. The women take a first long drag of the usual menthol cigarettes, hold their breath, and exhale with sighs of pleasure. The smokes are taken normally in silence, as if the women are escaping in their minds to someplace else. The women smoke quickly and always down to the filters, lighting the second cigarette with the butt of the first.

Women are rarely late for smoke breaks because it is the only regular opportunity for many of them to feel the outside air, an opportunity available only to smokers. Victoria broke down and joined the women for a smoke one time just to get outside, but doing so made her ill and she never returned. Needless to say, the practice of rewarding smokers with time outside of the house and excluding those who do not smoke harms the residents. It encourages tobacco smoking, undermines women's health, and places a financial burden on women with very limited financial means.

Theorizing about smoking from a gendered perspective, some scholars position women's cigarette smoking as a function of patriarchy (Annandale, 2003; Greaves, 2003; Jacobson, 1981). Walsh and colleagues (1995) describe women's smoking behavior as shaped by sex role stereotypes, reproductive division of labor, inequities in that division of labor, and gendered advertising and appearance expectations. Other research shows that smoking is often linked to traumatic experiences, including women's adult and childhood victimization, as well as substance abuse, which is often a coping mechanism for sexual, physical, and emotional victimization.[1] These traumatic experiences are common among women in this study and many others in trouble with the law, lending some support to the argument that cigarette dependence—and the practice of encouraging continued dependence at Alpha Omega House—can be aligned with patriarchal domination.

MORNING MEDITATION

Unless they are out of the house for treatment or another activity, all residents including "Blackout girls" participate in morning meditation. On this occasion, Mimi, Laurel, Rosa, and Billie create a circle in the living room with the plastic chairs Rosa retrieved from the dining room. From the monitors' office, Mimi has checked out a stack of books and morning meditation instructions written on tattered yellow legal paper. Rosa takes the books on her lap and opens each to the page corresponding to today's date. One book is daily inspirations for Overeaters Anonymous (OA), one is daily inspirations published by Alcoholics Anonymous (AA), and another is *Chicken Soup for the Soul,* a collection of inspirational quotes. Mimi holds the yellow pages and begins by reading aloud the instructions for meditation: "March 7. The key is willingness." Rosa shuffles the books to find the OA book and reads a short passage. The other women together mumble, "Thanks for reading." Mimi and Rosa together recite two prayers required during morning meditation. One ostensibly created by Alpha Omega House staff and called the "We Can" prayer reads: "We are too quick to resent and feel what we suffer from others, but we fail to consider how much others suffer from us. Whoever considers *his* own defects fully and honestly will find no reason to judge others harshly" (emphasis added).

Calling to mind a college sorority, the house prayer is accompanied a house pledge designed to support a sisterhood of women in transition. This one is called the Alpha Omega Pledge. It reads: "I am the butterfly built from the cocoon of the Alpha Omega. I symbolize rebirth, renewal, and complete transformation."

Rosa then reads a short passage from a book titled *Courage to Change.* Billie is intent and quiet, concentrating as if she is hoping to glean strength from the words. Rosa speaks slowly, struggling with pronunciation. "Thanks for readin,'" says Billie. Rosa hands the book to Laurel, who takes a turn at the next passage in the book. "Thanks for readin,'" says Billie. Rosa is nodding off, her head drooping to the side.

Billie is upset. She is having a hard time coping with her confinement, saying aloud, "I coulda done my ninety days in jail." She feels tricked by agreeing to serve a year at Alpha Omega House rather then to complete her jail time. Her start has been very hard. She compares her recent Blackout experience, which ended this very day, with the isolation cell in jail called the hole: "The hole was not this bad. I did thirty days in da hole, 'n got a ninety-day hit for a fight that was worth it."

Rosa is now fully asleep in her chair. A monitor enters, wakes Rosa by nudging her shoulders, and issues her a verbal warning and a three-dollar fine for falling asleep. The monitor leaves. Rosa turns to the others, laughing, "Why didn't ya'll warn me she was comin'?" Billie continues to sob and says, "I can't see stayin' through Blackout." Rosa replies, "You can do it; it get easier."

Today is Laurel's "max date," which is the latest date at which the criminal justice system can hold her according to the conditions of her criminal sentence. She says to the others of her impending departure, "I got money on the books, but they keepin' my money from me. They givin' me da pinch on the last day." She feels double-crossed. Leaving with less than two hundred dollars and having to wait for the remainder of the money to be mailed to her by staff, she is concerned about how she will provide for herself with no job and no stable residence. Having observed and overheard Laurel through the security camera poised high on the living-room wall, a monitor returns to the room and reprimands the women: "You supposta be meditatin,' not talkin.'" Mimi turns to Billie, who is new to the process and laughs at the irony of the statement, "Now it's at least five minutes of silence, like we don't do enough of that all day." Disgusted, the women sit in silence. Laurel looks worried and angry. Rosa has again fallen asleep in the chair, but her large body prevents her from sliding to the floor. Mimi nudges Rosa's head upright. Billie is crying.

Morning meditation should be an opportunity for women to prepare emotionally and spiritually for the day and the challenges that await them in real life. Instead, it is nonproductive. Adeline says: "It's the same books. I've been here for not even a month 'n I'm goin' a little nuts that it's the same books. Chicken noodle soup for the soul, AA. What the fuck does Overeaters Anonymous have to do with comin' outa prison 'n gettin' help we need? We gotta say that We Prayer, the Serenity Prayer. We should be sayin' what's on our mind, like give testimony. That would be more productive than readin' the same shit 'n saying the prayers."

MANDATORY CLASS

Amelia announces, "Going down!" as she makes her way to the basement. Violet follows with Adeline. Simone, a woman in her early sixties is the volunteer who provides a mandatory one-hour weekly "class" to residents. She distributes word-search puzzles, fruit, a board game, and photos of the women she snapped the week before. Candy and Laurel each take a puzzle as Rosa and Phoebe set up a board game. Simone opens a book and reads aloud the conclusion of *Anne Frank: The Diary of a Young Girl*. Phoebe and Rosa play Sorry, Candy and Mimi look at the photos, and Henrietta eats a tangerine. Laurel grabs a banana, removes new dentures that fill the once-gaping hole in the front of her mouth, and silently motions a performance of fellatio as she mouths "blow job" to Mimi. Candy has lost interest in the photos, and Laurel stares blankly as she listens to the story of the young woman in her own experience of imprisonment. Raquel enters, sits, and leaves moments later without saying a word. Phoebe and Rosa begin a second game of Sorry. Grace works intently on a crayon self-portrait. Mimi stares at Simone, who continues to read. At four-thirty, the class has ended, and the women return to the living room.

This routine is repeated every week. Simone is steadfast in her commitment to offer the women relief from the drudgery of their days at Alpha Omega House. She offers no treatment in the criminological sense to assist offenders in need, but the women enjoy her presence because it gives them a break in their days that seem to blend into weeks. Still, listening to a woman narrate or working on a puzzle is no proper treatment for the women's major needs. Clair, for example, was sent to Alpha Omega House in the very early stages of her jail stay, so she was still feeling the horrible pull of her crack addiction. She has been out of Blackout for two weeks and desperately needs help from someone who can relate to her. She cries out for a person to talk to, someone other than another suffering new girl, and someone other than a staff member. The monitor's call her to their office and tell her to calm down when she calls out. Today she has just returned from the local hospital, the "psych jawn" as the women say, where she spent three days on suicide watch. Clair says she needs to talk to an addict who knows what it is like to go through withdrawal, not go to a class where she colors pictures.

We sit there and color in puzzle pictures, seriously? What is that? I don't get it. She's not an addict. Miss Tennille is not an addict, Miss Monica not an addict. Half of these monitors are not addicts. You have to be an addict to know what an addict goes through. What will they do if they see me layin' down on the floor in my own puke as dirty green as that rug right there and you can't move. We need help. This place in here is not designed for junkies. We need to be in a facility where we have NA counselors 'n AA, 'n mental health, dual diagnostic, 'cause half of these girls in here are on mental health due to their addictions. So it's like they don't understand when we're like acting out or when we're frustrated. It's because we're not gettin' what we need.

Having advanced to Zero, Candy is itching to get out and rebuild her life. She knows that she needs help with her drug addiction as well as with other issues in her life, but instead she sits idly in the living room day after day, waiting for her opportunity to work in treatment. She says, "Why do I gotta keep waitin'? That shit don't make no sense. They should send my ass right on out." But women on Zero do not leave the house. Their multiple treatment needs remain unaddressed, and they have to glean whatever they can from classes, such as Simone's.

MONEY WEEK

The sound of the intercom breaks the stillness of the living room as women on Zero and beyond are called to the monitors' office one by one. Twice a month, the women are allocated spending money drawn from their personal accounts held by Alpha Omega House. The amount of money a woman receives through "revenue withdraw" depends on her phase of stay. "Blackout girls" get no money. Women on Zero get ten dollars for the month, and C Level, B Level, and A Level residents get fifty, seventy-five, and one hundred dollars respectively.

The money in these accounts comes exclusively from welfare (roughly $205 monthly for each woman) and, for some women, from Supplemental Security Income, which amounts to a bit more; none of the women at Alpha Omega House are earning money from employment. Women on Zero are also set up for benefits commonly known as food stamps. These funds, along with the welfare and SSI checks that are sent directly to the reentry center, are distributed to the women in the form of prepaid credit cards with a PIN number. Even though this organization receives grants and other funding to operate Alpha Omega House, staff retain women's food-stamp allowances and roughly 20 percent of the women's income to help offset their housing costs. What remains goes to women's "allowance"—fines and court costs, and savings. It is customary that participants in community-based correctional programs, including reentry centers, contribute to the cost of their participation. For example, inmates participating in Bureau of Prisons reentry centers pay 25 percent of income generated from fulltime employment to offset the cost of their participation in the reentry centers (Federal Bureau of Prisons, nd). It is also customary in correctional settings that correctional authorities oversee inmate accounts. In prisons, for example, inmates do not handle money but draw credit for commissary and other items from their inmate financial accounts.

A moment after she leaves, Adeline returns to the living room with a broad smile. She stands in the doorway and proudly stretches a five-dollar bill between her two hands before tucking it into her bra. Although Adeline received ten dollars, she owed the house for tampons she purchased as well as fines she incurred while in Blackout and, most recently, for having her shoes out of place in the closet. Smiling, she caresses the bill, turning it over to inspect each side, and says, "It's the first money I've held in my hand since 2009. I got five bucks. It's my allowance for two weeks. Thank God I don't smoke!" Adeline had spent the previous two years in prison, where handling cash is prohibited.

Not long after Adeline held her first allowance, she advanced a phase and began to get twenty-five dollars twice a month. Still, the money was not enough. Since being released from prison, Adeline works hard to reconcile and reconnect with her mother and to stay connected with her daughter, whom her mother has been caring for. She does this chiefly through letters and phone calls, since her mother's work schedule usually prevents her from visiting on the weekend. Adeline says: "Wit dis I have to buy soap powder, all my personals, tokens [for the bus], treats from the machine, 'n phone money. Not to mention fines. If I don't have phone money, I can't talk to my family."

Just as in prison (Hairston, Rollin, and Jo, 2004), the payphone at the house is expensive. A ten-minute call to her mother's cell phone costs Adeline $5. But if she wants to write her daughter and keep in touch with friends, she also has to purchase stamps. When has to travel outside she needs bus fare. She also has to pay staff for fines. With spending money of about $12.50 for the week, she'll be left with less than $8 for the personals if she decides to make the call, and this doesn't even account for the petty $5 fine imposed for not washing the dishes well enough. All of the women complain that their "allowance" is just not enough. Phoebe needs new jeans because she has gained weight, but she also needs paper for writing letters, soap, and bleach for the wash. But the pocket money she gets on C Level is already spent before she feels the cash in her hand. She says:

> If you need something, they won't let you take anything out of your savings to get it. They give you just a little bit of pocket money, and you gotta buy all your personals, cigarettes, clothes, everything wit that pocket money. It's not enough. I get twenty-five dollars every two weeks, cause I'm on level C. I need new jeans 'n shit, but I can't afford that. I got holes in these jeans 'n they're so tight 'n whatnot, but I can't get them, 'cause I have to buy deodorant 'n soap, toothpaste and whatnot, so I'm clean. I just gotta suck it in 'n hope the shit fits.

Everything a woman needs she must purchase for herself unless staff permit her family to bring in clothing and hygiene items. Women can make purchases at a store once a month for items like laundry soap, personals, and other basic items, but that is a reward that can be taken away. Sometimes women need tampons or bathing soap between outings, which are available at the house "commissary," as the women call it, but prices are expensive. The house charges one dollar each for tampons and sanitary napkins; enough laundry soap for one load of wash is another dollar.

The distribution of money in personal accounts held by Alpha Omega House leaves all of the women feeling exploited and confuses some who can't calculate exactly how. For instance, Henrietta loses much of her allowance to fines. She rushes to Rosa with a pencil and piece of paper—a Request to Staff Form—she will use to lodge a complaint. She asks Rosa, "Can you say: 'Why I don't get all my money?'" Rosa completes the form, and Henrietta signs and tells me that she will hand it in to the monitors later. Without knowing how to read or calculate where her allowance money is spent, Henrietta assumes the staff steals from her. Henrietta had handled her own finances before she came to Alpha Omega House and cannot understand why she is prevented from doing so here. Candy was able to manage her money in prison, drawing credit from her inmate account and adding to it from the various jobs she held there. The other women share these frustrations and say they should manage their own money.

Research has shown that offenders, particularly women, often lack financial skills that can get in the way of successful reentry (Koenig, 2007; Wilson and Anderson, 1997), and they would greatly benefit from financial programming that can help them to live independently upon release (O Brien, 2001). As will be discussed, employment is an essential part of the successful reentry experience but entirely absent at Alpha Omega House, where none of the women in this study were employed or earning incomes through employment. Even in the absence of income through employment, women at Alpha Omega House prepare a weekly "financial plan" consisting of a budget for toiletry items and travel expenses (tokens and passes), and they are encouraged to "work out a financial agreement to pay all fines and restitutions." But the women say they should have more responsibility to manage the money in their accounts that is not handed over to the house for room and board. As Candy explains, Alpha Omega House is a perfect place for women coming out of prison to be introduced to managing their own financial lives. She says: "If this is a transition place, why they in control of our money? Why's that? Ok, we got a welfare check. Fine, take money for rent 'n food, but the rest oughta go in my pocket, *my pocket,* not in a fuckin' vault. I've neva been in a place where you don't have no control of your money. All they want is to keep us down." Adeline adds: "We can't hold our money? How is that gonna help me? I lived a life where I worked, a single mother. I paid bills, 'n here I'm gettin' taught that this is how you do it? Now, I'll tell you how I did it. I was well dressed, 'n my freezer was full. Here, they intentionally keep you down. It strips you, it takes what we already had."

The argument Candy and Adeline make is a good one. Women in this transitional period of life should be encouraged to move toward financial independence, but the model in place prevents them from taking on this challenge. Money week should be an opportunity for the center to offer financial skills services for women. Take Rosa, who at this money week is distributed fifty dollars, but she owes twenty-five to the monitor for Avon products she ordered. Ten more dollars are given to Laurel and Henrietta to reimburse them for cash she borrowed to maintain costly cigarette habit. This leaves her fifteen dollars. She'll spend more than six of that for a pack of cigarettes today. For the next two weeks, she'll have less than nine dollars in her pocket. She might even be in the red, "endin up owin' 'em money for da fuckin' fines I'll catch next week." Rosa knew that she would be allotted this fifty dollars and perhaps she should have budgeted better before she spent the money on Avon products. But how she spends money at Alpha Omega House is just a reflection of how she managed money on the outside. She depended then as she does now on a monthly government money card and would spend most of it before she had card in hand. But on the streets she would earn back that cash selling her prescription medication and other drugs as well as merchandise she "boosted" from stores. She wants to manage her money, but she needs to learn how to do it legally and effectively. She and others agree that teaching women good financial decisions, budgeting, and planning should be part of the reentry experience.

DINNERTIME

The intercom sounds, "It's dinner time," and women move quickly for the food. On a table in the kitchen a monitor has poured clear plastic cups of sugary fruit drink next to plastic dinner plates. The plates are small, but heaping with food. As at other meals, women each take a blue plastic chair from the stacks against a wall and sit at one of two eight-foot plastic tables. This evening's dinner consists of fried chicken patties, heaping portions of white rice mixed with corn, and two slices of white bread. Though sitting with "Blackout girls" is frowned upon, Grace takes her place at the end of the table where the girls normally sit, the one pushed up against a wall. Rosa, Laurel, Phoebe, Adeline, Henrietta, and Candy sit at the main table, located in the middle of the room. They are seated as if they were students taking a test, one space between them. Rosa is not interested in her second chicken patty, and Grace notices. She asks, "Ya eatin' dat?" "No, Grace," Rosa says. "You take it." Taking a quick glance to the doorway and chancing that a monitor is not observing remotely from the camera perched above, Rosa forks the patty over to Candy, who takes it with her fingers, spins around and reaches over to Grace, who leans over and grabs it with a paper towel. "For tonigh[t]," she says, smiling as she tucks it into the pocket of her flowery medical scrub shirt, caring little that monitors may have observed her by the security camera. Like every meal, dinnertime is focused on consuming the food. It is not a time to laugh and lounge, to reflect on the day, have discussions, or socialize. Dinner is eaten fast because, the women say, they are hungry. Once they have cleared their plates of food, Laurel and Adeline head into the kitchen for cleanup chores while "Blackout girls" return to their isolation; other residents move across the hall to the living room and wait the call for smoke break.

The last of eleven statements in the house's "client bill of rights" reads: "Clients have to right to nutritious food." Most residents agree healthful meals with fresh vegetables, fruits, and green salads would be a nutritious diet, yet many complain they are denied access to healthy foods. Breakfast usually consists of fried eggs and bacon with white bread and coffee. Lunch can be hot dogs on white buns or soup and grease-filled grilled cheese with Kool-Aid or soda. Dinner is always a heavy carbohydrate-and-fat-filled meal with heaping portions. Meat and at least one slice of white bread are served at every dinner along with a sugary drink. Common dinner combinations include fried or fat-soaked chicken served with canned corn mixed into white rice, ribs and mashed potatoes with canned string beans and bacon, lasagna, or stew over white rice. It is not beyond the realm of the reasonable to say that the women suffer oppression through poor nutrition.

Food at Alpha Omega House is purchased in bulk and normally in frozen form. Residents rarely if ever get fresh fruit. Salads and fresh vegetables are almost unheard of. The diet provided is high in fat, starch, and sugar. Residents want better food. Violet says: "I like fresh vegetables and the only vegetable they give you is corn out of a can. I think we should have salad everyday. I haven't had any fruit since I been here. Why can't I drink milk at dinner? I think we should have a choice of what we want to eat, not what they want to feed us.

Even though each woman hands over upward of two hundred dollars each month for food through her allotment of food stamps, the residents contend that their input about food is not considered. While some people might argue that the women are still in custody and should not determine what they eat, participating in meal planning is not just a privilege. Amelia sees it as an opportunity for women to learn and practice responsibility. In fact, meal preparation is one of the essential elements of therapeutic community treatment, according to De Leon (De Leon, 1997). Amelia says: "We should be doin' the cookin' and plannin' the food. Every week everyone should be able to take the kitchen like a restaurant 'n cook what they want. We could learn 'n teach each other."

One of the more troublesome aspects of the food service involves women with medical conditions requiring special diets who worry their dietary needs are unmet. Henrietta feels the effects of poor nutrition. She says tearfully: "The food is nasty 'n right now I'm diabetic. They not even givin' me my food. I don't get no diabetic food here. They get my food stamps, no diabetic food at all. I had chocolate puddin' for two weeks. Yesterday I said, Please, can I have somethin' else? I don't have no choice 'cause I be hungry. And my health comes before anything. I be havin' headaches cause my sugar be up."

In addition to exacerbating medical problems, the sugary beverages and fat-soaked high carbohydrate and high-salt content food causes women to gain weight. With limited leisure or enjoyable exercise, women's bodies undergo obvious and rapid transformations at the house. Mimi says half jokingly that staff intentionally make women "fat" and unattractive. She says, "I grew from a size 5 to a 10. They got me fat 'n I can't do nuthin' about it. I'm bustin outa these clothes. I ain't got no clothes that fit. And then they fine me for showin' cleavage. What am I gonna do, not eat?"

According to convincing arguments by Freeman (2007), poor nutrition encouraged and supported by governmental and other institutions is structural oppression and profoundly affects traditionally subordinated groups. Arguing that food oppression is also racial and class oppression, Freeman describes how limited public-assistance money for fresh foods, race-based marketing, and the proliferation of fast food in poor urban areas, including schools, harms minorities. Further supporting the argument, Freeman connects health problems like diabetes, obesity, and heart disease with types of foods and how food is prepared (particularly deep-fried foods, starchy foods, and sugary drinks). Taking a similar approach, Eisenhauer (2001) describes how social forces exacerbate the problem of poor nutrition and corresponding declining health among minorities and cautions against looking at the problems from a behavioral perspective. The same arguments can be made here. Taking personal choice out of consideration, when an organization limits access to healthful foods for women, it participates in their oppression and domination.

LADIES, IT'S CHORE TIME

The hour-long chore time begins every weekday evening at seven o'clock. Now out of Blackout, women on Zero no longer clean the bathroom toilets or scrub the tubs—that is unless they are assigned those chores for punishments. With chores assigned by phase of stay, women on Zero may mop floors, scrub the kitchen stove, and clean the dishes, pots, and pans after each meal. Women nearing release have chores that take them out of earshot of the staff for the more desirable light duty work.

With the intercom call "Ladies, its chore time," women scatter from their usual positions in the living room and form a line at the janitorial closet. Some women are handed buckets with detergent and sponges or mops. Others are given rags and window cleaner or dusting spray. Rosa takes her spray bottle of disinfectant and paper towels. She sways over to the adjacent room and hits the power button on an old boom-box radio in the staff salon outside of Blackout. At maximum volume, Kanye West sings out, and Rosa moves her large body from side to side, spitting out the refrain of curses as she wipes the detergent off the fake leather sofa: "The night is young, what da fuck you wanna do, huh. The night is young, what da fuck we gon' do, huh." Her stomach falls out of her tight cotton shorts and two-sizes-too-small purple tank top when she takes an extra swipe around what looks like a foot-long knife slit in the seat that shows the yellow stuffing inside. Still swaying from side to side and bobbing her head front to back, she whispers the rap tune as she tickles a framed inspirational photo with a feather duster: "We in da time of our lives, baby." The intercom sounds: "Rosa, report to the monitors' office." She shakes her head and mumbles an expletive as she tosses the duster on the sofa and walks the hall answering the monitor's call. She returns and lowers the volume of the radio. Rosa was not fined for playing music, but was instructed to lower it. Only during chore time when the administrative staff is gone for the day could Rosa, or any other woman, ever get away with more than momentarily dancing, singing, or playing music outside of her bedroom.

Chore time takes women away from the sameness of their confinement, and they often use this time to try to lighten the mood. Grace is vacuuming the living room diligently as she softly serenades herself with a love song. She dances forward and back with her vacuum as a dance partner. Once she completes the vacuuming there, she will sweep the dining room and then polish it with Mop and Glo. She likes a shiny floor, but the women will tramp past her to the water cooler before the wax has a chance to dry, leaving a path of flip-flop prints. At the front foyer, Henrietta is wiping the table where the resident and visitor sign-in binders sit and will sweep the floor before she descends the stairs to sweep the hallway outside of administrative staff offices. Sometimes she sneaks into the phone booth area out of camera sight to sneak a whispered phone call to Jo-Jo, her "boo," when she is sweeping that area. On this night, Mimi has an easy chore because she is farther along in her stay; she cleans the laundry room in the basement where the women wash and dry their clothing. Laurel is about to graduate, so she cleans the conference room in the basement, washing down the tables with Pin-Sol before she vacuums the thin carpet there. She sets a worn-out AM/FM radio to the hip-hop station she wants—an added bonus of seniority.

On the main level of the house, Amelia is singing "wipe on and wipe off," exaggerating a circular wiping motion as she cleans the plastic on the picture frames along the main cinderblock hallway. Adeline's chore is to clean the stainless-steel industrial stoves and ovens, the refrigerators, freezers, countertops, and sinks. She also must sweep the floor and then mop with bleach. Adeline sneaks an ice cream bar she finds in the staff freezer, saying: "They used my fuckin' food stamps to buy shit for themselves. I'm takin' it." At that moment, Violet dances into the kitchen with her mop and her bucket of bleach and water, singing into the mop handle as if it were a microphone. With her mop in hand and the ice cream bar in her mouth, Adeline dances around Violet to the off-limits refrigerator, opens it up and grabs a handful of individual-sized coffee creamers. The pair momentarily interlock their arms and then toss back their heads as they "do shots" of creamers before dancing back to complete their chores.

Except for the "Blackout girls" confined to the bathroom for their chores, a similar scene of confined woman dancing through chores is repeated on the upper level of the house, where bedrooms are located. Phoebe sweeps the hallway outside of the bathroom with a large stiff broom to the beat of pop music coming from her bedroom radio. Candy dances past her and descends the stairway. Candy is assigned "man chores" as she moves from station to station, collecting trash from the other women's chores. Once she collects the trash in a large black trash bag, she walks to a dumpster outside and quickly returns under the watchful eye of a monitor.

Yet even as chore time gives the women at Alpha Omega House an hour a day of comparative freedom, the daily ritual subordinates them by reproducing a domesticity that subjugates women generally. The subject of domestic labor and women's corresponding subordination and domination is widely discussed in the literature.[2] In institutional settings, chore assignments in physical environments that resemble homes create an oppressive condition for women. For example, in her ethnographic study of homeless women, Harman (1989, p. 106) reports that "hostels replace traditional female roles by being modeled after homes and requiring women to do daily housekeeping chores. . . . In other words, they teach, foster, and reward domesticity."

As Hartmann (1976) points out in a discussion of patriarchy and division of labor, job segregation by sex evident throughout society originated with familial patriarchy and men's control over the labor of women and children. The purpose of job segregation and accompanying low wages for women's work, Hartmann contends, is to keep women dependent on men. When women marry men because of their dependency, their work in the household becomes domestic work and their absence from the labor market both weakens women's position in the labor market and strengthens patriarchy. Furthermore, by restricting women to domestic work and chore assignments, women do not learn skills that can benefit them in the labor market (Dobash, Dobash, and Gutteridge, 1986). The problems of domestic labor go even deeper when one considers historical race and class hierarchies (Anderson, 2000; Nakano Glenn, 1985). The fact that minority women were and still are employed as servants, laundresses, and cooks to perform low-level and onerous household work for white middle-class women perfectly illustrates how confining one group of people to menial labor frees up another group to supervise and to take on the more desired tasks.[3] Over time, the domestic division of labor among women would transfer to the paid labor market, fostering and maintaining an oppressive division of labor in larger society.[4]

The same dynamic is at work at Alpha Omega House where chore assignments determined by phase of stay reproduce sexist—and classist—divisions of labor. "Blackout girls" are forced to do the least appealing chores and those farther along in their stay, those closer to freedom, who arguably occupy a higher status within the house, are tasked with the least arduous chores.

Sexist stereotypes are also on display in the type of domestic work assigned to highly masculine women (see also Kennedy and Davis, 1993). Women appearing stronger and more masculine are often tasked with chores that involve lifting and require more strength; smaller and gentle-looking women work the lightest, most feminized chores. Candy complains that she gets the "manly chores." She says: "Dey got me workin' 'n shit 'cause I'm like a man." Since the very day she entered, Candy collects the trash from every garbage on each of the three levels of the house, including the fifty-gallon bag in the kitchen, and makes three trips out the rear of the building, down the steps, across the lawn, and past a parking lot where she heaves the trash above her head into a large dumpster. While the chore assignments change with phase of stay for other women, hers has remained the same. Candy is also routinely called upon outside of the designated chore time to change light bulbs, install window air conditioners, move furniture, and deliver groceries. She is not, however, the only woman assigned "man" work. Some women never use the feather duster or wipe picture frames, and others never take out the garbage. Just as chore assignments correspond to phase of stay, chores also correspond to a woman's physical strength and her perceived femininity. Except when Candy is sent outside to shovel the snow, cut the grass, gather the never-ending piles of litter, or sweep the stoop, women are not engaged in tasks that take them outside the house. Instead, they are kept inside and engaged in traditionally female domestic chores; they clean as maids would clean.

The women clean the building because they live in it, theoretically a practice in line with helping women prepare for responsibilities outside prison, but restricting them to this form of work, which is further segregated along stereotypical gender roles, perpetuates patriarchal forms of subjugation insofar as the women are reminded in a state-sanctioned institution of their proper roles in the domestic division of labor. All of the residents could share in some of the work done by Candy. Grace wants to do more skilled work, she says, to repair holes in walls or change light bulbs like she enjoyed doing when she was not incarcerated. And she and the others could climb a ladder and change batteries in fire alarms, mow the lawn, tighten the wiggly table legs, repair any number of damaged window screens, repaint bedroom walls, lay tile in place of the peeling linoleum floors, and any number of tasks that would not only improve living conditions and perhaps their self-esteem, but level out the division of labor present in this especially unequal domestic situation.[5]

LOCKDOWN

Like many women in the criminal justice system, residents of Alpha Omega House have significant medical and mental-health needs. According to research, rates of mental and physical illness are higher among women than men in the criminal justice system. According to one government report, the rates of mental illness in local jails are 75 percent among females and 63 percent among males, rates in state prison are 73 percent among females and 55 percent among males, and rates in federal prisons are 75 percent among females and 63 percent among males (James and Glaze, 2006). According to a report of prisoners returning from incarceration, women nearing release reported higher medical and mental-health conditions (77 percent) then did male prisoners (54 percent). In prisons, according to a Bureau of Justice Statistics report, more female prisoners (57 percent) reported having a medical problem than did males (43 percent) and a greater number of medical problems; 28 percent of female prisoners and 17 percent of male prisoners reported having two or more medical problems (Maruschak, 2008).

At Alpha Omega House, women's medical and mental-health needs are addressed partly through medication distributed in the mornings, sometimes the afternoons, and during a period women refer to as "lockdown." During this time the house is "in" or "closed," and residents are required to remain in their bedrooms unless they absolutely must use the restroom. This time is a good opportunity for women to meet privately, even for the briefest amount of time. Billie and Freya, who do not room together, have quick sex together in the shower stall. Candy sometimes meets with Mimi to discuss house developments that involve the women, like which of the new monitors seem to be willing to "look the otha way" or who might be carrying contraband. Others meet just for company and companionship, like Adeline and Laurel, who this evening are using hair remover to shape their eyebrows before the small cloudy bathroom mirror.

"Raquel, report to the monitors' office" sounds over the intercom. "Raquel gets her crazy meds," says Adeline shaking her head. After having recently moved to Zero and upstairs from Blackout, Adeline is housed with Raquel. Raquel seems the least physically threatening, but Adeline worries about her own safety, especially when she sleeps. She says:

> Raquel's drivin' me crazy. She don't stop talkin.' She talks to herself, she talks to the radio, lookin' at the radio real close 'n talkin' to the radio, to the books. I can't get no peace. She says that she is gettin' messages from the vendin' machine 'n the radio. She is paranoid schizophrenic 'n refuses to take her medication. [Adeline thinks Raquel hides her medications in her mouth then discards them when she is away from monitors.] So now I gotta live with her. I don't know if she's gonna snap one day, going through her moods and just start snappin.' People like that need to be housed by themselves like they do in jail.

The constant worry that Raquel will have an aggressive psychiatric episode creates tension and anxiety for Adeline, who gets little rest and looks for every opportunity to get out of her room. There is no other bedroom available. Two of the rooms along the hall are not being used; one is filled with cots, and another is more of a mess than any other of the rooms. She could room with Candy, but staff would never have that—Candy believes because they fear her homosexuality. Says Candy: "Dey don't room me with nobody 'cause they afraid I'll try 'n fuck her."

"Adeline, report to the monitors' office," sounds the intercom, and Adeline skips off, singing "time for skittles." Five minutes later Victoria is called. Victoria sighs as she slowly pulls herself from her bed and places her notebooks to her side. She makes her way down the hallway to the stairs, turning to peek inside bedrooms as she passes. Violet and Amelia are in their shared room listening to music while Amelia braids Violet's hair. Grace is standing outside Billie's door talking to her, which is a violation and gets the attention of a monitor one floor below. The intercom reprimands her: "No minglin.'" Grace walks to the bathroom while Billie pauses and then follows. The pair continue their talk in the bathroom. Leaving the bathroom, Laurel passes them in the hallway. She sneaks a peek into Rosa's room, where she finds Rosa playing solitaire. "Beat dat nigga!" Laurel shouts as she shuffles in her socked flip-flops back to her room and awaits her call downstairs.

"Grace, report to the monitors' office" is quickly followed by "Clair, report to the monitors' office." A daily ritual of medication is part of her life too. In addition to the pills for her Crohn's disease, Clair takes a host of medications. She says: "They got me on 750 milligrams of Depakote. It controls my moods, my mood swings. That keeps me at a good enough basis to where the racing thoughts aren't so strong. It's like a substitute for zannies [a tranquilizer similar to Xanax]. So on the street I would take *zannies*. I'm also on 600 mg of Seroquel, 500 mg of Trazodone."

Further down the hall from Clair's room, Mimi and Phoebe are writing letters and listening to music in their bedroom. Phoebe is composing a note to a new boyfriend who is incarcerated. She is summoned for medications next. Like most of the women here, Phoebe has a dual diagnosis. She is bipolar and lives with both depression and a drug addiction. She says:

> I got in an addiction to coke when I was seventeen 'n then the Percocettes 'n zannies and whatnot. I started heroin when I was twenty-one, snortin' 'n then shootin' a couple years later. So up until I got here, for heroin I was doin' like fourteen to like twenty bags a day 'n like five or six twenty-dollar bags of cocaine a day. And I'm a binge drinker. I'd just chug 'n chug vodka with it. I'm always depressed all the time. . . . I come from a split family 'n

whatnot . . . my father sells weed out of the house, and my mother is a drug addict. She finally got arrested 'n was in prison for three years. . . . my step-brother 'n sister tried to kill my mother on Christmas . . . I love my mom even though she abused me as a child. She has mental problems just as bad as I have mental problems and whatnot.

Phoebe gets up to leave for her medication. As she swings out of her room to the hall and toward the stairway, she sings a refrain from the Tupak Shakur remake of the song "Ooh Child": "Ooh child, things are gonna get easier. Ooh child, things 'll get brighter."

Taking a break from trying to read the Bible, Henrietta steps outside her doorway. Before she can say a word to Rosa, who is now straddling her own doorway looking to Henrietta's room, a monitor's voice rings out over the intercom: "No mixing." Another monitor quickly appears in the hallway and walks toward Henrietta, who pleads, "Don't give me no write-up." In room 7, Grace is one room down the hall from Henrietta. She stands at the threshold of her room with a drawing she's been working on and shows it to Billie across the hall in room 6.

After all of the other women, Candy is called for her nighttime medications. She pops out of her room where she was listening to heavy metal music and takes the stairs three steps at a time, yelling, "Comin' down!" as she hits the hallway floor below. She stomps quickly to the end of the hallway and rings the bell that is positioned on the wall to alert the monitor that a resident is present. "Come!" calls out a monitor. Around the corner in the monitors' office, Candy takes three pills and a tiny paper cup of water. She throws back the pills into her throat, follows with the water, and opens her mouth wide for the monitor to see that she has swallowed. Medication time is completed. Lockdown is over. The house is again "open."

MEDICAL TREATMENT

On one particularly hot summer day, Rosa explodes into an angry rage. Storming into the living room, shaking, she rants: "Dis place fucked up, dey need to shut dis fuckin' bitch down. Dis is fucked up . . . dey ramshacked my room, dey fuckin' stripped searched me. Is this even fuckin' legal? I didn't do nuthin,' I hate dis fuckin' place. I'ma roll some bitch. I'ma kill a muthafucka!"

Rosa screams the last sentence. She paces and mumbles, then sits and begins to massage her legs from thigh to knee as if to calm herself. In a moment, the intercom sounds: "Rosa, come to the monitors' office." Rosa curses through the second and third summons and is finally led away by a monitor. Rosa is angry at having been strip-searched in the basement. She had to undress to underwear and bra, as did some of the other women. It had something to do with the suspicion that a woman brought drugs into the house. Within minutes, Rosa returns to the living room visibly calmed. "Dey gave me some meds to calm me down," she explains. Sitting next to Phoebe on a sofa, she laughs. "I got borderline personality disorder with paranoia, bipolar disorder, 'n PTSD. Some other shit dey saying too. Sometimes I hear voices, 'n what's really fucked is that sometimes it's like I see it, like visual. I'ma kill some bitch one day," Rosa says. She bites her nails, returns to massaging her legs, and rocks herself as she does often when she is distressed. Breathing in and out deliberately, she closes her eyes and puts two hands out in front of her as if she is turning up the volume of an imagined radio suspended up high before her. At the edge of the sofa, her giant naked brown legs bend around themselves as she slowly glides back and forth to the sound of the music in her head.

In every situation similar to this one that I witnessed, the response by monitors was immediate, and results were often very much the same. At Alpha Omega House, as elsewhere, women are routinely medicated when they outwardly express anger and frustration. Shaylor (1998), too, notes that female prisoners who act out are all too often medicated as a form of social control.

Interestingly, a different pattern emerges when physical health is at issue. Mimi sits alone in the living room before sounds booming from the television. She leans to her side against the arm of the sofa to get as close to prone position as possible without violating the "no feet up, no lying rule." Mimi is recovering from a surgery just days before to remove hemorrhoids. She wants to be upstairs in bed, but despite her recent hospitalization is not exempt from the morning rule requiring all women who are inside the house to remain in the living room. She is having an especially hard time today. With a fever and severe pain, she worries about infection and is concerned about the quality of medical care she is receiving. She says:

> Remember, the people who work here, they were where we were, comin' out of jail most of 'em. And they're not really trained but giving us our meds at night, that's something serious. If you mess something up you can kill somebody. Just like Miss Wendy won't give me my Motrin for my fever to go down because I'm on pain meds. If I woulda known that, gimme the

Motrin and fuck the pain medication. I would rather deal with the pain, but the fever it starts to make you crazy; I'm dyin.' I'd rather get rid of the fever than the pain.

Like other women, Mimi is not permitted to possess medication. Instead, her over-the-counter and prescription medication are held in the monitors' office and dispensed only by the monitors without medical training. Moreover, residents at the house cannot arrange themselves to see physicians. The women must submit a ticket to speak to staff in the administrative offices and then wait for the administrative staff to arrange the medical appointment on the their behalf. This protocol is similar to what Acoca (1998, p. 62) refers to as a "sick call" system used in prisons, where all women regardless of the emergent nature of their medical issues must first seek approval to seek treatment from custodial staff that have no medical training. By the time Mimi is trying to make herself comfortable on the couch she has been waiting for three hours after submitting a ticket to speak to staff and contact her doctor about the medication. It will be three more days until she is seen by the administration in the offices below, and by then her condition will have deteriorated to the extent that she is transferred to the local emergency room. Complications of her surgery cause a high fever and serious infection requiring hospitalization.

There are other examples of inadequate medical care. Henrietta has Lupus, but is not sure what that means, so she asks: "I drinks 'n I got mental problems, but what is Loops? They wanna send me to the gyna-con-ogist for test-is. They say I got Loops. They say it's like ammonia." She was also recently diagnosed with diabetes, "sugar diabetes" as she calls it, but is given the same foods and sugary snacks as the other women. With a hospital band still on her arm from a visit to the emergency room the night before, Henrietta is upset that the actions of monitors put her in great harm: "I was at da hospital all night. I kept askin' for my medications. Where's my sugar diabetes medications? But dey never filled my prescription. Dey given me da wrong foods. I get scared. Dey finally call a cab 'n take me to da hospital 'cause I was almost in a diabetic coma."

Victoria also has medical needs requiring close monitoring. She has Sarcoidosis, an immune disorder, as well as high blood pressure and asthma. Like Henrietta, she is concerned about the distribution of medications and the staff's failure to meet her ongoing medical needs: "I have asthma, the sarcoids, I have high blood pressure, I have carpel tunnel, 'n I have acid reflux. I got lung disease. And these monitors try ta tell people what I should 'n should not take. These are prescriptions. That I don't like. They not no doctors. They need a nurse on these premises at all times. Somebody get hurt bad up in here, what are they gonna go? Nothing, nothing."

Victoria's worry that monitors will not be able to handle more emergent medical issues is sensible. Two weeks later at bedtime, Billie is having an asthmatic seizure as she climbs the stairway to her bedroom. Her body collapses on the steps. She is convulsing and drooling from her mouth as she stares ahead, the whites of her eyes showing. Her forehead is bleeding from the fall. Her body becomes cold and still. Grace rushes to comfort her, whispering her street name: "It okay, Marie." "Somebody get a monitor! Call 9-1-1!" shouts Freya. Twenty minutes later, the siren of an ambulance sounds near and then fades into the distance. Candy laughs: "Dey fuckin lost!" Momentarily the sound returns and quickly vanishes. One monitor is on the telephone informing administrative staff who have left for the night, and the other sits with Billie with her hand on Billie's back. "The ambulance must be lost," Mimi says. "Somebody go outside." The residents cannot leave the building and the monitors are otherwise engaged. I run outside into the dark winter night and flag the ambulance in the cobblestone street. Paramedics enter and then take Billie away, with Mimi as escort. The pair returns by taxi in the early morning hours.

The scene that unfolded that night on the stairway is often repeated in different ways. On another occasion, Freya had a medical emergency—severe anxiety, because she thought her medications were "mixed up." In a more serious case, Phoebe was rushed to the hospital after passing out and turning blue during a Narcotics Anonymous meeting in the living room. Another incident sent Adeline to the emergency room after her third seizure in one day—the consequence of a brain injury that was the result of repeated beatings to her head at the hands of her last boyfriend. She worries that monitors will not know how to help her the next time. Rosa fell on a front step of the house and broke her foot. Clair suffered for days without medications for her Crohn's disease when she started Blackout and was hospitalized for a short time as a result. In each of these occasions, the women experienced what they say is less-than-adequate medical care and potentially dangerous delays getting the right medical treatment.

These anecdotes raise two interrelated concerns. Women at Alpha Omega House, like many inmates in correctional institutions, are denied the ability to manage minor medical issues for themselves, in a pattern of disempowerment that Acoca (1998) calls the denial of self-care. Close to home, the residents are in a key transitional period of their criminal justice sentence, and many will continue to face the same medical issues when they graduate the program. Transferring the responsibility to medically care for minor needs, as would the average person, would assist them in their return to normal life.

Compounding this issue is a correctional environment that historically and legally permits lower standards of medical care for correctional populations (Vaughn and Carroll, 1998). Medical treatment in prisons is said to represent "penal harm medicine" when medical personnel in correctional settings adopt a punitive correctional ideology (Vaughn and Smith, 1999), and penal harm medicine for women has been well documented in the literature. Increasing the damage of punitive medical treatment is the fact that many women in trouble with the law are in poor health to begin with (Messina and Grella, 2006; Watson, Stimpson, and Hostick, 2004). Nonetheless, women's medical conditions are often undertreated or untreated in correctional environments (Wilper et al., 2009), and women inmates experience barriers to access of medical services including preventive and emergent care (Law, 2009), as well as unnecessary delays getting treatment, negligence in care, and overall inferior health care.[6] For example, a re-entry study reports that 60 percent of women leave prisons with chronic physical health problems and most never received treatment while in prison (Mallik-Kane and Visher, 2008).

While I do not contend that the medical care provided at Alpha Omega House is deliberately harmful, it appears to be subpar. Limiting women's ability to care for themselves medically and placing the burden of medical screening and emergent medical care on monitors whose job responsibility is foremost the supervision of residents is a matter of negligence that does harm women. In addition, unnecessary delays in providing simple medical treatment and access to specialized care, which adds anxiety to residents' already heavy emotional burden, further complicates women's medical health.

OPEN HOUSE

It is 9:15 p.m. and the "house is open," which means the women may return to the living room and the ever-present television. Some women almost always remain in their rooms, like Raquel and Freya. An open house also means that the women may use one of the three basement payphones. As usual, Grace, Phoebe, and Candy move quickly to the basement stairway, shouting, "Going down!" as they reach the steps. Laurel missed her chance by just a minute and waits. Candy calls her wife's family as a third-party way to communicate with her imprisoned wife. Phoebe phones her drug dealer, who is also sometimes her boyfriend. Grace calls her "huban," who is not actually her spouse but a man she met through her unpaid work internship. She says, "We pray getha, ree Bibe [read Bible], eh nigh." "Time is up, Grace," calls out the monitor over the intercom. Grace climbs the stairs and returns to the living room, passing a smiling Laurel, who takes her place at the payphone. Laurel calls her youngest son's father with whom she has a strained relationship, but whom she hopes will give her a room when she is released. She can be heard crying and pleading to him: "It be for a fuckin' little bit, nigga." Henrietta is last to the phone. Tonight she calls her wife, Jo-Jo. Worried that Jo-Jo is cheating on her, Henrietta can be heard whispering, "I love ya, please don't get no otha pussy." Monitors carefully regulate the fifteen-minute calls women are permitted during this time. Henrietta's time is up, and the intercom sounds: "Henrietta, report to the living room."

WEEKENDS

The house is quietest on weekends, when administrative staff and the regular weekday monitors do not work. This means women enjoy fewer write-ups and confrontations. Some women are even permitted to leave the house unsupervised. Depending on her phase of stay, a woman might be permitted what is called a "day pass" to attend an NA or AA meeting or a "home pass," which is permission to visit family for several hours and intended for residents to secure housing. Once a month the women are escorted by van to shop at a local store or to attend a movie. Upon return, they are met with a search and sometimes a drug test. Mimi was given a day pass to attend a Narcotics Anonymous meeting and took full advantage of her time outside. She skipped the meeting and sat on a park bench in the sun for three hours. When she returned, she says, the monitor on duty "didn't like the way I talked to her." Consequently, Mimi was tested for drugs by a urine screen. It "came back dirty," meaning it showed traces of drugs. But a retest the following day by Mimi's probation officer was "clean," indicating the first test might have been a false positive. Even so, Mimi will have to "give a urine" for the next couple of days to satisfy staff that she is complying with rules against alcohol and drug use. The inconvenience, Mimi says, is well worth the freedom of the day pass.

Another special privilege on weekends is a bedtime curfew later than eleven o'clock for women out of Blackout. Saturday nights, women may watch movies until one o'clock. Both the original and the recent remake of *Texas Chainsaw Massacre* are playing on this Saturday night. Most of the crowd has gathered in the living room. Rosa and Henrietta sit together on a sofa and prepare to play

Sorry. Billie takes a seat and holds a throw pillow close to her chest. Phoebe, Mimi, and Adeline squeeze into the small settee between the two doors to the hallway. Raquel is there, dressed all in black as usual, but she eerily roams in and out. Candy is lying on the filthy carpet, holding up her head with her arms as if she is about to start a sit-up. Grace, Freya, and the others have decided to pass on the first showing and spend time upstairs in their rooms. Amelia is braiding Violet's hair in their shared room, while Freya writes in her journal.

As the movie starts, the women fantasize about eating ice cream and the flavors they would select if they could. This conversation leads them to consider what to purchase from the vending machine, which is now open. But since money week is not for another three days, most of the women have no change to spend. Rosa presents a dollar from the band in her shorts, and Adeline pulls a quarter from inside her bra. They select Pop-Tarts and a Snickers bar, which they share with the others, all standing in the dining room because food is off-limits in the living room. The conversation shifts from "bein' broke" to "dat moon outside we can't get ta see." Tonight is the night of the "supermoon," a rare occurrence when the moon is closest to the earth and appears as a large orb lighting the night sky. The event will not recur for another twenty years, but the women can only get a blurred glimpse of it through the cloudy living-room windows because they cannot step outside, not even for a moment.

Movie time in Alpha Omega House is nothing like the quiet stillness one might envision of the living room in an abbey. Rather, it is more like a crowed urban theater with rowdy patrons talking, laughing, and cursing as the film shows loudly before them. The odd thing is that it is also very bright—the three four-foot-long overhead florescent lights may never be turned off. Two hours pass from the start of the first movie, and the monitor appears at the entrance to the living room, lips moving as she silently counts the women. Headcounts like this take place throughout the day and night. Before a quick intermission and bath-room break, the second movie begins, and so does a game of dominoes between Henrietta and Billie. Then Rosa and Henrietta clandestinely sneak in a rummy game, using the faces of the domino tiles in place of playing cards because rummy is banned as a form of gambling. The women lounge in their usual attire, sweat pants, T-shirts, and flip-flops, though Rosa dons her usual tight cotton shorts and skinny tank top. They get as close to lounging as they possibly can without actually lifting their feet from the floor because no one wants to give up the little money she has for a fine. As the last of the characters are stalked and murdered by a crazed lunatic, the second film ends just before the 1 a.m. curfew. The women

slowly make their way upstairs to their bedrooms, calling out "Up!" and "Goin'
up!" one by one.

Weekends are not complete without conflict. The argument tonight is between Candy and Billie. It starts when Candy, lying on the dingy carpeted floor,
reaches up and grabs a pillow that lies next to Billie, who is sitting on the sofa.
Billie had her own pillow, yet objects to Candy taking another. Mumbling ob-
scenities, the pair skirmishes back and forth. Rosa and Henrietta are sitting closest to them but ignore them and continue to play their game. Adeline turns from
the television and shakes her head. Having overheard the shouting, the monitor
calls out over the intercom, "Candy, report to the monitors' office," and soon,
"Billie, report to the monitors' office." Moments later, the pair returns with no
trace of conflict between them; the argument is over. A more serious conflict
involved Freya and Adeline the weekend before. Freya had had her feet up on the
couch, which is a rule infraction. "Being a new girl, just out of Blackout, maybe
she didn't know," Adeline had thought and told Freya, "We're not supposta put
our feet up." Freya turned and said, "Fuck you, bitch, don't fucking tell me what
to do," and turned back at the television. Adeline popped to her feet in front of
Freya. Bitch is a very serious insult at the house, and Adeline yelled, "We don't say
that here." Before Freya could reach her feet, Candy quickly intervened, pushing
Adeline back and telling Freya, "Ya'll, she was just tellin' ya something." The
monitor appeared in the living room asking, "Is there a problem? Do I need ta
shut this house down?" Adeline and Candy returned to their seats, and Freya
went to her room. The quarrel is over, but any potential for a positive connection
between Adeline and Freya is entirely erased.

WEEKEND VISITS

"Ding-dong . . . pop." On any other day, this sound can only mean a resident is
back from an appointment, a volunteer has come to run a class, or a staff member
has arrived for her shift. But today, the sound could also signal the arrival of a
family guest. Once cleared by administrative staff, family approved for visits are
permitted to enter throughout the day without appointment. Women who have
advanced past Blackout are now eligible for visits.

"Henrietta, report to the monitors' office." Henrietta is out of her usual sweat
pants and stained, overly large white T-shirt or her dark blue medical scrubs;
today she is dressed in a feminine top and black slacks. Her hair is not a purple
mess like it had been the day before; her newly dyed black hair is a tight cornrow
braid, and she is wearing makeup. Her nails are colored in different shades of

blue. Henrietta pops up, smiling, and heads out to meet her guests. She greets her daughter and "grandbaby" with a nod and then walks them into the dining room where they briefly embrace. Henrietta takes three blue plastic chairs and sets up a game of Sorry that she retrieves from the living room closet. Her grandbaby asks for a snack, pointing to the vending machine, but Henrietta has to say no to him even though she wants to give him the crackers he asks for. It is still too early in the day to use the vending machine, and she cannot risk getting another fine because she already owes Rosa three dollars. Henrietta and her family visit for less than an hour, talking quietly and drinking water from plastic cups as they play the game under the watchful eye of the security camera. Henrietta only partly observes a cardinal rule: no physical contact during visiting hours. Then it is over; Henrietta walks her family to the end of the hall, stopping to ring the bell next to the monitors' office. The monitor appears, signs the guests out, and sends them on their way. Henrietta's smile turns flat as she walks toward the living room.

Saturday and Sunday afternoons from one to five o'clock are open for family visits that, sadly, the women rarely receive. Laurel talks about her family, including her mother and her sister who do not support her and who never visit, as well as about her ten children, who have never visited her either. Mostly, she accepts the blame for her broken relationships with her children and her touchy connection with her mother and sister. Still, she hopes for reconnection. She says: "Family is everything. It's so important. It's fuckin' lonely in here. You're in different worlds. You need letters, you need visits just to cope. You need them to pick up da phone 'n say, 'I love you, it's gonna be ok.' . . . You get dressed, ya wait for people to come, dey don't show, you're devastated. Wash your hair 'n then you wait for da bell to ring. And every time da bell rings, ya look 'n its not your person, it hurts. It makes ya depressed."

Just as most women never get visits at Alpha Omega House, women who are incarcerated infrequently see family or friends. In fact, a national survey of prisoners indicates that more than half of female prisoners never see friends or family, including their own children (Hairston, Rollin, and Jo, 2004). One Bureau of Justice Statistics report shows that 54 percent of mothers in prison never had visits by children (Mumola, 2000), and research by Celinska and Siegel (2010) reports that 41 percent of mothers in prison and 75 percent of jailed mothers received no visits from their children while incarcerated. As is often the case with women who are incarcerated, visitation by family and friends for women at Alpha Omega House is often hampered by transportation difficulties, restrictive rules, and the punitive nature of the correctional environment, as well as by reluctance, particularly on the part of child caregivers, to expose children to the correctional environment (Block and Potthast, 1998; Celinska and Siegel, 2010; Siegel, 2011). But the causes of the estrangements are often more personal. Citing their own choices, particularly their substance abuse and destructive behavior patterns, women at Alpha Omega House frame lack of visits as a consequence of distance in their personal relationships with parents, siblings, and their own children that occurred before their incarceration. Phoebe's troubled family doesn't visit. Candy has no family to come; her father and mother are deceased, her brothers have been murdered or are serving lengthy prison terms, and her wife is in prison. Billie has no one but her husband, who has never visited. Freya is estranged from her son, having relinquished parental caregiving may years before. Violet's family does not come, she says, because her drug use has created so much tension and distance there. Amelia has a young baby being cared for by his grandmother and Amelia's sisters, but none of them visit. Keira's daughter is an active drug user lost in drugs on the streets. Clair's husband does not visit, but she is able to maintain some connection to her children through supervised visits. Mimi's daughter (who will later become a resident of this reentry center) is in jail. Henrietta is the only resident visited by family more than a handful of times.

DISCONNECTED RELATIONSHIPS

Laurel is slouched on the sofa and dressed in the usual two-sizes-too-large men's white T-shirt and sweatpants with white tube socks and flip-flops. Her prison-issued rosary dangles over the lined paper in her hands as she writes one of her younger sons a letter. Max is newly incarcerated for drug and gun charges. She looks over to me and says as she reads her writing: "I tellin' him you ain't no boy no more, you doin' man things sellin' drugs 'n guns 'n bullets, 'n now ya gotta dig in deep 'n take it like a man. I wanna see him, go set him up wit what he needs. But I can't do nuthin' ta help him from here."

To write supportive words is all Laurel feels she can do for her son, but she has to do it secretively due to rules on inmate-to-inmate contact. Laurel continues with tears: "That still my nigga, my son. I got ta still be there. He my son. I gotta tell him dis 'cause he in God's hands; there's nothing I can do for him now. There's nothing else I can do. I can't help him 'cause I'm locked up in here. It's killin' me."

Max is not Laurel's only child with troubles. Two other sons are serving long prison terms for gun and gang crimes, but it is Laurel's youngest daughter's situation that is hardest for Laurel to handle. Paris, age twenty-four with two babies, is an active crack-cocaine user. The last Laurel heard, Paris was running the streets, bingeing on drugs. Laurel's concern for the well-being of her daughter is evident as she contemplates the selfless act of absconding to help Paris. She says: "My baby is out there on da streets, she's in abandoned houses gettin' high 'n I'm in here. It kills me to be in here. It takin' everything for me to stay here 'n not go find my daughter. The power for me to stay in here, I gotta sit on my hands 'n not do nuthin' 'cause I'd go up state row, 'n I can't help her in jail. When I leave here, I can help her find a shelter. It takes everything for me to stay. I just sit on my hands 'n just think about where she at, think if she dead."

Laurel is far from alone in her worry about family outside Alpha Omega House walls. Mimi also has loved ones incarcerated; her only daughter and her long-term boyfriend are both serving time. Like Laurel, she is not permitted physical, telephone, or mail contact with either of them and feels "cut off" and frustrated that she "can't help anybody from in here." Other women have loved-ones incarcerated with whom they cannot communicate, which they argue further harms them because connectedness in relationships is central to their lives and their emotional well-being. Especially for women who are mothers, the strict rules of Alpha Omega House and county and state prohibitions on communication between inmates criminalize what Celinska and Siegel (2010, p. 461) call "mothering from prison" strategies like mail and telephone correspondence.

Stress from disconnection in their relationships is a common problem for women at the reentry center, just as it is for women who are incarcerated (Bloom, 1995; Tuerk and Loper, 2006). All of the women at Alpha Omega House suffer disconnection or interrupted ties with people essential to their lives. For example, Phoebe has no family incarcerated but worries about the health and welfare of her mother and, especially, her young siblings who are still young children. She has always taken on a caretaker role in her family, protecting her young sisters from the volatile home life. No one can take her place, she reasons, because her two oldest siblings have active drug problems, her mother is a cocaine and alcohol abuser, and her stepfather is an alcoholic who physically abuses Phoebe's mother and the older children. Even though Phoebe knows she must focus on her own recovery and hope that her family can overcome these troubles, her concern about the health and welfare of her family might sidetrack her recovery. There are countless other stories. Rosa's grandmother has late-stage cancer, and Rosa is hurt that she cannot be with her. Billie's grandmother passed away suddenly, but Billie was in Blackout and not allowed to attend the funeral. This sent her in an emotional tailspin. Clair is separated from her children who are temporarily in the custody of her ex-husband, and she struggles to cope with what might become a permanent change. Like Laurel, Keira suffers by not being able to actively intervene in the life of her daughter, who is glorifying the street life, smoking wet, and turning tricks for drugs and money. Just as parental incarceration and disconnections in relationships affect loved ones on the other side of prison walls, particularly children,[7] the women worry that their family and friends are also negatively impacted by their absence.

In addition to the obvious need for changes to policies regarding communication between residents of Alpha Omega House and loved ones outside is the need for relational programming for women. According to Bloom, Owen, and Covington (2005), gender-responsive strategies for women under correctional supervision require programs to promote and foster women's relationships of importance, that is, with children, families, significant others, and the community. Stemming from empirical research,[8] this principle is based on the idea that some men and many women, including women in trouble with the law, demonstrate a relational way of being, often understood as a feminine psychology or, more specifically, as a voice of care. Compared to others, those who demonstrate this psychology in their attitudes, behavior, and values are more relational in their lives, thoughts, and interactions, and they place great value on maintaining ties in relationships of importance, and they privilege the emotional as well as physical welfare of others. As an illustration, Clair defines herself in relational terms and is harmed by separation from the community outside, but more importantly from the disconnect between herself and her new husband, her children, and her incarcerated sister. She says of her inability to help her husband maintain finances: "I'm disconnected from the outside. Just because I'm in here doesn't mean my life out there has to stop. I have responsibilities. They are taking my checks, 'n now my husband is havin' trouble payin' the mortgage. I have to deal with it, but they don't let me." Her children, too, suffer because of the disconnect. She says: "I got a letter from the foster parents sayin' that they want to get rid of my middle daughter. My three kids are supposed to be together. I can't do anything about it from here. This is the hardest thing. I just wanna leave. I almost walked out last night." And not only are Clair's children at risk of losing one another during their time in foster care—a common problem for incarcerated women (Schirmer, Nellis, and Mauer, 2009; Moses, 2006)—her relationship with her incarcerated sister is also at risk: "We can't write another person in prison, but it's my sister. I don't think it's right. If you find a friend in prison, and it's really hard to find a friend on the streets much less prison, you should be able to keep in touch if you want. Relationships are so important when you have a good one."

Any behavior or practice that disconnects women from relationships they care about and every impediment to strengthening these relationships is a form of oppression. While the stories of separation might be different, the root of the problem is the same: women at Alpha Omega House are deprived of relational programming that could help them to maintain connections and demonstrate care in their important relationships. Laurel is not permitted to communicate with her son. Billie cannot visit family during a funeral. Clair cannot assist her husband with the management of her home, communicate by mail to help her sister deal with the hardships of jail life, or comfort her children who might be separated from one another.

Familial relationships during confinement function to preserve the family unit, promote the well-being of members, and facilitate reintegration (Hairston, 1991). But many residents of Alpha Omega House are prevented from contact with family by a narrow conceptualization of the family by the reentry organization that reflects a traditional definition—a woman and a husband in a legal marriage, plus a woman's children. This rule favors traditional heterosexual marriage over same-sex relationships and women not legally married to their male partner. While the function of the relationships—support and love—remain the same (Treuthart, 1990), same-sex couples and women in nontraditional "marriages" with male partners are denied rights and privileges afforded to women in traditional family relationships. For women at Alpha Omega House, these prohibitive rules mean that visits from friends and same-sex partners as well as common-law partners are cut off for the one year women are residents. The extent to which these rules are commonplace for women in reentry centers is not known, but the women at Alpha Omega house see the threat to their relationships as deliberately and overly oppressive. Billie says of the man whom she loves and to whom she is "married" but not legally: "How you gonna tell me I can't see my husband? I'm married. How you gonna tell me I'm not married? And I don't think that's fair. He hasn't been allowed to see me. Especially in a situation like this, you're not allowed to get no visits. It feel awful and I think its wrong for them to do this to us."

Henrietta is permitted visits from her husband to whom she is legally married (he has never visited), but she should also be able to see her wife, who holds her heart. The disconnection between them worries Henrietta, and the stress of worrying that her wife may not stay faithful much longer causes Henrietta to say she might just end the relationship and become "strictly dickly," that is, entirely heterosexual. By having relations only with men, Henrietta reasons, she will maintain an emotional distance and cheating will not hurt her nearly as much. She says of her troubled loss of connection and communication with Jo-Jo, her "boo": "My boo was in da hospital for a couple days 'cause she ate somethin' bad. I ask her maybe you ate da wrong pussy. I don't trust her. I think she cheatin' on me. I understand dat she out dare, she doin' her 'n so she might be layin' down wit someone."

Still, Henrietta loves Jo-Jo and wants that connection with her and other dear friends. She compares house visiting rules with those of jail:

> I want Jo-Jo to come here, but she can't. Nobody come in here but my grandkids or my daughter—that's it. If you was in jail, you could have all the visits in jail, all you want, all ya got to do is show your ID. It's worser here; it's worser den bein' in jail. The only ones dat can come is your children 'n your grandchildren, 'n your husband. Dat hurts 'cause I got friends wants to come 'n visit me but dey can't. Dey say, What kinda program is dat? When you was in jail, you could have everybody come see ya. My boo should be able to visit us, you got a boyfriend, dey should visit too. You need you family. I have to meet my boo sneakin' to see her. That ain't right. It hurts, it hurt me, make me sad, cry, 'cause I can't have my wife 'n visitors da way I likes to have. Dey make me happy, bring life to me. But here you sad everyday. Every day you sad. I'm depressed all da time, I swear to God I am, so bad it's a shame. I wants to run away but I can't do it, 'cause I don't wanna go back to jail 'n get no three years added.

Candy has a similar problem. Her wife, Valencia, is incarcerated. The two met when Candy was serving her fifteen-year prison term, and they have been a primary couple for more than nine years. While Candy might have a girlfriend for sex here and there, Valencia is her family, her wife, and her responsibility, as she sees it. This separation burdens her so much that she contemplates committing a crime so that she will be sent back to prison where she may be able to find Valencia. A year ago she did just that: she violated parole to be sent back to Valencia. This time, she tries to convince herself to break up with Valencia: "I have emotional distress 'n don't know what to do. My wife want me to come back ta prison, ta say fuck everythin.' She want me to get locked da fuck up. I did it before. Now you don't mess with Mommy Valencia; she'll shoot you in a minute, she don't give a fuck. But I wrote her a letter through my stepdaughter, told her I wanted to split." Being separate from Valencia is hell for Candy, but breaking up may be even more harmful than getting reincarcerated, Candy explains. Her wife's reply to the break-up letter made her feel even more anxious and confused. It reads in part: "You ain't leavin' 'cause I'ma kill you first. I'ma cut you throat, bitch. You dead if I hear you wit anotha bitch. You my wife. We die togetha."

IDLENESS

Research has shown that idleness structures the inmate experience for many offenders in jails and prisons,[9] but idleness runs counter to both the philosophy of reintegration and the therapeutic community model. If the purpose of a reentry center is to bridge the transition from a highly controlled environment of jail or prison to independent living in the community, then activities of everyday social life should be central to the women's daily routine. Not only should the center be making every attempt to nurture the women's emotional network of friends and family, provide job skills and opportunities, and offer housing assistance and individualized treatment programming, Alpha Omega House should also be supporting constructive leisure activities. To assist residents in their lifestyle change, routine activities should be used, according to De Leon (1997), to minimize boredom and negative thinking. But to the contrary, the house severely restrict opportunities for physical, emotional, and intellectual activities and quality leisure. Idleness is the dominant theme in the everyday lives of women at Alpha Omega House. This no doubt constrains their reintegration, further frustrates them, and reinforces a culture of oppressive confinement. As Candy puts it: "In jail you're shut off but we have freedom. Here, we're shut off 'n we have no freedom." The primary activity available to women at Zero Level is watching television, and it structures everyday social life at Alpha Omega House.

Just as they were shocked at the isolation of Blackout, "Zero girls" become quickly frustrated. They expect that they will now be able to take action through a regimen of treatment or be assisted with job placement, but instead they wait—and this waiting creates tension and stress that is palpable in the living room. Just a week into Zero, Adeline blames staff for the lack of movement toward her reintegration. She feels "duped" and betrayed, saying: "I'm frustrated. I see it for what it really is. You try to ignore it, but it's all about them, the people runnin' this place. This place is nothin' to do with us, nothin' to help us. We just sit around. I wanna get out there 'n do stuff for myself."

Aware of Adeline's frustrations, even though she is much further along in the program, Mimi remembers her own experience in Zero limbo. She says of the constant waiting that still structures her days: "I think that this experience is supposta be helpin' us to get out into the world. Don't keep us in here on the couches all day. How therapeutic is that? Let us get out 'n do things; let us go find a job. We should have a curfew."

Participating in public life is a part of healthy living, but the residents say restrictive rules and limited programming prevent them from doing so. While women further along in their stay might be permitted to ride a bicycle in warm weather for an hour each week with a volunteer group, none of the women are ever permitted to go outside for a walk or to enjoy time in the outdoors alone or unsupervised with friends. Except when they are at scheduled appointments, on a rare group visit to local stores, at the annual or semiannual private picnic on the grounds, the women remain physically isolated inside the building. The lack of sun shows on the women's faces, especially in the summertime when even the darkest face appears oddly pale. Spring is the toughest for the women to endure, especially when the warm breeze pushes through the living-room windows. Adeline feels that she should be allowed outside for fresh air and sunshine, even if it means she is confined to the stoop or the front yard. She says, "I'm not gonna run, all I want to do is sit in the grass." Even while she was in jail, Adeline was permitted outside for leisure time.

Laurel, who has been out of Zero for some time, still languishes in the idleness that continues to structures her days as she prepares to graduate. Her remark about leisure and other activities for women is telling: "It's worse than jail here. In jail I worked, I went to school; you use da phone, have visits, everything. Walk around, go to da gym, play ball, workout. You do everything. Here, you do nuthin.' You sit on the fuckin' sofa all day. Watch TV 'n do nuthin.'" This near-constant confinement and lack of activities contribute to stress and anxiety. Laurel continues: "The devil makes idle time, loves da idle time. My mind runs 'n thinks bad things. The more I think about good things for myself, like tryin' to buy da house, like the Facebook 'n email, da more I want to get outa here."

Laurel's illustration of women sitting idly on the couch all day is mostly accurate. Aside from the occasional class or group meeting in the house, activities are restricted. While permitted to play certain board games, to write in journals, and to select from the mostly fiction and religious books in the living room, they are prevented from possessing electronic devices, using computers, or playing cards. Rosa says these prohibitions prevent her from using her mind. She argues: "Dat's another rule I think is pretty stupid. Like we can't play no cards here? Like who does that? Why not let us play cards just for fun? Why not? You use your brain. Dey got dem computers downstairs 'n we can't use 'em. We just do time. Time all day, we got time all day. We sittin' around doing *nuthin.'* Dis place is doin' nothin' for me. I sit around 'n watch TV all day, 'cause dats all I'm allowed to do. I could do dat at home. Dey got nuthin' for us here."

With little else to do, the women are channeled into heavy television viewing, and this effectively transforms the living room from what could be a spirited, progressive center of interaction after a day of reintegration activities to a prison that dulls, stresses, and controls. Like the others, Henrietta feels entrapped. The alternative, at least in the evenings, is sitting alone in her room. While she never learned to read, she enjoys playing cards (banned in this house) or board games. But when board games become monotonous, she is forced to choose between the passive activity of looking at a television or sitting alone in her room. She says: "I watch television. What else can I do? You can't do nuthin' in here. I watch television or go upstairs 'n lay in bed. I stays in my room, ya know. I don't read. I got nuthin' to occupy my mind. Dey don't have no kinds of activities. Like when you was in jail you could play cards, spades, pinochle, you can't even do dat in here. It makes you think, like strajety [strategy], 'n somethin' to pass da time away too 'n enjoy. It's a terrible thing 'cause you can't get your mind goin' in here."

The ever-present television and absence of productive, mindful activities are intellectually harmful, complains Henrietta. Adeline adds: "There is no way to use your mind. The TV's always blastin.' Can't get away from it . . . [it] can make you go crazy." Similarly, Amelia says of her mental state while watching TV: "I'm in my head" and this "screws with your mind." For Clair the television "just makes you space out." Further aggravating this milieu of social and intellectual idleness is a house rule that prohibits conversation before the television. This rule of the General Conduct and Behavior Rules reads: "Talking in front of the television or changing the channel while the group is viewing a movie or television is not permitted." Even if the women wanted to break the no-talking rule, the deafening volume prevents private conversation.

Even though the women sit together before the television, media viewing can be isolating, further adding to women's frustrations. Television viewing is known to foster loneliness (Rubenstein and Shaver, 1982), as it is a passive activity requiring little or no structured action or independent thinking (Bryant, Carveth, and Brown, 1981). It can also be physically harmful, as research links heavy television viewing with obesity (Foster, Gore, and West, 2006) and cardiovascular problems (Wijndaele et al., 2011) in adults. The content shown on the television is also problematic, as it often portrays stereotypical images of women and femininity—the highly sexualized and painfully thin female agent in a crime thriller and the troubled and weak woman in a made-for-television crime drama. Such sexist programming, according to research, can have a negative impact on women, affecting their body images (Halliwell, Malson, and Tischner, 2011) and sex-role attitudes (Ross, Anderson, and Wisocki, 1982).

Television viewing is sometimes said to benefit prisoners by helping them cope with prison life (Jewkes, 2002; Vandebosch, 2000; 2009). It can be used to pass idle time, provide distraction from the everyday monotony, connect inmates to the outside world and reduce feelings of isolation, contribute to feelings of safety and autonomy, even improve their lives through instructive media content. However, Vandebosch (2000) points out that benefits to television viewing and the negative effects in television dependency are also functions of alternative activities. Candy says, describing her need for alternative activities and the effects of inactivity and the relentless television: "They won't let me work, but I asked if I can go volunteer feedin' da homeless people. I ask if I can go to a meetin.' No, I can't leave. All dis fuckin' just sittin,' sittin' around doin' nuthin.' Dis is what we do all da fuck every day; sit in front of da TV. I been back since ten-thirty. I went to welfare. I left outa here at seven-thirty. I'm back 'n gotta sit here. I'm about to snap out like I did yesterday."

As I have discussed, women Alpha Omega House have very little in the way of enjoyable leisure activities and a considerably limited amount of time in treatment programming for their multiple treatment needs. Inmates who are without alternative sources of leisure are what Vandebosch (2000) calls a "captive audience" who become media dependent. And to their advantage, correctional officials use media to "normalize" confinement so that inmates accept imprisonment as natural (Jewkes, 2002). At Alpha Omega House, heavy television viewing, idleness, and accompanying social isolation reproduces the repressive and punitive confines of prison and strengthens penal power.

Resistance

Sitting in the living room as if she is waiting to be called for a job interview, Billie is in her first days of Zero. She is dressed this morning in a professional skirt with black high-heeled open dress shoes and an outdated light blue satin blouse buttoned around the neck with ruffles—just because she could, now that she is no longer restricted by the dress code of black. Her hair has been "dun up" by

Amelia; the hair grease holds her short crop up and to the left side of her head, accentuating her strabismus. She even holds a small black purse, which is a rarity at the house because monitors keep women's purses used outside. Billie sits and waits, doing time in the living room in dramatic display of a woman out of place.

As a woman stuck in a state of limbo between Blackout and the business of reintegration, women on Zero spend their time mostly idle. While they may discard the black clothing and leave isolation in the Blackout room behind, hold a couple dollars in their bra or pocket, or break up their day by stretching their legs going up and down the stairs, Zero is not much different than Blackout. In fact, women spend hours of unstructured, idle, "in our head" reflection under rule of quiet. "Zero girls" are confined to the building and do little more than sit. Their routine is eerily similar to the daily habits of the monastic nuns of yesteryear who would sanctify their day in prayer and silent thought (Evangelisti, 2007; Walker, 1999). But nuns gathered in thought before the cross; here women pass time in the living room before the constant noise of the television.

Knowing this second month of reentry programming is not likely to be much different than the last thirty days, the women employ various coping mechanisms to get them through. How they deal with Zero is partly dictated by the constraints and opportunities of that level of confinement: as we know from the literature, resistance strategies correspond to available alternatives, social position or status (Hunnicutt, 2009; Jurik, Cavender, and Cowgill, 2009), and the level of repression experienced (Scott, 1985). Women no longer sleep their days away as they may have in Blackout, because they are also faced with new constraints: rules now require that women remain in the living room for most of the day. None of the "Zero girls" escape as many "Blackout girls" did. Realistically, the housing assignments and physical condition of the building limit the women's opportunities to jump. Even if a woman can make it out her second-floor window, the fall could kill her. If she was determined to escape, a woman might simply walk out the front door past the monitors on duty.

Nevertheless, new routines at the Zero Level open up new opportunities for resistance.

OUR SISTERHOOD

As women who are now actively interacting with the others in the house, "Zero girls" become more active participants in a culture of resistance, offering them some measure of relief as well as new coping strategies. While the women are members of many different cultures outside of this reentry center, their primary community (Cox, 1989) is inside this patriarchal setting and as such, its culture plays an important role in socialization of its members. Part of this culture involves learning rules and expectations such as never to trust staff, support one another, do not draw attention of staff, do not mingle with the staff, and respect one another. Women distance themselves physically and symbolically from authority, what Collinson (1992; 2000) calls "resistance through distance." Through a continuous cyclical process moving with phase of stay, the newer residents of the house participate in a tutelage by women before them who pass along these cultural values and support their resistance efforts. While the house intends to build a sisterhood of confined women—the Alpha Omega sorority—through its daily regime of prayers and pledges, the informal sisterhood built on resistance triumphs. Mimi says, "We have a sisterhood, but it's our sisterhood, not theirs." She positions herself as role model as she socializes "new girls": "They want us to be role models to the new girls in their way, but I ain't gonna lie. I hate this place 'n I tell them. I tell them, jail, you might want to be goin' in 'n out, but once you come here you'll never want to come back. It's so bad you never want to return." Mimi will not become a role model in "in their way," teaching compliance. Rather, Mimi explains how it really is and how "Zero girls" might find relief through their own sisterhood of mutual support that binds women in a shared identity with a common purpose to manage the conditions of their subjugation through resistance.

Two important points about this sisterhood of confined women are noteworthy. First, while the women share a space and a status and are brought together by a shared experience, their sisterhood is not one of loving connections and kindness. It is built out of necessity and involves a certain measure of interpersonal mistrust. Candy explains this quite plainly as she tells how she and other women help the "new girls"—that is, "Blackout girls" and "Zero girls"—by giving them what was given to them at the start, like shoes, cigarettes, and advice: "We care about how each other takin' it, but don't think I wanna be your girlfriend. Bitch I don't give a fuck about you, just listen to what I gotta say or take dis shit I'm givin' 'n get out my face. We just make sure dey ok."

Passing along advice and helping new members settle into the group helps to convey the attitudes and values of the sisterhood and to build solidarity in resistance. But individual members retain emotional distance, autonomy in this case, that fosters their personal determination and control. Some women say they do not trust others. This finding has been reported elsewhere of imprisoned women (Greer, 2000; Kruttschnitt, Gartner, and Miller, 2000). As the women have learned throughout their lives, mistrust is "a life lesson when you're dealin wit da 'hood." For many of the women distrust started early in life—the first time she was abused or when her parents abandoned her—and is reinforced when adult relationships fail and friends turn away, from the dog-eat-dog world of crime to the tense confines of jail. Clair particularly distrusts women, because she has experienced so much disloyalty. She says:

> I've never had a real friend, because you can't trust. I can't trust another female. I don't know what it is. After being in jail around them 'n in rehabs with all women, I've learned that women have a tendency to talk. They like to gossip, they like to talk. You got girls, even in jail, that I got high with, dope sick together, throwin' up for hours together, then they go to jail and they talk about you, forgettin' where they been. . . . You learn that you can't trust your own family, you can't trust friends. It eats me alive. That's why I can't make no good friends here. You're on your own. I came in this place by myself 'n I'm leavin' out those doors alone.

Clair last comment is especially telling. She knows that while she might have help along the way from other similarly situated women, she is ultimately on her own. Accordingly, she also knows that her success is also ultimately in her hands. Adeline agrees with Clair about the difficulties of having trust in a captive population of women and the importance of being individually responsible: "Girls do get close 'n they do support each other sometimes, but that same person that's huggin 'n holdin you when you're crying is the same person that's gonna be talkin' about you two days later, runnin to the cops [i.e., the staff]. And when you don't have nuthin,' you got nobody. It is one man, one armband. That's what we say, which means that name that's on our armband, our identification band, 'n that's all we worry about, ourselves, one man one armband. That's the new way it is. It may have changed. Back in the day maybe women stuck together, but today everybody is thinking about themselves.

Although this is not the street and not the jail, the women bring their inhibitions, fears, apprehensions, and assumptions to this new setting. They live by the motto "one man one armband." This is not to say that the women never get close to one another. Indeed, they do develop relationships and bond to deal with pressures of confinement, but they remain guarded and learn how to connect in meaningful ways while protecting their self-interests. For instance, Henrietta and Rosa are the closest of friends. They rely on one another emotionally and to pass the time. They play board games together, console each another, and have each other's back. Yet, they are still defensive of their own interests. Says Henrietta: "I can't talk to da girls, can't talk to da monitors, 'cause it gets back to everyone. Dey snitches in here. I tell somethin' to one uh da girls—like my daughter gave me thirty dollars for a cheese steak—'n dey tell da monitors 'cause dey jealous. Me 'n Rosa close, but I can't even trust her. Everyone's out for theirselves in here.

Rosa agrees with her friend. She loves Henrietta but trusts only herself and sometimes that is even hard for her. She says, "I love Henrietta, but when it come down to it I don't give a shit 'bout nobody but myself. I take care uh myself. Just like on da street an just like in jail: trust no one." Lovers do not even really trust one another here. Billie and Freya "hooked up" when they were in jail, but Billie ratted on Freya to staff when she learned that Freya smoked marijuana when she was out of the house for an appointment. Freya's continued commitment to Billie might not make much sense to an outsider, but Candy sheds light when she explains why she will not leave her wife despite separation by prison walls. She says of Valencia, "I don't trust Valencia. We been together nine years. She says I leave her she'll kill me. Mommy Valencia ain't fuckin' around. I keep her close 'cause she dangerous."

While women who are "roomies" might develop close bonds or small groups might forge allegiances to improve their conditions and reduce oppression (see also Pheterson, 1986), the culture of mistrust and need for autonomy prevents women from fully relinquishing themselves to group alliances or the dictates of a sisterhood. But even in this environment of women clinging to their independence, group cohesion is fostered when participation in the group matters, especially when its culture is secretive or oppositional (Fine and Holyfield, 1996). This is the case at Alpha Omega House where participation in the group benefits women by uniting them in a shared struggle against oppression. As DeKeseredy and Schwartz (1997) demonstrate in their research of sexual assault on the college campus, peer support maintains unity, fostering an oppositional force against behavioral constraints. And women unite against oppression and domination as part of their sisterhood at this reentry center even within a culture of mistrust. Just as they have on the streets, in their relationships, and when they were behind bars, the women continue to live by the expression "one man, one armband." As Rosa tells it: "It's you 'n only you doin' da time." In the end, each woman is solely responsible for her own future. This leads to the second important point: the group culture values individuality. As is the case with other group cultures that support collective efforts against oppression and accommodate individuality

(Sonn and Fisher, 1998), the sisterhood of the women at Alpha Omega House promotes individuality over collective action in resistance to domination and oppression, and its primary function is to support individual efforts at resistance.

DISTANCING

Now that she is out of Blackout, Victoria is able to select a book of her choice from the wall-sized bookcase in the living room. Although rules prevent her from being alone in her room during the daytime where she would much rather sit alone, Victoria spends hours in the living room, carving out a private space in the public sphere while reading or planning her future in her journal, Today she reads a romance novel about a woman working to free herself from captivity. She says: "I'm still tryin' to deal with this, with being locked up. What helps me to deal is to spend time by myself. That's the only way to cope. That's the only way I can cope."

Victoria's behavior represents intellectual resistance as she keeps her mind active, escaping through fantasy to pass the time, and performing symbolic resistance as she claims private space. Her opposition is similar to the strategy of "resistance through distance" and may be likened to "cognitive escape," where oppressed individuals separate themselves emotionally through dreams of escape or planning in their minds lives following release.[10] The boundaries Victoria creates between public and private are apparent; she sits apart from others in the living room on a wooden chair, close to the television and away from the others, encircling herself with books and other possessions such as her journal, her water bottle, and a sweater. She incorporates these objects to create and protect space. Victoria's intention is not to change the behavior of others or to challenge organizational rules, but to free herself mindfully from her oppressive conditions as she attempts to normalize the conditions of her confinement. Thus, she is rebelling when she appears to be conforming.

As is the case throughout the reentry center experience, Victoria and other women within this household structure puts to work a strategy of distancing by creating physical and symbolic boundaries in place or space to exercise autonomy (Edwards, Collinson, and Della Rocca, 1995). Alternative constructions of place can be created as resistance even in the highly controlled correctional setting where inmates create personal boundary space real and imagined (Harvey, 1993; Sibley and van Hoven, 2009). Consistent with the idea of avoidance, "resistance-through-distance" (when individuals stay away from individuals or situations that create tension and prejudice), and "avoidance protest" (when subjugated individuals remove themselves from oppressive conditions), my effort here is to illustrate the physical, emotional, and behavioral tactics of distancing that the women use to resist oppression and domination in this domestic sphere.[11]

Grace relies on emotional and physical distancing to relieve herself of entrapment more than she uses any other strategy. Like Victoria, Grace complies with rules and regulations but resists through emotional and behavioral escape. When the rules permit, she avoids the crowd in the living room, preferring her personal private space upstairs, spending her time listening to love songs, rearranging her furniture, and petting Oscar the house cat. She creates a "defensible space" (Willcocks, Peace, and Kellaher, 1987) using methods of everyday life (Turiel, 2003), even in this public place of constant surveillance. Laurel also likes to listen to music in her room even though any station she finds is always static-filled. Billie, Freya, and Candy share her appreciation for music as a mechanism to manage anxiety and "get away." Phoebe, Grace, and Adeline especially like to use art as an alternative to constant close interaction and the idleness of the living room. Laurel and Rosa routinely switch to speaking Spanish in conversation when monitors enter the room to keep their conversation private, a strategy Spanish speakers often use in response to language oppression (Cobas and Feagin, 2008). All of these examples are similar to "active disengagement" (Fleming and Sewell, 2002), which is complying without conforming.

In addition to these methods of distancing themselves from the everyday hardships of their reentry experience, the women also put to work other routine distancing strategies, such as daydreaming or "avoidance coping," and playing games and gambling. Game playing has been shown to reduce monotony and establish a sense of normalcy in groups under oppressive conditions and to ease everyday social class struggles of working-class women.[12] As an example, Rosa and Henrietta routinely spend hours in the dining room or the living room shifting between two board games. They are complying with rules, but distancing from the isolation and idleness of Zero. But the repetitive play of board games becomes dull, so the women subvert house rules to stay sane: the pair keeps dominoes and a deck of playing cards hidden away in Rosa's room and surreptitiously play them when away from cameras and out of earshot of monitors. Subverting both the prohibitions against gambling and mingling in another resident's room, they meet regularly during lockdown in Rosa's room, "the gambling room," to satisfy their competitive urges and their desire to, as they say, "use our minds" strategically. The sisterhood supports their resistance. Rosa says, "We always have a lookout for staff. We have signals we use to communicate." Sometimes Rosa and

Henrietta risk playing in the dining room in plain view of security cameras and passing monitors, but they use cards from board games to make it appear they are playing a simple game when they are actually playing rummy. Rosa and Henrietta enjoy doing this because they fool the monitors, Henrietta says, "They watchin,' but dey don't know what we doin."

PRAYER AND THE HOLY ROSARY

Before coming to Alpha Omega House, Victoria was not particularly religious; she did not attend religious services or sit in prayer before her crime. In fact, she had never held a Bible or read Holy Scripture. Yet Victoria would come to seek relief and personal strength in prayer and the religious symbols of faith so closely tied to this building's past. Almost from the start of her term in prison, Victoria resists through prayer, seeking relief from her feelings of demoralization and her impulses to strike out against monitors. She describes how prayer helps her to cope with oppression and domination of her confinement and subjugated status:

> I have had enough of bein' aroun women 24/7. I've had enough of bein' told what ta do, what I cannot do, when I can get up, what I can eat. I've had enough of that. I have to pray from the time I get up in the mornin' so that I can get through it. I do what I have to. I just do it 'n get it over. I have to survive here. I don't wanna be goin' to these classes, I don't wanna be getting up five-thirty in the mornin' 'n all that, but I do it because it needs to be done. I pray on it. I pray, 'n the Bible says to respect authority figures, 'n this is what stays in my mind. This is what I need to do, to keep me from snappin' out. I am a kind, considerate person, but jail has made me a little bit harder 'n it takes a lot for me to keep my temper in here . . . This is what stays in my mind. If I get out of here, they will neva be able to tell me what to do again, they will neva ever be able to control me, to tell me what time to get up, what time to eat, chores, not even a day off.

Victoria relies on prayer to maintain control of her present and to "survive" by guiding her conduct as she acquiesces to some demands, and she believes that if she continues to maintain control her future freedom is assured. In fact, positive religious coping is often sought out by individuals to achieve emotional comfort and personal control during times of stress and when dealing with constraints over behavior.[13]

Unlike Victoria who has come to seek relief through prayer by way of her confinement experience, Freya has always seen herself as a spiritual woman. Carrying over from her days in Blackout, Freya resists the emotional discomfort of Zero idleness and the constant weight of her subjugated status as confined criminal woman. Part of her strategy is to use prayer to accept her status with deference while holding on to her personal identity. Doing this enables her to maintain calmness and to retain strength through her use of agency. Says Freya: "My spirituality is an assurance, a comfortable place within myself that I go to when I feel trapped or controlled. There's nuthin' like a weak and humble spirit. But you don't humble you'self so much that you give up your whole self. This is strength."

Particular religious coping methods are reflected in these narratives. They include "reappraisal of God's powers," used to channel power to influence a particular stressful situation, "collaborative religious coping," seeking control and problem-solving with God's guidance, and "self-directed religious coping," which is seeking control through personal strength and initiative (Pargament et al., 1998, p. 711). Consistent with the women's reliance on personal agency, their religious coping only rarely reflects "deferring religious coping," which is a passive strategy that puts a situation in God's hands. But this strategy too can be helpful. Henrietta provides an example. Henrietta sees herself as a spiritual woman, having regularly attended church service before her incarceration. Although she has never learned to read, Henrietta holds the Bible and flips through its pages, trying to glean strength. She seeks God's intervention to "hurry up and get me out here," unlike Victoria and Freya who seek guidance and support to resist their confinement effectively. Henrietta says: "I tries to read. I pick up the Bible 'n tries to read. I use my mind to pray to God to hurry up 'n get me out here, that days go by quicker than I 'spected, 'cause it drivin' me crazy, we all bein' all up in theyself 'cause of this place, it's not right." In addition to prayer or contemplation, Henrietta surrounds herself with religious symbolism. Her room is adorned with rosaries, as are many of the others, and one half of her dresser holds her Bible and devotional pictures or prayer cards atop a simple cotton doily. It is the images and symbols rather than text that benefit Henrietta.

While the women who occupy this building now are different from those of days past, one symbol that remains a central part of everyday life at the house is the rosary. Brought into Alpha Omega House from jails and prisons by the women, the simple strings of beads ending in a crucifix adorn the bedrooms; some women have three or four hanging throughout their rooms. The women do not pray the rosary as the Catholic nuns before them did. Nor is the rosary necessarily a representation of their religiosity. Rather, it offers women symbolic protection and hope. The cross is typically a symbol of peace (Watt, 2003; Wills,

2006), and the rosary beads convey strength and resilience to the oppressed, particularly in the strength of Mary (McClain, 2003), to whom most of the traditional prayers are devoted. To Adeline, the rosaries "are very symbolic. They protect me from the demons around me. In jail, it's an evil place with lots of evil shit going on. Here, I don't know what's going on." Nonetheless, manipulating religious symbols to guide social interactions and conditions is a help (Few, 1995).

Most of the time when women are in Blackout and at Zero Level their rosaries are worn around the neck and outside of the clothing, just as they were worn on the outside of the nun's habits (Kuhns, 2003). Some women wear two, even three rosaries. Victoria's rosary was a gift from her "cellie" in jail. She uses it in her own method of prayer and feels a close link to Jesus when she holds it. That link, she says, affords her protection and courage helping her "deal." She says:

> It helps me. I hold Jesus close to my heart. I hold him in my hand, and I pray, and it helps me, 'n plus I look at his face. I'm tellin' you. If it wasn't for him, I would neva be able to sit here calmly 'n talk to you, because I still feel like I'm in a nightmare. Am I makin' myself clear? I've never been through anything like this, neva. My whole life is gone, my whole life. My whole life as I knew it before, it's gone. It's gone. Somebody who's never been in trouble before 'n all of a sudden I got this harsh sentence. This helps me deal.

Though the rosary begins as a symbol of strength and courage for the women, it soon becomes stigmatizing (Wills, 2006). The black-plastic rosary is well known in the surrounding neighborhoods as prison-issued, the women explain, and its presence risks the women being stereotyped and judged. Laurel consigned her rosaries to her bedroom wall after a stranger on a bus commented on them and inquired when Laurel had been released from HSC (the local jail for women). She says: "I put 'em in da room. I hang 'em up. 'Cause everywhere I go dey say, You were locked up? How long were you locked up? I wanna go out dere 'n not have people know I'm locked up."

And like Laurel, other women who advance in phases of stay tuck away the rosary when they leave the house, and after a time the symbol of strength and peace becomes an adornment on their bedroom walls. Just as the color of black sets "Blackout girls" apart, a rosary worn outside of clothing easily identifies women at Zero. Adeline wears two rosaries as she sits on the settee in the living room with Mimi, who wears no rosaries. Victoria wears her rosaries, as does Billie and Violet, who are also on Zero. Phoebe is past Zero and so are Henrietta and Rosa, whose rosaries adorn their bedroom walls. Though still near to them, the rosary is replaced by other methods of resistance when women move from Blackout through Zero and onward.

Stepping out of Blackout after passing the Blackout test, Victoria puts a precious gold stud earring into the holes of each ear as she climbed the steps to her new room upstairs. Like Victoria, Adeline rushes to reclaim her femininity and individuality when she reaches Zero Level, placing two small barrettes neatly in her hair when she awakes each day. Violet emerges from her new room on the second level as a Zero resident with bright red lipstick. "It makes me feel good, like a lady," says Amelia, who has tossed the black clothing and likes to dress in low-cut tops, wear makeup, and "do" her hair even if she plans to sit by the television. Billie's feminine routine is the most dramatic; she is fond of wearing business suits with high heels when she sits by the television, even though she will not be seen outside the house.

Other common routines when the house opens at the end of the day include manicuring, nail painting, eyebrow waxing, and hair braiding. On this particular Saturday evening during the showing of a horror film, Rosa returns to the living room with another part of her right ear and her chin pierced. She likes to wear large hoop earrings, but those are banned, so she settles for studs borrowed from Mimi. While she abides by this rule, she does subvert the makeup rule by wearing a thickly drawn, dark lip liner around her brown colored lips. Adeline and Violet also get new piercings on this evening, and before the end of the night, Phoebe shows off her new naval piercing compliments of Amelia. Henrietta had never before her confinement experience pierced any part of her body, but now has a nose piercing, compliments of Rosa, and wears in it a simple gold-colored stud. "It make me feel good," she says of her decision. "Dey don't like it," suggesting that her actions also function to subvert authority.

While women are not subjected to the rule of black when they reach Zero Level, they are limited in what they can wear and how they appear by formal and informal rules. Staff routinely counsel women about their clothing (the women say they are "constantly hassled") to dress in simple attire that is neither too feminine nor too masculine and to limit jewelry and makeup. Just as the workplace dress code limits self-expression (Bartlett, 1994), so do restrictions on dress and appearance at Alpha Omega House. Written and unwritten regulations on appearance also regulate sexuality and reproduce normative assumptions about women. In response to these particular threats, women assert their identities through some feminine routines that are in line with rules and regulations of the house, others that push the boundaries of dress and appearance, and a few that subvert rules altogether. The women may select clothing that monitors criticize as "provocative" dress on weekends when administrative staff is not on duty. They often defy rules regarding hair with "extravagant hairdos" and "hair coloring" prohibited at all phases of stay.

When women step out of the normative, oversized white T-shirts and sweatpants that conceal their shapes and push the boundaries of dress, they are met with counter-resistance in the form of complaints and demands (the dress is "inappropriate," "slutty," "provocative"), reprimands (to "dress like a lady"), as well as fines and write-ups. Phoebe likes to display cleavage and wear low-cut tops because she likes to show her body. Mimi does too but has "caught" more than one fine and write-up because of her insubordination. She cares little about these repercussions and continues to resist. Candy also dresses to accentuate the female self, but in her mostly masculine way. Candy has been counseled time and again by monitors and especially administrative staff to dress "less manly and more like a woman." This repeated attention to Candy's dress and appearance and attempts to strip her of her own sexuality is a futile attempt to impose heterosexual norms (Skidmore, 1999). At first Candy did accommodate by using a strategy known as "passing" (Kanuha, 1999), which can involve performance of a gender identity as a way of disguising one's sexuality as response to oppression (Ginsberg, 1966), or by "role flexing" (Shorter-Gooden, 2004), which is dressing more like others to diminish bias and fit in. She donned a pair of purple eyeglasses, eliminated the chunky gold cross on a chain, shed her trademark workboots for no-nonsense black shoes, and replaced her baggy jeans that showed her boxer shorts for fitted, creased slacks with a tucked shirt of arm length that covered the scars and tattoos to her wrists. The most revealing transformation was the softer, safer look of her growing Afro hair that made her appear more female. But the performance did not "feel right" she says. The change lasted only days until Candy was back in the clothing that matched her feminine style and sexuality. She clearly subverted the unwritten appearance regulation designed for her and its accompanying assumptions about homosexuality. Her most defiant move was a haircut, returning to the look she had on the day she arrived seven months earlier—a very close shave. She says of the change, "They ain't gonna like it 'cause it make me look like a man, but fuck 'em." Complete with her forearm tattoos in plain view and a large men's watch on her wrist, workboots, and showing boxer shorts, Candy reclaims her identity.

Feminine routines such as I have described are efforts by women using the female body as the site for resistance to reclaim autonomy (Shaylor, 1998), reassert their identities, and resist the stereotyped norms about their behavior and sexuality. Similar findings that women strive to reclaim their autonomy by negotiating regulations on their appearance are reported elsewhere among women workers regarding makeup and dress as well as residents in other domestic social contexts who ritualize routines of feminine appearance to escape the surveillance culture and reproduce home.[14] The feminine routines are everyday forms of resistance that, though often subtle and situational, can help women to assert power (Abu-Lughod, 1990), even while they follow rules regarding dress most of the time. The give and take the women display regarding regulations on appearance and dress are "patriarchal bargains" (Kandiyoti, 1988), allowing them to glean what they can from the patriarchal system through feminine routines while acquiescing to its demands most of the time.

GAY FOR THE STAY

Candy rubs the name tattooed in prison ink across her forearm—VALENCIA—as she talks about her incarcerated wife. "She my wife, Mommy Valencia. We been together nine years ... She upstate waitin' for me." Just then, a resident named Charisse appears. Called "Half-Back" by the women because her large bottom appears to take up half of her back, Charisse pokes her head into the living room on her way to the stairway to her room and pouts to Candy, "I neeed some money." Candy turns and asks, "Why?" "I just need some money. Gimme some mon-ney," replies Charisse, grinning as she seductively glides her generously endowed breasts against the trim of the hallway door. "I'ma get ya," Candy concedes as she dismissingly waves Charisse away and shoots a devious grin my way.

Candy is a lifelong lesbian, what Ward and Kassebaum (1964, p. 167) term the "true homosexual inmate," and Charisse identifies as heterosexual, but the pair share a consensual sexual relationship. Of course, all sexual or romantic relationships between women are strictly prohibited at Alpha Omega House. This type of relationship is a method of resistance—for Candy to her deprivation of sex, so she says. Charisse gives Candy sex. Candy gives Charisse a bit of pocket change and is ready to "protect her back" if need be. Charisse is what the women refer to as "gay for the stay." That is, she takes on homosexual relationships with other inmates during her incarceration while she lives a heterosexual life outside of confinement. She is what Ward and Kassebaum call the "jailhouse turnout." Upward of 90 percent of the women in prison who engage in homosexual relations there do not identify as lesbian but adapt to prison life in this way. In this house of confinement and in the local area, Charisse's role is of a "commissary whore." A term brought over from prison, a commissary whore relies on another woman for money and "commissary" items like cigarettes and candy in exchange for sex (see also Greer, 2000). Candy could be called a "block slut"—a woman who is normally lesbian who provides sex to commissary whores in exchange for goods and services. Clair explains the setup: "Commissary whore is a girl that goes into jail 'n she has nothin,' 'n she sees this other girl who plays as the jail's slut, the block slut, because she's sleepin' with all these girls 'cause they're gay for the stay. She goes 'n befriends that person 'n that person likes her, so that person starts buyin' her stuff off of commissary: food, coffee. She's trickin' for whatever. Just like tricking with a sugar daddy on the street. It happens here too." In Candy and Charisse's case, their relationship is not based foremost on romance but on other needs: economic, sexual, even the need for security.

Other women in the house are also involved in consensual sexual relationships. Henrietta, a lesbian, says she has sex with Candy from time to time in the shower but keeps it secret from her closest friend at the house, Rosa. Billie and Freya, both bisexual women, carried over their jail relationship to Alpha Omega House until Freya had sex with Henrietta. Other women have sexual encounters as well. Having never before been incarcerated, Victoria was unaware of and surprised at just how many women enter into these relationships but now understands that same-sex relationships are common among incarcerated women and this pattern carries over to the reentry center. She says: "Half this place is gay like in jail, half of them is gay. Some of them have men, husbands, 'n they have girlfriends too. They so many of 'em here."

Homosexuality among female prison inmates is well established in the literature.[15] Different studies estimate the prevalence of homosexuality among women in prison at 30–45 percent (Hensley, Tewksbury, and Koscheski, 2002; Owen, 1998), 60–70 percent (Ward and Kassebaum, 1964), even 95 percent of incarcerated women (Giallombardo, 1966). Homosexuality is said to be an emotional coping mechanism to the deprivations of prison life—including isolation, loneliness, and distance from loved ones[16]—involving women who may or may not have had lesbian relationships outside of prison. It may also serve economic functions (Greer, 2000; Propper, 1978), such as described between Candy and Charisse.

At Alpha Omega House, a few sexual relationships occur between lesbian women, more happen between women who live bisexual lives, still others involve lesbians and heterosexual women, but very rarely do women who are heterosexual outside of this environment enter into sexual relationships with one another. A woman may become "gay for the stay" to compensate for a lack of intimate connection and affection with partners outside the house, but at this reentry center women enter into these relationships knowing they are temporary; women are not gay for the stay to find a life partner. When they leave the confines of Alpha Omega House, the women say, they plan to return to their relationships of preference. But while they are at the house, homosexual relationships help some of them cope with stressors of their confinement experience.

TRADES, SWAPS, AND BARTERS

"Hey, playa!" yells Candy as she jumps from a living-room couch, meeting me at the entrance to the room to shake my hand. Hers was not the simple handshake one might envision between acquaintances. Candy's motion was more like the action of a windmill, with a windup starting with her arm behind her shoulder, then overhead and down as she grabs my hand with a vicelike grip. "Playa," she repeats as she slowly and dramatically slides her large hand out of mine to get a better view of the orange running shoes on my feet. "They's nice, they my color," she says as she looks into my eyes, smiling. She asks, "They's my tradeoffs?" Candy wants to trade her jeans and black sneakers for my running shoes. She kicks off her shoes, unbuckles her belt, and slides off her jeans expecting the swap to happen.

A week earlier while in the living room on a Saturday night I said, "Nice jeans Candy." She rose from the couch, kicked off her untied men's workboots, unbuckled her belt, unzipped her jeans and slid them off, throwing them to me in a heap at my feet. Standing momentarily in boxer shorts and her workboots, she is hooted and hollered at, the women laughing at her skinny legs before she turns to head upstairs, shouting, "Going up!" on the way. She returns clad with below-the knee gym shorts a person might wear to play basketball. But before she can sit, Mimi shouts to her, "Hey Candy, nice shorts!" and the women all laugh as Candy strips off the shorts just as she did the jeans, throwing them to Mimi before heading back upstairs. Candy returns a short time later with a new pair of jeans. Mimi rises from the settee, strips her baggy gray cotton gym shorts and replaces them with the pair from Candy. She tosses Candy her shorts.

Trading clothing is something the women tend to do a lot, under different conditions. It happens immediately when women leave Blackout. Women on Zero need tradeoffs to put together a wardrobe, unless they feel like staying in blacks. But all of the residents participate in tradeoffs. Shoes, flip-flops, and hoodies (hooded sweatshirts) are popular. Costume jewelry is very commonly swapped too. Laurel traded Mimi her Westville housing projects hoodie for a pair of dress shoes—a real win for Mimi, because Westville is said to be one of the most dangerous housing projects, and showing off that hoodie will bring her a lot of respect outside this house. Adeline traded Phoebe leather sandals she got in a trade from Laurel for an Avon necklace with a heart pendant. Phoebe has new eyeglasses, traded from Candy for a sweatshirt with plenty of holes and sneakers without laces. One of Mimi's favorite tradeoffs is a pair of homemade shorts cut from men's insulated cotton underwear traded to her by Clair in return for a light winter coat. Candy likes shoes, sneakers, and anything masculine. It doesn't matter if the shoes are new or badly worn—what matters is that they are different from what she currently wears. She has no money to buy shoes because what little she does get goes to the payphone to call her wife's daughter, for cigarettes, and to pay her for fines.

Sometimes the women swap temporarily. Mimi is wearing a borrowed necklace from Billie. Adeline has pants from Mimi in exchange for a zippered blue sweatshirt. On graduation day, a woman might give away her belongings to those who remain, partly to leave a legacy at the house. A woman named LaToya left a pair of jeans and a couple of tank tops to Laurel. She also gave Grace a pair of slippers. Charisse left Candy a pile of clothing. In addition, women barter with services. Phoebe is wearing a T-shirt from Henrietta in exchange for a nail polishing. Mimi always has her nails freshly painted and trades T-shirts and costume jewelry for the labor. Henrietta likes to braid hair and trades this service for jewelry and nail polish. Sometimes she banks her compensation for a more desirable reward, such as shoes. Keira gets clothing and jewelry as payment for braiding hair. But for coloring, which is prohibited and therefore risky, Keira's compensation could be the more coveted items such as money, cigarettes, and shoes.

Women's possessions are limited. They might carry a few belongings from prison or jail, like photographs of children from years before, cards received while in prison, letters from lovers, and poems. On her first day Adeline put it this way: "I came from jail to the convent, and I brought what I had on: my rosaries, a Bible, a radio, and a comb. This is all I got." In addition to the things the women carry in with them, the staff provides women with a bar of soap, bottle of deodorant, a plastic black comb, and a bath towel. In addition to the so-called setup of personals, the women might get a piece or two of clothing from the piles of donated clothing in the basement if they are lucky enough to find a staff member willing to help. The rest of what the women might possess—sneakers, jeans, pencils, notebooks—is normally delivered by an immediate family member in the form of a "drop-off." Once able to leave the building, women may bring in additional possessions they call "pick-ups" from the outside. Contraband smuggled in under the radar of the staff, pick-ups are risky, exposing the women to fines and other punishments if detected. The tradeoff, swap, and barter systems are the most common methods the women use to acquire possessions at the house.

According to Acker (1988), women participate in relations of distribution to increase their control, resist, and survive under economic oppression within a household, trading labor and services with their wage-earning for economic support. This perspective on economic exploitation in patriarchy and capitalism helps to make sense of the ease with which women at Alpha Omega House trade personal possessions with one another. While one resident is not necessarily submissive to any other resident in these exchange bargains, the need to survive is the same. Their behavior of trading, swapping, and bartering allow the women to attain services and possessions they could not otherwise. It is also how they are able to resist not only the surveillance and economic constraints of the halfway house—they cannot leave the house or afford to pay for a manicure and pedicure at a local shop—but also a mechanism for them to replicate everyday life. If they are not stuck with the same clothing or shoes and their hair is trimmed, they are not stuck in time.

HUMOR

It is a Saturday and opening night of "Skittles and Beer," performing live before a roaring crowd of five residents in the living room. Skittles refers to the candy-like look and colorful variety of commonly abused prescription pills. While they have no musical skills, the performers—Violet and Adeline—drum on pots and pans taken from the kitchen along with their aluminum lids and wooden spoons as they sing phrases from a well-known Michael Jackson tune. "Beat it, beat it, yeah, beat it, beat it!" they screech at a level much higher than the song's intended pitch. This provokes dancing and cheering in the crowd until two monitors squash any further deviation from the no-talking-in-front-of-the-television rule. Even though their resistance was met with counter-resistance, Adeline and Violet made their humor work effectively to interrupt the otherwise dull evening, to bond with others, and to glean power. Even the name of the band—Skittles and Beer—is an effort of resistance.

Humor as a resistance strategy of oppressed and marginalized groups, including women, has been reported elsewhere.[17] For residents of Alpha Omega House, humor functions allows women to temporarily escape the confines of the house, its control, and the idleness of the everyday. Of the lingering sameness of her Zero Level experience, Adeline says: "You gotta make jokes; you gotta make the day go by or you'll go crazy." Henrietta always relies on laughter when she is in distress because it helps to calm her. Candy likes to horseplay with all of the women because it energizes and gets her "away from dis shit."

Humor also helps the women to bond with one another or boost group solidarity, as reported elsewhere (Gilbert, 2004), and to distinguish themselves from those who dominate. But humor has other functions. It is a way of stepping away from a real situation, an uncomfortable and subjugated position into a "creatively distorted" reality (Dubberley, 1988), temporarily altering power structures and relations. It can be a subversive tool in its capacity to point out the absurdities in a context of oppression and to weaken the dominant ideology by ridiculing those who dominate (Gillooly, 1991). The women routinely clown around when they are forced to participate in groups and classes they say are belittling, and they mock and joke when they feel bullied by treatment providers. Freya, Clair, Adeline, and Mimi use parody and crack jokes aloud in their frustration at being routinely summoned by monitors over the intercom.

Humor can also be thought of as a mechanism for women to take control of themselves in contexts where they have little autonomy. As Barreca (2013, p. 56) points out, "Prolonged and outright laughter shows that you are able to let yourself lose control, if only for a moment, and therefore surprisingly illustrates how very much in control of yourself you really are. If you laugh at your enemy, in other words, you are in the position of power." This ability to assume a position of power, even if it is momentary, is perhaps the most important function of resistance through humor used by women at Alpha Omega House.

SECRETIVE COMMUNICATION

As described above, practices and rules of Alpha Omega House regulate women's behavior by restricting communication with people who live outside of the reentry center and those who are incarcerated. Only "immediate family" may visit. A woman may have a visit from her siblings, children, parents, or husband. She may never have a visit from a close cousin, aunt, or uncle, from her same-sex spouse, or from a man she has failed to marry but calls husband. Zero Level affords women no opportunities to subvert these communication restriction, but once women pass on to C Level, they may be able to make secretive contact with those loved ones who are prevented from visiting. They may use the telephone to maintain contact, but doing that becomes costly. Mail is the most commonly used method of communication with loved ones outside of the house, but even this approach prevents women like Henrietta, who is illiterate, from meaningful correspondence with her partner.

Rules of Alpha Omega House also prohibit telephone and mail communication between incarcerated persons, and many jail and prisons also restrict communication to family in the community. As women under this custody status, residents experience these regulations as harmful to their relationships and personal growth. Candy cannot maintain contact with her wife through legitimate channels and neither can Keira, because those partners are incarcerated. The same rule applies to Mimi, who had not been permitted to speak to her boyfriend during his incarceration and still cannot communicate with her only child who is imprisoned (because of a no contact order by the courts). Laurel is not legally permitted to speak to her son or to write him while he is incarcerated. The rule also applies to Phoebe, whose sister is jailed and whose boyfriend is in prison.

Though face-to-face visits are not possible, the restrictions on relationships with a partner, child, or friend who is incarcerated can be subverted at Zero Level and beyond. As Adeline says: "There's always a type of way to get around stuff." The women primarily resist by using two strategies. Secretive and covert, these communication strategies are "hidden transcripts" in which resistance is expressed "offstage" by those who share knowledge of and participate in the practice (Scott, 1990). One strategy involves three-way telephone calling that requires assistance of friends and family on the "outside." Because jail and prison inmates cannot receive incoming calls but may make outgoing calls, women invoke the help of someone in the community able to merge phone calls so that the women are able to speak directly to their loved ones and friends who are incarcerated. The person who is incarcerated in jail or prison must initiate the call to a third party. At the same time, the Alpha Omega House resident must make a telephone call using the basement payphone. The third party then merges the two calls. For instance, Mimi is restricted from communicating with her adult daughter who is in jail. To get connected, Mimi and her daughter both make payphone calls at a certain time to Mimi's boyfriend, recently released from prison, who joins the pair using a three-way calling feature on his telephone. But this strategy requires perfect timing and is therefore unreliable. Adeline says: "Sometimes it don't work 'cause they [third party or inmate] might not get to the phone or you end up waitin' for the phone [in the basement to make the call]."

With few economic resources to feed the costly telephone and the practical difficulty in successfully timing phone calls, women turn to mail communication as the primary strategy to subvert restrictions on communication with incarcerated loved ones. Like the telephone, mailing under the radar requires a willing third party—in this case another resident who has passed Zero Level and may leave the house. Residents send covert mail in two ways. They may mail letters directly to the person who is imprisoned and use a residential return address so that when the letter arrives at the jail or prison, it is not identified as originating from a correctional institution. But women cannot mail these letters through normal channels—by handing them off to monitors—because the false return address will be detected and the recipient's address will be identified as a jail or prison. Thus letter writers must rely on other women with travel privileges to mail the letters when they are outside of the house. Residents who are able to assist say they always help because the sisterhood at the house requires this mutual assistance, and they too benefited from the help of more senior women when they were at Zero Level.

Phoebe writes her new prison boyfriend using this method. Keira uses this strategy too. And Adeline explains how this approach enables her to subvert rules and communicate with her former "cellie," who is serving a life sentence in prison. She says: "You can't write no other prison 'n they can't write here. It's like that in all places. Like you can't write from jail to jail. I write her too, but I just gave it to one of the girls to mail it outside 'n put another address in the top corner. This place ain't gonna stop me from stayin' in touch."

People in the community also help residents of Alpha Omega House correspond with friends and family who are incarcerated. Someone in jail or prison might mail a letter directly to the third party in the community. The third party discards the inmate's envelope and any traces of jail or prison markings, reseals the letter in a fresh envelope, marking it with a noninstitutional return address, and mail the letter directly to the intended recipient at Alpha Omega House. Adeline explains how her former cellie sends her letters from prison using this method: "She mails her mom a bunch of letters for different people and her mom remails 'em to everybody, so she [the inmate] shoves 'em all in one envelope so she only uses one stamp, 'n then her mom does her the favor 'n remails the other stuff. So, we stay writin' each other." This method works for Adeline and her friend, for Keira and her wife, Mimi and her daughter, Phoebe and her boyfriend, and for Laurel and her imprisoned son.

Another though less commonly used third-party approach involves both mail and telephone contact. Here, inmates mail letters intended for Alpha Omega House residents to a third party in the community. Once they believe letters are received, the residents use the basement payphones to call the third party, then listen to the inmate through the voice of the third party who reads the letter aloud. Candy prefers to communicate with her wife this way, because it is safest, she reasons, and she is able to stay connected with her wife's family. She explains: "I writes the letter 'n when I go out, just drop it in da mailbox. Her mail don't come here. She sends to her daughter, 'n I calls 'n [ask] my stepdaughter to read it." This method necessitates planning and timing. Candy sends letters to Valencia using a fabricated return address and drops the letters in a postal box when she is outside running errands for house staff. She has to anticipate when Valencia's return letters will arrive and when to make the call to her stepdaughter. But having made initial contact, the pair can more easily plan for future correspondence. Valencia mails her daughter letters for Candy twice each week. Candy then calls Valencia's daughter at a planned hour on weekends to hear what Valencia had to say. This method works; Candy says her correspondence with her Valencia has never been detected.

Like workers in organizations who use covert strategies to resist organizational control (Mumby, 2005), residents at Alpha Omega House demonstrate their agency using covert and nonconfrontational forms of communication resistance. While secretive telephone and mail communication do not directly challenge organizational control, the women's resistance undermines control in practice, enables the women to maintain connection with loved ones, and further supports the resident oppositional sisterhood.

FOUR

C LEVEL

WITH BLACKOUT PAST and a month served on Zero, women are eager to advance to C Level. Normally three months in duration, C Level rewards women with fewer restrictions and increasing freedoms. Now socialized into the customs and culture of the house and its formal sisterhood, Adeline, Billie, Freya, Clair, Violet, and Amelia are some of the women who move to C Level. With this move, the women step up a notch in status, normally leaving their chores to Zero girls for slightly better ones, and they are now provided fifty dollars per month spending money, which is quite a change from no money at Blackout and the ten dollars they received on Zero. These are some of the formal benefits of advancement to C Level. Informally, women who move to C Level are more senior members of the house, and with this seniority, they are now able to enforce over Blackout and Zero girls their preferred seat location in the living room. They also pass along their advice and resistance strategies to women at the earlier phases of stay who are still learning how to negotiate Alpha Omega House. Advancement to C Level makes women eligible for treatment and programming outside of the house in the form of intensive outpatient programming, popularly called IOP, at various local agencies. This treatment and its accompanying unsupervised travel are their greatest privileges yet, but new constraints are also imposed, for example, pat-down searches when they return from the outside and substance-abuse testing when staff suspect alcohol or drug use. When they are not at IOP, C Level women continue to participate in the groups or classes that take place at the house.

As described earlier, Alpha Omega House advertises treatment opportunities in a therapeutic community (TC) setting. TCs are popular for substance abusers,

and they stress self-help as well as personal and social responsibility as participants move toward prosocial lifestyles, attitudes, and behaviors in a structured,
treatment-oriented setting. According to the National Institute on Drug Abuse
(Hanson, 2002, pp. 1–2), effective TCs involve both "rehabilitation—relearning
and re-establishing healthy skills and values as well as regaining physical and
emotional health"—and, for individuals who have never lived healthy lives,
"habilitation—learning for the first time the behavioral skills, attitudes, and values associated with socialized living." The TC approach at Alpha Omega House
is what De Leon (1997, pp. 1–2) describes as a modified therapeutic community;
its substance-abuse focus is modified for a special population in a special setting,
that is, women in a prison reentry center who have a broad set of treatment needs.
The essential elements of the therapeutic community according to De Leon involves treatment of the "whole person" (p.4). Thus, rehabilitation focuses on the
individual's psychological status and lifestyle through cognitive-behavioral and
other approaches, and the individual's personal characteristics, including education level, self-esteem, responsibility, and financial self-reliance. Key to successful
treatment is the "community approach," which involves peer involvement and
functional and productive activities targeting social and interpersonal skills,
financial planning, family involvement, and housing assistance.[1] Like reentry
centers traditionally, employment is of primary importance in the modified TC
(Inciardi, Martin, and Surratt, 2001).

The treatment opportunities advertised at Alpha Omega House—in house
and through community referral—incorporate many of the traditional TC
elements:

- Drug and alcohol treatment in group therapy, individual therapy, psycho-
  therapy, and family therapy
- Educational experiences
- Housing assistance
- Family reunification when possible
- Self-esteem and interpersonal skill building
- Financial planning

In addition to advertising itself as a therapeutic community, Alpha Omega
House promises gender-responsive strategies for women returning from prison.
These include parenting classes, women's health classes, literacy training, and
job-skills training designed to help women become "independent and responsible

law-abiding members of the community with the capacity and confidence to care
for themselves and their families."

The first part of this chapter describes women's actual experiences of treatment programming at Alpha Omega House in IOP in the community and classes
at the house. Just as women experience new routines when they advance reentry-
center phases, their opportunities for resistance also change. As they participate
in the three months at C Level, women rely on the resistance strategies that
helped them to cope with the constraints of Blackout and Zero, but they are
now able to put to work new methods. The second part of this chapter illustrates
the common resistance strategies that characterize women's C Level experience.

Intensive Outpatient

It is 8:30 a.m. on a gray Monday morning in the dead of winter. Rosa completed
her morning exercise and ate a quick breakfast. She will skip morning meditation
because she has "outpatient" today. She heads to the front door, but stops short
of the hallway to alert the monitor of her presence. She rings the bell and waits.
One minute passes, then two. "Come," replies a monitor, and Rosa steps into
the monitors' office. There, Rosa shows the monitor the money she will carry
out with her; the monitor records the exact amount, which will be compared
to the amount with which Rosa returns. The monitor retrieves Rosa's winter
coat, her Alpha Omega House identification card, and her almost-empty pack of
Newport cigarettes. Rosa then signs her name, writes down her destination, and
records the current time in the gray binder marked "resident log." Expected back
by 1 p.m., Rosa quickly heads out the door. Her destination is within walking
distance, just short of a mile away, but residents are instructed to take public
transportation. The bus ride there will take almost an hour and a half.

Rosa is not wearing her usual skin-tight gray cotton shorts and undersized tank
top because it is close to zero outside. Instead, she sports a body-hugging gray
cotton sweatshirt with sequins on the zipper and even tighter matching sweatpants with a white sneaker on one foot and a black medical boot on the other
for her still-healing broken toe. She wears a tight-fitting down vest over the en-
semble. Standing under the word CONVENT, etched in the marble over the door,
she lights a smoke even before the door clicks shut. Taking her usual tiny steps,
she makes her way up the walkway and through the wrought-iron gate, where she
pauses to drag on her cigarette. Sliding across the icy sidewalks never cleared of

snow from a storm three days earlier, she throws her butt away as she tiptoes into the slushy cobblestone street beside honking cars and passing busses. It takes Rosa ten minutes to walk the fifty yards to the bus stop, where she lights another cigarette and then snuffs it out before boarding the bus, putting the half-smoked butt back into her pack. Rosa pulls herself into the bus and hands over three dollars—good for the one-way ride on that bus and a transfer to another. This leaves Rosa with about five dollars for the next two weeks. She will have to borrow bus money from staff for the next two trips to her IOP and repay it during the next money week.

The scene passing outside the bus window is one of inner-city decay characteristic of this urban neighborhood. Visible to the bus rider are open-air drug selling and drug use, boarded-up row homes, graffiti-covered metal gates across closed storefronts, the occasional pilfered automobile, and backpacked children on their way to school. Rosa points to the places along the way that are good for selling drugs and talks openly about which of the "meds" she takes every day are "hot" products in today's drug market; "zannies" could fetch her upward of twenty dollars a pill. A woman sitting in the row behind Rosa taps her shoulder with blackened fingers under her fingernails, a sure sign of drug injection. "Ya got any works?" she asks Rosa. This is street lingo for drug injecting paraphernalia. "Nah," Rosa replies, turning her head toward the woman momentarily. At the fourth stop, Rosa steps off the bus to make a transfer for the next bus going west and lights the last barely smoked cigarette. The smell of marijuana is strong in the air during the wait on this busy street corner with other riders waiting for the transfer, passers-by begging for money, and hustlers selling pirated movies, bottled scents, single cigarettes called "loosies," and drugs.

After a short trip up the avenue, Rosa arrives at an old brick structure housing various social services for adults. She smokes another cigarette before joining a small group in the waiting room for "Possibilities," a program for women with mental-health and substance-abuse problems who are on probation, parole, or residing at a reentry center. A young child accompanying one of the women is running around the room and jumping on and off chairs. Laurel is also there, having taken an earlier bus. One woman says she is from a different reentry center in the area, and the rest say they are on probation or parole. As the women wait for "group," talk turns to topics from last week's session and other women who are in trouble—"all smoked up" from getting high on drugs, back in jail because they "caught a new case," or "on the run," having absconded from programs since last week. At 10 a.m. a social service worker leads the women down a narrow hallway to a small, windowless conference room where everyone takes a seat around an oval table. A counselor escorts the young child into a play area.

The session begins with Rosa discussing her lonely weekend without visits and her worries about how she will handle home visits at the next phase of her stay. Last week when she rode the bus back to the house, a woman asked her where she could buy some "wet," Rosa's favorite drug. The exchange made her nervous, she tells the group, because having been a constant abuser for more than twenty years since the age of thirteen, her mind immediately sped to that familiar feel of the first inhale. She worries about how to avoid the ever-present pull of the drug in her 'hood. The idle time at Alpha Omega House does not help to free her mind of this worry. She says "And dat place ain't doin' nuthin' for me. We always stuck in dat fuckin' room." She pushes her chair back from the table. "Dat's all I got." Rosa offers just a hint of her struggles at this group therapy session, because "you never know who gonna talk shit behind ya" or "disrespect ya" face to face. Just last week a fistfight broke out across the table between two women when one interrupted the other.

Rosa looks to the woman to her left who begins with how hard recovery can be. Crystal is a middle-aged woman who has been caught like the others in a continuous cycle in and out of the criminal justice system for drug-related crimes. After her testimony, she spends the rest of the session texting with her phone in her lap, interjecting from time to time with comments like "uh-huh," "yeah sista," and "dat shit fucked up." Loretta, a fifty-ish black woman with a platinum wig and bright red lipstick talks of her struggles with a thirty-plus-year crack addiction. She is a former resident of Alpha Omega House, or "the convent house," as she calls it. Between answering texts, she tells the group she hopes this is the last time she ever has to get clean again. She says, "I done played out, I ain't got no more play at it." The last time she used was with her daughter the weekend before. She says of that day, "My daughter got one dick in her mouth 'n another up her ass wit her six-year-old dumb-bitch daughter walkin' around singin' Beyoncé. Dat shit fucked up," she says; "dat little girl a bitch, she a dumb bitch, constantly singin' da same song."

Mac sits next to Loretta and shakes her head. She is a tough-looking woman in her late twenties with her neck and all visible parts of her arms and hands covered in classic grayish prison tattoos. Her testimony is bittersweet; she was reunited with her brother and sister with whom she lost touch after her own incarceration, but the meeting was to say goodbye to her mother who was comatose from yet another drug overdose. Across from Mac and sitting next to Rosa is a woman with heavy black makeup underlining her eyes, accentuated by hair extensions that look like long red and black ropes hanging from her head. Her tongue ring is visible when she speaks about how she "caught another case" for shoplifting while she was on parole and is probably headed back to prison. Beside her is a twenty-something woman wearing a bright pink sweater and a black hajib. Her head points down to a phone in her lap that beeps incoming texts throughout the session. Then Laurel from the Alpha Omega House takes the floor. She starts with complaints about the routine of idleness structuring her days, "doin' nuthin' all day" and her frustration with "bein' locked up in there." For the past several months, she has struggled with her youngest son's incarceration and her inability to visit him. "Dat still my nigga, my son. I gots to still be there. But he in God's hands, there's nothing dat I can do for him now," she cries. "He be okay, Laurel," Crystal says. "He gotta figure dat shit out for hisself," adds Loretta. "Um-hum," Mac adds. "How was your week, Quintera?" asks the moderator, turning to a young, very masculine woman dressed in an unzipped sweatshirt with a tank top over a flat chest and Dickies construction pants with unlaced men's workboots. Her shaved head makes it even more difficult to discern her gender. Newly released from jail, she tells the group that she is "grateful" to be back with her girl. As Mac nods her understanding and Crystal offers an "uh-hun, sista," the social worker notes the hour and dismisses the group.

Rosa and Laurel return to Alpha Omega House together before 1 p.m. Like everyone else who leaves unsupervised for IOP, the pair is under strict instructions to travel directly to and from treatment in an allotted amount of time. Any diversion is a "deviation" punishable by write-ups, fines, reprimand, drug testing, restriction, or even discharge. As Rosa flings her smoldering butt at the building's façade, and Laurel points a middle finger toward the front door and remarks, "Takin' one last muthafuckin' breath," and then lowers her finger to ring the doorbell. "Ding dong, pop" sounds the door, and Laurel pushes it wide. They step inside and immediately sign back in, being sure to note the current time. Having also returned from IOP moments ago, Candy is getting searched. She raises her arms up and out as the monitor pats her down. Candy is dismissed, and the monitor moves to Rosa as Candy disappears in the hall yelling, "Goin' up!" "Shakin' out," Rosa sings as she lifts her sweatshirt and bra, leans forward, and shakes so that anything hidden between her breasts and the bra could fall to the floor. She pushes up her shirtsleeves, then pulls out the insides of her pants pockets. She raises her left leg and draws her pant leg to her calf but needs to grab the wall to balance her body. "Awright," says the monitor, and Rosa lifts her right leg. The monitor takes a close look inside Rosa's medical boot. "Did'ja buy anything?" the monitor asks. "Nah," answers Rosa, who hands over four bills and the coins from her pocket. The monitor will compare that amount with what she recorded when Rosa left. Had Rosa purchased anything, she would have handed the monitor a receipt showing how much she spent so that her "book" would be balanced. Rosa then hands over her identification card, her down vest, and her pack of Newport cigarettes. Sighing loudly, she makes her way in tiny steps to the living room as Laurel steps before the monitor.

Searches like this occur whenever a woman reenters the building, even after being sent outside on the grounds to pick up litter. Nothing can be brought in from the outside: no cell phones, no extra money, no less money without a receipt, no cigarettes, no drugs, no alcohol, no food, no candy, no clothing, no books, not even a clover found growing in the abandoned lot—nothing at all.

The group session attended by Rosa and Laurel is the most common type of treatment IOP program attended by the women and key to the therapeutic-community approach. Otherwise known as a self-help group or life-skills group, it is also a very common form of therapy for criminal justice populations. Participants in each session carry on the "treatment," and a moderator—in this case the social worker—guides discussion. This type of therapy focuses on peer involvement in learning new adaptive attitudes and reactions to common problems and emotional as well as behavioral triggers that sustain drug use and criminal activity. According to research, the cognitive-behavioral approach, which varies in setting and structure, is effective at reducing recidivism (Cullen and Gendreau, 2000; Gendreau and Goggin, 1996).

Alpha Omega House, like many criminal justice agencies, brokers treatment services to community agencies. The IOP attended by Rosa and Laurel is one of several programs that collaborate with the house. Every woman who makes it to C Level is placed into IOP at one of several privately operated programs in the community. Some programs offer a generic set of services for women, such as group therapy and life-skills programming. Other programs are geared to more individualized needs, like parenting or woman abuse treatment, as well as to particular crimes, like prostitution. The IOP attended by Laurel and Rosa is geared to women with children and those with substance-abuse and mental-health problems. It offers treatment primarily through the group sessions, but women also meet with a social worker and other IOP staff for one-on-one counseling as well as receive psychiatric assessment. The IOP also advertises childcare, education, employment, housing, and financial-planning services. Depending on her particular program plan, women can attend group sessions or other programs two, three, or even five times each week.

Without data on the IOPs, it is hard to say just how effectively these interventions are carried out. But they advertise therapeutic approaches known to be effective for criminal justice populations: they are community-based; rehabilitative in nature; focused on criminogenic needs like substance abuse, mental health, and woman abuse; and they include multiple treatment modalities, such as group and individual therapy (see Cullen and Gendreau, 2000). Discussions with the women who participate in the IOP programs suggest they do benefit from them. As a group, the women look forward to getting out of the house for the treatment and say their therapies are beneficial. Rosa likes to attend because she can "vent," and Clair is glad she can "be led by people who know about addiction." IOP helps Candy cope with her history of violent victimization as well as her proclivity to resolve disputes with violence, and Phoebe says she is "happy" to attend substance-abuse group "with other junkies" because it is a supportive and caring environment to "talk about problems and whatnot."

Classes in House

While most of the women who make it to C Level enjoy finally getting to participate in IOP at some point, their involvement takes them out of the house just a few hours each week. This means they are still primarily exposed to the conditions at the house and treatment offered therein. At Alpha Omega House, women's treatment is not structured as one might expect in a therapeutic community, which at its most basic level should treat the whole person (De Leon, 1999; Schram, Koons-Witt, Williams, and McShane, 2006), or in a reentry center, with meetings, job assignments, recreation, counseling, and other activities scheduled throughout a regimented day. Rather, women wait in long periods of idleness for volunteers to bring treatment to them in the form of half-hour or hourlong classes.

This section describes two such classes. One is called Houses of Healing. A college intern runs the other. As will become clear, treatment at Alpha Omega House is poorly conceptualized, badly structured, and runs counter to the principles of effective intervention.

HOUSES OF HEALING

It is quiet in the living room in spite of the blaring television on a dim winter Wednesday afternoon. Grace, Henrietta, Rosa, Laurel, Phoebe, Candy, and Mimi are slouched in their seats, talking loudly over the crime-scene drama playing out on the television. The intercom sounds, "All residents report to the living room for class."

Just then, a middle-aged white woman with graying hair and pursed lips walks quickly into the room, placing two paper grocery bags on the chair beside me. Standing, she starts firmly, "I am here for a healing class. These chairs need to be arranged in a circle. I want you to move them now."

"What class?" Mimi and Laurel ask simultaneously.

"Huh?" asks Henrietta.

"I will tell you when I am ready," the woman snaps back, raising her voice and then moving to the television. She fumbles with the remote control as she tries to turn the television off. She continues with her back to the women, "This class is Houses of Healing." She turns to the group with her hands on her hips. "This involves self-work, homework."

"What the fuck," Candy utters.

"It is emotional healing," the woman announces. "You will work through traumas from childhood." She takes a seat and gathers papers from one of the bags.

The last comment raises eyebrows. The women are unnerved. Henrietta crosses her arms. Candy laughs out loud and then sighs. Grace shakes her head no. It is not the first time a stranger with a "mandatory class" has entered this room without the women knowing what is about to happen. Their defenses are up now.

Phoebe crosses her legs saying, "Fuck this."

Rosa adds, "Ya gotta be fuckin' kiddin' me."

"Are you a therapist?" Laurel asks the woman.

"No," she replies.

Phoebe asks, "And *you* want *us* to spill out everything that hurt us in our lives and get this out and then what?"

The woman sits and stares before answering, "You have to work through the problems in your life that caused you to be here."

"You kiddin' me? You think I'm gonna talk to you about *my* childhood?" Laurel retorts.

The woman replies as she fumbles in her bags, "It will not be easy, it involves self-work and it will be hard, but I promise that it will pay off."

Laurel pauses and then compares the task to a never-healing wound and growing more agitated with every word:

> "It's like a scab. I want it to heal. I don't wanna keep diggin' at it. You wanna dig at it. *No,* it gets crusty, 'n ya dig 'n it gets infected again. 'N da thing is, alright so shit happened, fucked-up shit. I can't let it keep fuckin' wit my future. If I keep bein' followed by it, I'm never growin.' So stop pickin' at me, Lady, I'm not your fuckin' scab. No, I'm not doin' all that. *Stop.* People want to keep pickin.' Dat shit happened like fuckin' four decades ago. Get da fuck outa here. That's how people stay sick 'cause people tellin' them all da time that's because of this, because that happened."

She stands and bows and then returns to her seat.

Phoebe nods her head up and down in agreement as she uncrosses her legs. Mimi is silent. Candy agrees, "Ya got dat shit right." Henrietta says, "Fuck dis." Rosa just stares. Grace looks nervously at the others.

The woman continues shuffling papers from her bag, dismissing Laurel's comments: "You have to participate. This is a mandatory class. This is a class for prisoners. You are prisoners. It is designed for prisoners."

"Whaaaat!?" Laurel and Candy shout at once.

"I dote wan be he [here]," Grace adds as she shakes her head back and forth like a toddler not wanting to eat.

"Dis bullshit," says Henrietta.

"I'm so fuckin' angry," Laurel says. Rosa is now shaking her head with her arms crossed over her large body. She tips her head up with her chin out in a posture of toughness. Mimi is just glaring at the woman. Phoebe and Laurel exchange complaints. Candy rises to leave but turns back and sits.

"Stop the cross-talk," the woman demands, then continues, "It is a two-hour thirteen-week mandatory class. You have to do it so let it go. Let the hostility go. This is about helping women heal. I guarantee you that if you do the 'self-work' then you will see personal growth. Take a packet of information." She hands me a pile of stapled papers with the title page reading "Hostile, Controlling, Angry" in large print and gestures for me to pass them along.

Laurel and Henrietta leaf through the pages. Phoebe is fanning herself with her packet and again crosses her legs. Mimi is just holding her packet still agape.

Candy has her packet rolled up as if she is ready to swat a fly. Rosa flips through the pages. Grace places hers on the floor at her feet.

"Let's read on page eighteen," she says as she turns to Henrietta.

"She can't read," says Laurel.

"Then she can be read to by another person," says the woman.

"No way," snaps Henrietta proudly. "I ain't havin' no one read ta me. I ain't a chile."

Grace cannot read either. She mumbles as she rises and walks out of the room. Phoebe has found a pen and clicks it in and out above her head, uncrossing and crossing her legs. Sitting next to her, Mimi continues to watch the stranger with the mandatory class.

"Ah, fuck it." Rosa jumps in and starts to read very slowly as she struggles with the words: "Personal sub-personalities are things that we use to express ourselves, but which are not who we really are." She rubs her forehead and stops.

"Is controlling one of your sub-personalities?" Laurel asks the woman, and laughter fills the room, easing some of the tension.

"No, it is my teacher's role," the woman quips.

"Weeelll," Laurel begins with her hands out, gesturing to the woman, "I commend *you* for wanting to work with *prisoners*."

Candy jumps from the couch, pointing her finger to the woman as she yells, "People always classifyin' us as prisonas. We in society. People always use dat term ta classify us, 'n it wrong, we are not prisonas no more. We in here 'cause we about to be livin' out there. Don't call us prisonas." Candy appears to be on the verge of tears or a violent rage. She stands motionless, piercing the woman with her black eyes and then returns to her seat.

The woman looks blankly at Candy and then quickly demands Phoebe stop clicking the pen and Laurel stop "cross-talking" to Mimi.

"I done," Grace says as soon as she happens back into the room. She turns and walks out again.

"Fuck dis," said Henrietta.

"What you do in this class is up to you," the woman continues.

"You come in here disrespectful 'n want us to talk to ya 'bout things that happened to us?" Phoebe asks, dumbfounded.

Rosa is reading the packet of information in her lap. Mimi is shaking her head. Laurel is laughing nervously with Candy.

"What do we get outta this, a 'tificate [certificate]?" asks Henrietta as everyone but the woman breaks out into a roar. This is an inside joke; after completing any "class," say Bible study or learning about contraception, a woman is awarded a paper dollar-store Certificate of Completion with her name scribbled across and an "official" signature of house staff. Henrietta continues, laughing, "What my reward is?"

"There are no rewards," the woman replies looking down at the stapled packet in her lap. She then asks aloud, "Who am I? I want to ask you to go around the room and say who you are."

"Yeah, who are you? I'm Laurel. You never told us who you are," asks Laurel.

Looking away from Laurel she says, "My name is Olga. *Now,* who are *you?*" she continues, asking Henrietta to begin.

"I'm a skip-a-frinic [schizophrenic]," says Henrietta, and the laughter begins again.

"Say what?" replies Laurel, "Skip to France?" and the laughter grows louder.

Rosa is more serious. "Ok, I am a daughter, sister, granddaughter, niece, 'n I have a nephew dat I love."

"*No,*" interrupts Olga, "just tell about *who* you are."

"I *am* tellin' ya. Don't interrupt me. Ya asked me and I'm tellin' ya," replies Rosa loudly. "I'm a recovering addict," she continues.

Olga interrupts Rosa again, raising her voice, "*No, stop,* don't say that."

Rosa does not have that tattoo of bloodied fists on her bicep just for kicks; it is a signal of just how tough she is. She sits up in her chair, tightens her chest, and shouts back as she points a finger to Olga, "Don't ask me da fuck again! You're rude. Don't ask me *nuthin.*'"

"Okay, next?" Olga continues as she dismisses Rosa.

Henrietta starts, "I'ma motha, sista, grandmotha, wife, woman. I'ma nice person when ya getta know me," she adds, laughing.

"*Quiet,*" Olga orders Henrietta.

Mimi finally speaks, "If she don't laugh, she gets angry. That's how she deals with stuff that bothers her. You should let her laugh," she warns.

Grace reenters and sits on a small wooden chair safely squeezed between two sofas close to Rosa on one side and Candy on the other. She says nervously, "I got eigh ki [eight kids], uh, ni ki. I'ma how-key [housekeeper]. I hate he [here]. I try do beh [best I] can."

"I got fake teeth," Laurel blurts as she flashes the middle finger with both hands as if to signal a gang sign. Candy and Henrietta laugh aloud. Phoebe nudges Laurel in the ribs giggling.

Unaware of my presence as researcher and assuming that I too am a resident of Alpha Omega House forced to take part in this mandatory class, Olga turns to me and asks who I am. Before I can speak, Laurel shouts to Olga, "That my nigga, Double O-G." Grace sings loudly, "Ga[il] in da hou[se]"!"

Then Candy raps, "I'm someone who made a mistake, went upstate'n now 'bout to hit da gate." She then says seriously and sternly to Olga, "I gotta do what I need ta do, I'ma human bein,' a woman, so please don't classify me as a prisonar. I ask you *please* don't do that."

Laurel announces like a robot, moving her head with her shoulders as one back and forth, "I am convict number 748666 [her actual prison identification number]." Phoebe chuckles and Candy howls. Having emotionally checked out, Rosa has been flipping through a book she grabbed at random from the bookcase behind her head and says to herself, "This fucked up."

Laurel continues, "I'ma good mother, a comedian, a great person 'n I sell drugs, I like suckin' 'n fuckin,' *the end.*" Laughter erupts in the room. Pointing to Mimi, Laurel adds, "'n she a pimp." More laughter fills the room. It is another inside joke about the brothel Mimi ran from her home with her daughter, managing the work of several sex workers. She could be called a pimp, but she prefers the title "madam."

Mimi takes over: "I am a mother, a grandmother, a bartender. I was a madam. I am a nice person. I love animals 'n kids." She smiles and turns to Phoebe who continues to click her pen.

Phoebe says with arms waving, "I am Phoebe Colleen Costa. I have ADHD. I am very stressful, I am a smartass better than a dumbass, I am bipolar. I am a hot shot, hot shit, hotty with a body, a recovering addict, daughter, aunt, sister, granddaughter. I crash cars." The room again fills with laughter.

Olga shouts, "*No,* tell me *who* you are."

Leaning out of her seat, shouting directly across the room to Olga, Phoebe says, "I *am* telling you who I am."

Candy jumps in and demands to Olga plainly, "Who are you?"

Olga replies, "I already told you. I am teaching this class." She rises from her seats and hands each woman a workbook titled *Houses of Healing: A Prisoner's Guide to Inner Power and Freedom.* She continues, "The class begins each week with meditations, then I will give you a lecture. Then we will have an inner process and then reflection." She stands in front of Rosa, and asks Rosa to continue with the reading.

"No," Rosa replies. "I told ya. No, don't ask me nothin.'"

The room is silent with tension. Laurel continues where Rosa left off. She then offers her view of the reading:

> It says basically dat hostility 'n the other sub-personalities are bad. I say no. I learned how to be rough, tough, 'n hard, 'n that's who I am. I'm strong; I don't depend on no man, woman, or child for anything. Knowin' I'm strong keeps me safe. I'm not gonna allow people to step on me. Now, I love just as hard. If we hangin' 'n we got busted, I'm wit ya, we get booked together, wassup. If I bang with ya, we bang real hard. I'm a loyal friend. Ya use defense techniques to keep yourself safe, it make me a better person, I can see shit before da stink.

Laurel's last point is well made. The objectives of the class, it seems, is for "prisoners" to discard unproductive "sub-personalities" like anger, hostility, and deception in order to live emotionally freer and more wholesome, honest lives. And the rationale, it seems, is that if women like Laurel and the others really know themselves, including their flaws and the goodness within, they can re-form. Laurel's argument, however, makes perfect sense. She is well aware of herself, including her flaws. However, what the "treatment" defines as her flaws are really her strengths, because without her toughness or skepticism, Laurel would fail to survive in her social world. This class experience is an example of a gender-responsive strategy that is oppressive in practice.

According to the publisher, the book Olga used in this class is "a book for prisoners [that] addresses, in depth, the necessity of self-forgiveness and forgiveness of others—subjects that are often overlooked and misunderstood despite the fact that they are essential to the cultivation of empathy and emotional and spiritual maturity." One evaluation of a twelve-week course for incarcerated women based on this book reported no difference in measures (such as depression, anxiety, self esteem, and spiritual well-being) used to compare women who participated with women who did not (Ferszt, Salgado, DeFedele, and Leveillee, 2009). Like many other classes at the reentry center, this treatment approach seems to have failed for multiple reasons.

According to program administrators, Alpha Omega House contracted with Olga her volunteer services as well as the cost of program materials to provide this treatment over a period of months. While this arrangement is not privatization in the traditional sense, research tells us that the use of outside agencies in the administration of treatment programming in corrections raises concerns about program quality, program management, and accountability (Anderson, Davoli, and Moriarty, 1985). In terms of program quality, the instructor is an outsider disconnected from the experiences of the women and the real challenges they face in their reentry. She "can't relate," as Laurel says. "She don't know us," Candy reasons. To what extent Olga was exposed to working with correctional populations or trained on the use of the book and any accompanying curriculum is uncertain. But what is known is that Olga was not formally screened or interviewed by Alpha Omega House administrators. According to Cullen and Gendreau (2000), programs that involve untrained volunteers often fail because they lack therapeutic integrity. Furthermore, a study involving treatment program staff, prison administrators and women participants of treatment programs reveals the importance of treatment-staff qualifications and demeanor to the success of treatment for women inmates (Koons, Burrow, Morash, and Bynum, 1997). In the present case, the volunteer's demeaning and authoritative approach was nothing but abusive, and any positive benefit that could have been gained was lost. As Rosa explains, her "I'm better than you" attitude was perfectly communicated as it alienated women from the start.

THE VOLUNTEER INTERN

The doorbell rings. "Ding-dong" and "pop" sounds the front door. The intercom interrupts *CSI Miami,* just as it had three weeks earlier, as the women sit in the living room on an ordinary Wednesday afternoon: "Report to the living room for a class; all residents report to the living room for a mandatory class." The instructor is a woman named Davina, a correctional officer turned college student who is earning credits as part of an internship at Alpha Omega House. At first Davina is different from abusive Olga. Also a volunteer, Davina appears to be a strong woman who knows the 'hood, as she tells the women, and who can appreciate the challenges of being a woman in these tough neighborhoods. She offers no "class" in the formal sense of a treatment or education. Instead, as she explains, she plans to spend two hours every Wednesday afternoon to encourage the women to reform themselves and lead forward-moving lives; she comes as a friend who can listen and share her positive experiences.

Waiting at the doorway to the living room, she asks the residents if she may enter the room—a positive first step—and then introduces herself. She takes a seat in one of the wooden chairs along the windows and tells about her youth in hard circumstances and her "reformation" in young adulthood. Sitting on the edge of her seat, she turns toward Rosa and Candy and continues with strong words of encouragement: "You got to keep focused, keep going, knock 'n knock that door until you're ready to kick it down when you want to move ahead, let things go, work out problems, take advantage of any little bit of somethin' that they have to give you here."

The women are listening and some are interacting with Davina. For the next half hour, she keeps the attention of the women, even energizing them. She asks if she may return next week and does, every week for two hours to sit with the women in the living room and discuss with them life's challenges. Some of the women were encouraged too, especially Candy, Rosa, and Billie.

But it soon becomes apparent that Davina is not much different from Olga. She fails the women on two fronts. The first is her attitude and approach toward "treatment." The following exchange illustrates the problem. Candy, Phoebe, and Mimi are in attendance. Davina has introduced the session's topic as "responsibility" and begins by posing a question to Candy:

"What would you do if you found a wallet on the street?"

Candy replies, "I'd fuckin' take it."

"No," says Davina. "That's the wrong answer. You're not supposed to take it."

"No, I'd take dat money," Candy asserts.

"That's the wrong answer. You don't take the money."

"Yeah I do," said Candy.

"No, you shouldn't take the wallet," Davina says.

"Okaaaay," replies Candy sighing and smirking.

Davina continues, "What would you do if someone stole money from you and a friend said they knew who did it?"

"I'd kick dey fuckin' ass," announces Candy proudly smiling.

"No, that's the wrong answer," says Davina.

"You steal from me, I kick yo ass," Candy says. "I'd kick da bitch's ass," Candy repeats.

"No," says Davina, "that's the wrong answer."

"Fuck dat. Dat bitch be beat. I'd kick her ass," says Candy.

Mimi leans in to Candy and whispers, "Give the answer she wants so we can get outta here."

This treatment approach is not likely to change Candy's sense of personal and social responsibility or change her behavior. Davina might have wanted to help Candy make better moral choices and control her emotions, but she is not professionally trained or equipped with life experience to "rehabilitate" Candy. The second reason this intern from "da 'hood" fails the women is that she acts in a way the women will interpret as disloyal. The first tip-off is that she begins to spend more time sitting in the monitors' office with staff. Then she gives orders to women during chore time, even walking the upstairs hall, enforcing the no-mingling-in-the-hallway rule during the dispensing of medication when the house is "closed." Phoebe explains that she has changed her mind about Davina: "I thought I liked her at first, but then I seen a whole different her. It's hard to explain 'n whatnot. She come across like she nit-pickin,' like her body language, 'n she walked around here the other day like she was workin,' like she worked here 'n whatnot. Like checkin' shit out, 'n she not 'posed to be doin' that. That's probably why they have her in here—to spy on us 'n whatnot. She don't have no trust at all."

The others also note that Davina's attitude and behavior have become more like that the monitors' and not those of a kindred spirit trying to help. Laurel says, "She get up in our shit," meaning she is nosy and inspective. Perhaps Davina's past as a correctional officer worked against her too. Adeline refers to her as a "white shirt," the term for cop or staff member, and Candy says Davina is on a "power trip; she an officer 'n she ain't here to help." The fatal mistake that Davina makes that solidifies the impression that she is, as Mimi says, "against us," is telling the monitors that Phoebe has candy in her room. Even if Phoebe is not reprimanded or fined for this infraction, betraying trust makes Davina a rat, and a rat can never regain trust. When trust is lost, any potential of treatment will also vanish.

Not all of the volunteers who come to Alpha Omega House in the name of treatment act in ways that abuse and dominate the women. Some are inclusive, trustworthy, and honest women who seem to work hard to make a difference. But a positive and caring volunteer can only do so much to help women with broken lives reenter society after incarceration. Even if their intentions are otherwise, women like Olga and Davina cause actual harm. And for Alpha Omega House staff to allow abusive treatment to recur is a failure at the highest levels.

Unmet Needs

The roster of treatment services advertised to the women at Alpha Omega House is impressive and highly desirable, since residents have needs in a variety of areas. Quite a few of the women actively sought out the house as a treatment option because of its promised gender-responsive offerings, and many others agreed to placement rather than serving out their sentences when they believed they would get the help they needed. But as the basics of program evaluation and policy analysis remind us time and again, what appears on paper can be quite different than actual practice. Candy explains:

> Dey look good on paper 'n dat's it. This is nowhere to be rehabilitated. There's no structure here. There's nuthin' here. Dey need more meetins, dey need people ta show up, dey need people who don't think we less then them. Dey need everything dey put on dat brochure. Dey don't have none of that. Dey don't have life skills, dey do have parenting—but dey don't do nuthin,' that domestic thing—dey come when they wanna come, dey have this lady come dat reads damn books. Dey have bike ridin'—that's a good exercise, but how's dat gonna help me? We don't even have a "big book," no NA books. 'n what da fuck is a wallet on da street hav'ta do wit me livin' outa here? Ain't nothing happenin' there.

Although a Christian Bible hour offered weekly by committed volunteers, short bike rides led by a local group, or being read to by Simone (as described in chapter 3) might for some of the women provide an hour's distraction from their normative idleness, the women lack continuous and focused intervention that would support IOP treatment. As evidenced by their everyday routines, the women experience almost no maintenance for IOP treatment when they are at Alpha Omega House. In fact, everyday practices and services at the house work against the comprehensive and continuous delivery of services one might expect of a rehabilitative and reintegrative setting. According to Petersilia's review (2004) of what works in prisoner reentry, effective treatment programming should encompass 40–70 percent of the offender's time during the course of the program. But some women at Alpha Omega House attend actual IOP programming for as little as two hours weekly during the three months of C Level and subsequent phases and, by my observation, fewer than four hours weekly of dedicated classes in-house.

The following discussion describes the women's frustrations in the treatment planning at Alpha Omega House, namely the lack of wrap-around services and individualized treatment, women's inability to participate in choices about their own treatment plan, and the slow pace at which women are placed into IOP programs. All of this demonstrates how the subordination of women and their needs is fostered at Alpha Omega House in their transition from punishment to community life.

Rosa attends IOP group three times each week, but worries about having enough support at her six-month juncture at Alpha Omega House. She attends the mandatory classes, like Simone's reading class and Davina's internship, and she is mandated to the half-hour-long parenting class. IOP a few days each week helps her, but Rosa needs more. She says: "It ain't preparin' me for nuthin.' All dis place givin' me is parentin' classes 'n for what? I don't even fuckin' have kids. I don't have no kids. All dis place givin' is parentin' classes. Dat's all dis place offers me. So really, dis place ain't doin nuthin.'"

Like Rosa, Clair wants focused help with her addiction when she is not at IOP. Mimi wants a job. Laurel needs help to make better relationship choices and stay away from the drugs. Phoebe cannot seem to resolve childhood trauma on her own or quit her heroin and cocaine addiction without close monitoring and guidance. Grace has major treatment needs and wants to live independently. Henrietta should learn to control her anger. Billie wants to read. All of the residents have individualized needs that require much more intervention. Mimi knows that building comprehensive treatment plans based on individual treatment needs is a starting point for effective correctional intervention.[2] She says: "Each person is an individual here. You can't give us all the same stuff. The only thing good is when ya go to outpatient, they ask what ya need. It should be individualized for each person. Like you need domestic abuse, you need this outpatient plus meetings, you need a job search. We are not discarded people. We need treatment. We shouldn't be thrown away."

Part of giving women treatment they need is to give them a voice. Like Mimi, Freya knows that generic treatment does not work for everyone and that women need individualized programming. Giving them a say about this treatment is key, she says: "Instead of workin' with me 'n appreciatin' my input 'n things that I feel would help me as an individual, don't group me 'n throw me into some class that won't help me. I know how to put on a condom. I am a drug addict, 'n I need NA. I know that. I'm not stupid."

While IOP is said to start when women move from Zero to C Level, women often wait in limbo for a month or longer for that treatment to begin. Adeline has been on C Level for more than a month and still has no treatment plan. She says, "Getting' domestic counselin' is not happenin' 'cause I'm not a priority. I'm not an addict, so they ain't helpin' me." So her days are spent locked inside, away from help she desperately wants and needs. She does participate in the parenting class, however. She says of that:

> I'm thirty-three years old 'n they are teachin' me how to use a condom. It
> was pretty funny, though, with the dildos 'n all. They were blue 'n pink, 'n

some had dolphins on 'em. We all got a kick outa it. But shit like this happens all the time. Last week they made me go to an Alcoholics Anonymous meetin.' Why? I don't have a drinkin' problem! We do word search puzzles every week. Why? I need domestic violence counselin.' It's dumb. I gotta go 'n get help for stuff that I don't need help wit, but I can't get help for the shit I do need help wit. This is all part of the system. This stinks.

Adeline never got help she needed while in prison, and Alpha Omega House fails her too, as she is channeled into classes that set her to work playing with condoms, learning about how to overcome an addiction she does not have, and finding words in a puzzle. She says: "Like my whole case is the reason why I am here, the reason why the judge didn't put me upstate for life, 'cause he wants me to have domestic-abuse treatment, not for a narcotic or alcohol treatment. I'm starting to get worse again just sittin' around here. I need help. Everybody I look at looks like him [the man she loved and killed]. I need help . . . Like da main goal is to give you what you don't need. They *intentionally* want us to fail."

While she had a kindhearted sentencing judge who had the presence of mind to keep her out of prison and assign her to a reentry center funded to help rehabilitate women, she sits and waits, shut off from the world. Her treatment needs remain unmet, and she suffers as a consequence. Research also finds that unmet treatment needs create additional problems, such as institutional misconduct and failure on parole, as well as recidivism.[3] Though advertised as a reentry program that focuses on gender-responsive strategies, this study reveals glaring omissions in the treatment and services at Alpha Omega House for childhood and adult trauma and victimizations, education, a history of poverty, and a lack of marketable employment skills, among other problems.

Billie also waits for her treatment to begin, even though she was eligible to start IOP when she moved to C Level weeks ago. She also wants the educational opportunities promised, but she will never have those, nor will any other woman but for Rosa, the single exception. Waiting for her substance-abuse IOP to commence, Billie spends her days sitting in the living room in front of the television dressed as if she is expecting a job interview. She completed the usual ticket to speak to staff, but two weeks passed and she has heard nothing. She can contain her frustration no longer. Sitting in the living room dressed in a light blue women's suit straight from the 1980s with black flats and a purse at her side, Billie explodes in frustration, yelling, "I'm sick of dis place! I wanna blow dis place up! I'm fightin' my addiction every day. I'm in my head every second. I'm ready ta walk out 'n go. I'm ready ta leave. Every day I fight it. Dis place isn't giving me what I need. I've been sittin' her for three months, where's my help. I need help. Dey don't care."

Adeline moves to Billie's side and takes her hand. Billie sobs aloud and then screams again. Quick to respond to emotional outbursts like this, a monitor appears in the entryway to the living room, followed by an administrative staff member from the basement. The staff member turns off the television and sits near the door and away from Billie. She asks Billie, "How'd your day start?" Billie replies, "I was feelin' bad. I need help for my addiction. I fight it all da time. Why can't I go out for help? I'ma 'posta be gettin' IOP." The staff member asks if anyone can respond to Billie. Adeline replies honestly: "I tried to tell her to be calm 'n the feeling will pass. But I have to agree with her. Women are strugglin' with addiction. A lot of da women need treatment 'n some people are gettin' treatment dey don't need."

But the staff member corrects Adeline that even though Billie is almost four months into the program, she is not ready for IOP, and the only way to deal with this is to "tough it out," to be strong and self-reliant. She tells Billie: "You are stronger than any addiction. You have to wait. I would love to send you somewhere [for IOP], but what if you all up in your head 'bout what you wanna do? You gotta wait it out. Use this time to dream, ask yourself what would it be like if I gave into my addiction. You're gonna have to hold some stuff down. You're gonna just have to work it out. It's all about you. It's only up to you."

The staff member rises to her feet and takes her leave as Billie continues to cry. Adeline strokes Billie's hand. Mimi remarks: "Can you believe that shit? Isn't that the purpose of this place, to help us? If we could do it on our own, we wouldn't be here." In her comments, the staff member seems to be referencing the principle of self-help that is an integral part of treatment in the therapeutic community model. According to De Leon (1997, p. 4), self-help is a process of "incremental learning toward a stable change in behavior, attitudes and values of right living that are associated with maintaining abstinence." But to engage in self-help is to do more than to "wait it out" or "dream" or "hold some stuff down." Rather, a supportive environment of multiple interventions including work and educational and therapeutic activities structured throughout the day facilitate self-help, as do meetings, various groups, and seminars.

The lack of wrap-around services and individualized treatment, the women's inability to participate in choices about their own treatment plan, and the slow pace at which they are placed into IOP programs harm women at Alpha

Omega House in their transition from punishment to community life. Moreover, women are banned from using computers that can help them learn about the world, locate employment, or communicate with loved ones. They are not set up for paid work, as will be discussed in the next chapter. Those who are illiterate are not taught how to read or write and have no access to audiobooks or other accommodating materials. Women who struggle with addiction complain they are not provided enough exposure to Narcotics Anonymous or Alcoholics Anonymous programming. Nearly all of the women have been victimized as children or adults, but they receive no dedicated services outside of IOP to help them heal from those traumas. Though advertised, family reunification with people who really matter in their lives is not facilitated. As discussed in chapter 3, the women are not allowed to cook, plan their meals, or truly manage money. They have little say in the IOP treatment they are assigned and no input into which reintegrative services could really benefit them. These are the most obvious examples of how female oppression and domination is fostered at Alpha Omega House.

Resistance

With oppression comes resistance. As the nature of control changes for women at different phases of stay at Alpha Omega House, so do their reactions to control. During their time at C Level, women expect more in the way of comprehensive reentry services, but they experience a slow pace of treatment programming and a lack of comprehensive reentry services, which further stresses and frustrates them. In response, they rely on many of the resistance strategies they have used already and begin to employ new ones as they become possible. They use parody and humor to handle being pushed around, but they cannot pray away abusive volunteers.

Having already spent months at Alpha Omega House, C Level residents are fully integrated into the informal culture of the house and its corresponding sisterhood. The newfound integration of the women with fellow residents particularly supports three new resistance strategies: strike and refusal, sneak trips, and self-reliance. Resistance strategies used at this phase of stay are sometimes overt acts of defiance, such as confrontation, which tends to bring upon the strongest forms of counter-resistance. Women take advantage of their greatest freedom of C Level—getting outside for IOP—to care for themselves and others through sneak trips away from supervision and surveillance. Furthermore, the women's adage "one man one armband" demonstrates the power of their personal agency, expressed through self-reliance.

STRIKE AND REFUSAL

"Ding-dong," sounds the doorbell, quickly followed by the sound of the intercom: "Ladies, report to the living room for mandatory class." It is Wednesday evening. This means Davina is back. The women have had enough of Davina's "class" and strike collectively. Candy shakes her head, saying to Davina as she enters the living room, "You late; you not supposta come here now. You hour's up." Henrietta picks up from Candy and adds from the sofa as Davina stops in her tracks in response to Candy: "We ain't gotta take your class, you late." Arms crossed and shaking their heads no, Mimi, Adeline, Keira, and Clair silently agree as Davina scans the room. Davina then turns around and walks back to the monitors' office. The women's strike paid off. Though Davina's weekly presence at the house will continue, residents say they are no longer mandated to participate in her class, and Davina's movement throughout the house is now restricted. Laurel sees the collective resistance as a victory: "Dat bitch cop, we got her outta here. We let dat bitch have it last night, da way she be walkin' around the buildin' ya know. So dey [staff] told her she can't go upstairs 'n nuthin' else 'cept talk ta who wants ta, 'cause we said we don't feel comfy around her. We said she acts like a cop."

Even while the women at the house mistrust one another, they know that collective action is sometimes necessary. Mimi says: "Even though we don't all get along in here, we'll stick up for each other if an outsider does somethin.' We bicker 'n fight all the time 'n we might have bigger beefs, but let somebody else talk shit to us 'n watch what happens." The supportive connection inherent in the cultural sisterhood of the residents transcends relationship problems among them and benefits them all. It is the strength of the sisterhood's commitment to support resistance that makes the strike strategy viable. But because collective resistance strategies and openly defiant tactics are more often met with strong counter-resistance,[4] they are used less frequently.

Refusal to comply or cooperate is a related resistance strategy the residents use more frequently. When practiced by individuals resisting therapy, refusal is characterized foremost by emotional, mental, or social withdrawal, and noncompliance (Billow, 2007). Like the strike, refusal is directly oppositional and often involves collective action or collective resistance to remove problematic staff

(Jurik, Cavender, and Cowgill, 2009). The women successfully used refusal to remove Olga the abusive class facilitator. (To neutralize Davina, they used direct confrontation through collective action—the strike.) In Olga's class, refusal was communicated through withdrawal and noncompliance, in addition to parody and humor.

Most of the time, refusal to attend or participate in mandatory classes, to follow rules, or complete tasks occurs at the individual level. Morning exercise is so unpopular, for instance, that Rosa deliberately skips it even though she will "catch a fine" or "get a write-up" for noncompliance. If forced to attend mandatory classes against their will, as the women usually are, they know how to separate themselves emotionally even while they remain physically present. Clair's comments reflect the group's perspective: "You resist what you can get away with." Refusal practiced at the individual level usually yields little counter-resistance. The women who oppose the class called Bible study because of their faith, or morning exercise because they are ill, for example, learn that staff have little to gain by forcing them into participate. An often-refused rule is the requirement to announce use of the stairway to the bathroom and bedrooms. Women protest because the rule demeans them. Henrietta says, "Dey treat us nasty like we animals. Dey talk like we animals. Just like havin' ta say I'm goin' upstairs? Why do I have to say I'm goin' upstairs, 'n we live here? Dey disrespects us." It took Henrietta some time before she refused this rule because she was worried about receiving a fine, but she learns by the examples set by other women that she is unlikely to get anything but a verbal reprimand. Clair never really followed the rule completely. She says, "I don't say 'goin' up,' I just go up. What can they do?" And the verbal reprimands she "catches" are acceptable to her.

Refusal also takes the form of individual resistance when the women are instructed to perform a task or follow a rule they feel is beyond what should be expected of participants (Trethewey, 1997). Rosa refused an order by staff to "clean better" in the basement conference room. "I won," she says. "I told her I'm not doin' it, write me up, I don't care." She explains: "You know dey watchin' you in da cameras. Miss Wendy calls me up, tellin' me I gotta clean dem spider webs in da windows where I have ta literally climb on somethin' cause da windows high up. I said no. I'm not doin' dat. I told her straight up, I'm not climbin on nuthin' so my fat ass could fuckin' fall 'n break sunthin' else. I had just finished breakin' my foot here. Like no, I told her straight up. I thought she was gonna write me up for dat shit. She didn't." Rosa's resistance through refusal paid off.

Mimi is past C Level, but her situation also illustrates the point that the refusal strategy can produce change. Preparing for her upcoming graduation, she planned to resume work. Having cleared the arrangement with probation, she needed the okay of an administrative staff member to finalize the arrangement. A discussion about the job quickly turned sour as the administrative staff member threatened to sanction Mimi for her communication style. Mimi says: "Miss Prenice brought me downstairs 'n said, If ya don't communicate better—she's like—I'm gonna give you written essays to do. I said you could try; that's not part of my requirements of bein' here, doin' written essays. Go ahead, you can try. Watch 'n see if I do it, what are ya gonna do? Put me on restriction 'cause I won't write an essay?" Mimi's refusal worked insofar as she was not assigned the essay and not placed on restriction, but she lost too; her work request was not approved.

Both rebellion and refusal are overt forms of resistance involving action and opposition that are both visible and recognized as such by targets of resistance (Hollander and Einwohner, 2004). Collective or individual resistance efforts of this type at Alpha Omega House are sometimes met with counter-resistance; therefore, they are used strategically by the women when the context is right.

CONFRONTATION

Confrontation is another individual strategy used by women residents to meet their needs. It involves individual face-to-face conflict with monitors or administrative staff and can seen as aligned with resistance strategies such as complaints and challenge, fighting back, and confrontation with abusers that involves name-calling.[5] Women rarely use the confrontation strategy because it is usually met with the strongest forms of counter-resistance.

Confrontation is employed by residents of Alpha Omega House when residents experience what they call bullying behavior and humiliation by monitors. Bullying, which can occur between individuals at different levels of an organization's hierarchy (Hutchinson et al., 2006), occurs here between monitors and residents. Responding to behavior by monitors that she experiences as bullying, Phoebe reacts overtly and says: "I'm not gonna let people talk ta me like I'm a piece of shit." Normally quiet and compliant, Phoebe "mouths off" directly to authority when she feels belittled by monitors. In one instance, a monitor entering the living room at the start of her afternoon shift pointed to Phoebe and demanded that she go upstairs and change her shirt. "She musta been lookin' at the cameras for somebody to fuck with," Phoebe reasons. The monitor started directly toward Phoebe, saying, "It too tight, 'n your cleavage is showin' out . . . you supposta look like a lady." Interpreting this directive as offensive, Phoebe shouts back to the overweight monitor in loose-fitting medical scrubs, "Ladies have breasts. I have nice breasts, 'n I like showin' 'em. See, you don't like me. I don't like you. Don't talk to me 'cause you don't know how to talk to people." Phoebe then turns her head from the woman standing above her with arms crossed, dismissively staring toward the television. Shortly after the monitor retreats from the living room, Phoebe is called over the intercom to the monitors' office. "Fuck," she sighs as she pulls herself from the sofa and heads out. Her challenge to authority is met with a fine that Phoebe says is designed to "put me in my place."

Confrontation is similar to strike and refusal resistance strategies; it is a visible and known form of resistance, is interpreted as such by targets (Hollander and Einwohner, 2004), and is used when women object to participation or to rules. Those who use confrontation directly challenge authority. Take Victoria, an especially low-key, compliant woman, who can be quick to lash out when she feels disrespected. In the anecdote that follows, Victoria recalls an occasion before morning exercise as she nervously prepared herself to confront a monitor she believed had been needlessly bullying her for days.

> I remember sayin' to myself, put on your armor. Put on your armor for the battle. I was prepared because I was not gonna take it anymore; I said I'm not gonna take it from her anymore. I'm a grown woman. So when I got up that morning, I put on all my armor, 'n I mean like a stiff face. I was prepared for anything that come out her mouth. And when I went into the livin' room 'n did my exercise, I looked at her as evil as I could, 'n that's not like me. She didn't espect it. She knew, she could tell I wasn't gonna take it. I stiffened up, I looked right in her eye, 'n she could tell I was ready to fight. And she didn't mess me no more that day . . . I'm tryin' to be good, I'm tryin' to do what I'm told, but 'cause she got that little authority she could talk to someone like that? No. That's what I had ta do, that's the only thing dat stopped her. I had to get to that point ta stop her. That's a shame that I had to come up wit a attitude five-thirty in the morning, but that's the only way to get her to leave me alone. It's sad.

To "mean business," as Victoria says, the women have to prepare themselves—put on armor—to verbally confront supervisory oppression. The women know they need confidence in their own argument to both sustain their resistance and handle the counter-resistance they will surely face.

Victoria and Phoebe used minor forms of confrontation that under the right circumstances can bring about positive change. But when women take confrontation to the extreme and lash out verbally to staff, they can find themselves in serious trouble. Freya, whose discussion about her involvement in IOP turned into a screaming match with the executive director of Alpha Omega House, provides an example. Freya wanted more drug treatment through IOP, just one more day a week, and she thought the executive was being disrespectful, trying to pacify her with promises of more treatment to come and dismissing her before any progress had been made. Regardless of her criminal justice status, Freya says, she ought to be respected. So she fought back verbally. She says: "I felt that she was bein' very disrespectful to me. Not acknowledgin' that I'm a woman just like she is 'n deserves to be respected. Whether you're where you are 'n I'm considered a low-life to you or not, I still deserve to be respected."

Freya could have stated her discontent calmly, but she is naturally confrontational, using posture and tone of voice in everyday interactions that might border on threatening. Later that day, Freya and the executive director met again, and this time things got out of control. From one floor above, the back-and-forth yelling and cursing and something breaking could easily be heard through the cinderblock walls and over the blaring television. As Freya stomped away from the scene to her room as ordered, she poked her head in the living room and shouted to the others, "I woulda knocked da shit outta dat bitch outside here." Freya's verbal confrontation approached physical violence, a measure that means certain departure. She was discharged the next day.

Women stop short of physical altercations and the threatening behavior Freya displayed not because they are afraid of fighting—they are surely not—but because they have to protect their own interests. Freya was transferred to another community-based program, but had she assaulted the executive director, she most certainly would have been sent to prison on felony assault charges and sentenced for her failure to complete the reentry program. Candy knows herself well enough to accept that she must carefully regulate her emotions when interacting with staff. Here, she remembers a confrontation she had with a monitor who refused to allow her to take a smoke break after Candy missed the scheduled break because she was at a staff-member dinner: "She kept sayin' I couldn't smoke, dat I shoulda been there on time. She disrespectin' me. I told her to stop. I told her to stop disrespectin' me 'n treat me like a person. You treat me wit respect, I will respect you, but if you talk sideways to me, I will talk sideways back. If I was upstate, I woulda busted her face, forty-five days to lay down solitary. Fuck it. Gimme my smokes, roll 'em up, 'n chill. Fuck it."

In this event, Candy restrained from using physical violence only because her freedom was close at hand: "I woulda busted her da fuck up. I would fight the guards in prison 'n not give a fuck. But if I wanted to stay upstate, I wouldn'ta came out. I wouldn'ta waited to get all the way out 'n then go back. Not now, I controllin' my anger. Goin' back is easy." Wanting to salvage the years ahead and live in freedom, Candy relies on her vision as a restraining measure. She and the others know that verbal confrontation that borders on physical violence is a sure way to be "dishonorably discharged," as Freya was.

SNEAK TRIPS

The restraints on women's physical movement during Blackout and Zero limits options for resistance, but with C Level's opportunity to leave the house for IOP treatment, the women begin to exploit temporal and spatial opportunities and the break in constant surveillance. Residents employ several resistance strategies when outside of the house to meet their personal, drug-use, and economic needs, some of which I discuss in the next chapter. The women call one widely used strategy "sneak trips"; these mitigate the isolation of their confinement as well as the disconnection they experience in their personal relationships.

Clair is walking up the avenue from IOP to the bus stop where she takes the first of two buses back to the house. She passes Billie, who is smoking a cigarette and talking to another woman from IOP who is also waiting for the bus. Clair quickens her gait as she passes the bus stop and crosses the avenue. She has one thing on her mind—meeting her man. He is walking a half block behind her, hurrying in the same direction. Clair shoots a smile toward me and keeps her pace around the corner into the park woods and out of sight. The man follows. Clair reappears after fifteen minutes, crosses the avenue and boards the next bus.

Clair had sex in the park woods with her "sugar daddy," the man who was once just a "trick" but who has become something of a lover who tends to some of her financial needs. Later that day she says, grinning, "A girl's got needs." Clair is happily married, but she keeps close this man she met years before on the street when she began selling her sex for crack money. She elaborates on their mutually satisfying relationship: "I call my sugar daddy and say to him, Vin, I need money, and he's always there for me. It's a win-win situation. He uses me and I use him. All he wants is a companion, and he takes care of me and I take care of him. There is sex, but I know if I need him in other ways, he's always here."

Clair manages to meet Vin as well as her husband on other occasions while out of the house for IOP because her IOP rarely lasts for the scheduled two hours, and Alpha Omega House gives her more than enough bus travel time to get to IOP and back. The C Level opportunity for women to step outside the house is the key for most of them to reconnect with loved ones and, for some, to earn a couple extra dollars through sex work. The day Mimi's boyfriend was released from prison, she gave him sex, a "little summin' summin,'" behind a row house when she was heading back to Alpha Omega House from the IOP she calls "prostitution camp." Henrietta manages to visit her children and tries to meet up on the street with her girlfriend, Jo-Jo, at least once per week. Laurel routinely visits her husband on sneak trips. Sometimes women use the time and space away from the surveillance of authorities to benefit them economically by selling sex to strangers. Billie says of the first time she tricked on the way to IOP: "Yeah, I was walkin' to da bus, 'n dis man makin' eyes at me, said, Umm, ya got somethin' I want. Yeah, I say, what chew want me to do? Uh hun, we went in da alley." Billie hid the money she earned where a monitor could not find it when she returned for search—down her underwear.

Women also deviate to escape the dullness of the everyday, like Adeline who runs between the bus stop and her probation officer or between the bus and IOP to spend a few minutes on a bench in the sun or to take a stroll. "I would see my boyfriend," she says, "but I ain't got none. I killed the last one I had," she laughs. Violet uses the computers at the library to check her Facebook page when she is heading back from IOP. In this way, she is able to maintain a connection to friends.

Of the opportunities to deviate between appointments, Laurel says timing is everything, "When you see an opening, ya take it. If ya have to make a stop, make a ten-minute stop 'n keep moving." To make use of the time, women might take an earlier bus, walk faster, and leave IOP or other scheduled appointments sooner. Women also take advantage of good-natured workers at IOP, probation, and parole who might let them out of appointments early. Rosa says of the support she has from her IOP, "My outpatient is cool as shit. I do what I need ta do. I go there. I report. Den I leave a little early. They don't care 'cause I show up." Rosa likes to visit her mother and grandmother but, importantly, she and the others do not skip out on IOP entirely because they believe that the treatment helps them. While she is resisting through rule subversion as she makes the sneak trips while out of the house for IOP, her behavior also involves compliance or accommodating behavior, which is a common feature of resistance (Crewe, 2007; Gerami and Lehnerer, 2001). But the women's voluntary compliance says something even more important than that resistance and compliance usually exist together. It demonstrates that the women do not resist treatment that works, which implies that if Alpha Omega House were offering legitimate treatment services within the house, the women would not resist those efforts either.

For a long time, Mimi would just walk the streets, enjoying the freedom during the months she spent on C Level while her daughter and her boyfriend were both incarcerated. But when her boyfriend is released and her two days of IOP are not enough time for the pair to be satisfied together, Mimi uses another route: blank physician appointment cards routinely available at any doctor's office. She creates a fake appointment date and time and submits the appointment card to monitors along with a request to be released. This strategy works for Mimi because she has been dealing with health problems and routinely sees doctors. But lying to get outside is risky. Henrietta tried unsuccessfully to see her wife and "grandbabies," telling the weekend monitors that she had permission to see her grandchild in the hospital. After having been checked out of the house, Henrietta was moments away from stepping on a bus up the block before being "found out," led back, and placed on restriction in her room for the remainder of the weekend. Because of the risk of detection, rarely do the women use outright subterfuge to get out of the house.

To deviate successfully, sometimes the women also need the cooperative trust of another resident. As in the case of secretive communication, residents normally cooperate because the sisterhood among them requires this mutuality. Adeline and Violet feel their secrets are safe with one another when they use the library computers when their IOP gets out early, but trust is not always guaranteed. Violet says: "You gotta realize everyone ain't loyal. You gotta separate the loyal from the disloyal, the real from the rake, the fake from the snake." When Clair walked past Billie at the bus stop the day Clair met her sugar daddy, she later promised Billie money for her silence because, she says, she had a suspicion Billie would report her to staff. While Billie agreed to take five dollars to keep her mouth shut about Clair's deviation, she was not "real," as Violet would say; she was a "snake," and she reported Clair to staff, which cost Clair in-room restriction for the next two days.

These anecdotes constitute covert resistance (Hollander and Einwohner, 2004) using time (Nordstrom and Martin, 1992) and geography or space (Keith and Pile, 1997) through subversion of rules regarding travel and restrictions on physical movements. Like probationers and parolees who selectively subvert rules to manage the repressive aspects of legal constraints over their behavior (Werth, 2012), the women's behavior is not entirely oppositional. Rather, it involves rule-bending (Hutchinson, 1990) and some measure of compliance, as they normally attend IOP before or after their deviations.[6]

BARGAINING AND SELF-RELIANCE

Bargaining or negotiating for change is a common tactic many of the women use to minimize repressive rules and practices. Proposing better living conditions, healthier food, or a quick start to treatment and services is often the women's first try if find they are struggling over these issues. Sometimes this bargaining involves verbal negotiation about change and opportunity with relevant authorities (Kamphoff, 2010). For example, Henrietta wants a second helping of pasta because she missed lunch due to an outside appointment. She has not eaten in more than nine hours and will not be able to eat until morning breakfast unless she buys herself a snack from the costly vending machine. She normally accepts the rules about food consumption, but on this occasion she feels that she has a legitimate reason to bargain. She walks from her seat in the dining room to the end of the hall where she rings the bell for a monitor. When summoned around the corner, she asks, "Please can I have more pasta? I won't ask no more." But, the monitor quickly dismisses Henrietta, sending her back to the dining room. Her action failed. Like Henrietta, the other women quickly become frustrated by the extraordinary difficulty of having face-to-face time with staff that occupy the basement offices—those who can most directly effect change—as well as by the apathy staff show toward the women's requests when they are heard.

Collective bargaining at Alpha Omega House is about as effective as individual bargaining. For instance, with input from the other residents, Mimi has written several proposals to the staff for better scheduling of laundry time to reduce bickering about washer and dryer use. Mimi reports that she was told, "They'll call me down to discuss it." She says, "Right, like that'll ever happen. It's been two months already." On another occasion, Mimi, Phoebe, and Adeline (having been elected by other residents to represent their interests) submit a written request to the monitor on duty to meet with staff to discuss the residents' proposals for food service, an additional daily smoke break, and a daily opportunity to sit on the outside grounds of the house. After weeks of waiting, the women were told that a meeting would take place in the living room on a particular Thursday evening. On the scheduled day, the residents waited in the living room prepared for a discussion with written notes. But staff never showed. Mimi said later that evening: "They just got a monitor to say there isn't a meetin' after we sit here 'n wait 'n wait, 'n nobody shows." Mimi did not give up. She requested the meeting be rescheduled, which it was. What happened, Mimi said, came as no surprise to her at all. Almost two hours before the scheduled start time of the meeting, when many of the women were still out of the house at IOP, the residents were called to the living room over the intercom. Mimi swears this was done intentionally:

> They duped us, they said two-thirty 'n called it at one so that we would be unprepared. I wasn't even allowed to go upstairs to get my list of things to talk about. They wouldn't let Adeline get her notebook that had all the requests written down. Candy 'n Billie were still at IOP. We wanted to talk about better food, like gettin' fruits 'n vegetables 'n salads, 'n to go outside to grow vegetables, an extra smoke break. They didn't even have the same meetin' we thought. They came in 'n said this is a meetin' about rules 'n regulations, what we were doing wrong, what has to change. They talked about the toilets bein' dirty 'n how the girls argue over seating, that assigned seatin's not allowed. They totally fucked us over.

In this case, not only did staff counter-resist by failing to play by the rules, Mimi maintains that they manipulated the situation, using their authority to avoid confrontation and thereby twisting what could have been a productive gathering into punishment.

More effective than bargaining at Alpha Omega House is self-reliance, which involves rule subversion to improve a woman's life through treatment or other intervention. The following example illustrates this often used resistance strategy at Alpha Omega House.

Adeline knows from the last few months that what she expects—treatment for woman abuse and help to find work—is unlikely to occur unless she takes action. Her judge, she says, ordered her to Alpha Omega House for that very reason, but she says, "so far, I have not fulfilled his orders." She tries repeatedly to meet with staff but is not successful. With no access to a computer to search for treatment or jobs, or even a phone book to locate local providers, Adeline feels she has to reach to outside agencies for help. Even if Adeline had a telephone number for an IOP that could meet her needs, rules prevent women from using telephones during business hours. Adeline's mother helped by contacting local treatment providers on her behalf and relayed information to Adeline when they spoke on the telephone at night. Growing more and more frustrated, she says, "I am tired of smilin,' makin' it look like everything's okay. I wanna walk down there on Monday 'n tell them to give me the treatment or I'm walking out the door. Fuck this place." And Adeline did just that, walking past monitors to the administrative staff offices and demanding placement into treatment. She said: "I flew downstairs, not ringin' the bell, not askin' for permission. They chased me, but Miss Prenice put her hand up 'n said, 'It's okay.' I got what I needed." It worked, but only to a certain extent.

Adeline was placed into an IOP, but it was for substance abuse, not for woman abuse. Nonetheless, it was a partial victory, Adeline explains, because she took advantage of time outside two days a week, and she was able to "make moves to get things happenin.'" On her third day, she explained to the IOP staff that she believed she was wrongly placed, and she traveled across town to a program that her mother had found that better fit her needs. Adeline interviewed there and, with the help of her probation officer, was officially placed into that IOP. And Adeline was not finished. She knew that group counseling through IOP could be helpful, but she wanted intensive therapy. Rushing to a nearby public library after IOP, she accessed telephone numbers of local providers using the library computers and made payphone calls before and after IOP. She said, "I called like eight or nine numbers till I found a place that could take me. I hope it works out. I got an appointment tomorrow." It did work out. Adeline was scheduled for weekly intensive, one-on-one therapy with a psychotherapist specializing in woman abuse.

Because bargaining—collective or individual—is so often ineffective at Alpha Omega House, women pursue their own interests. Self-reliance as a resistance strategy is similarly reported elsewhere, for example among parolees who subvert rules to secure employment and move toward successful reintegration and positive change (Werth, 2012). Self-reliance can be aligned with "resistance through persistence" among organizational workers pursing their interests (Hearn, 2004). Even though rule subversion is sometimes considered lack of compliance and lack of commitment to change among correctional populations (Robinson and McNeill, 2008), my research shows that self-reliance through rule subversion can be taken up specifically to create positive change. It is a resistance strategy that clearly demonstrates women's ingenuity and the power of their agency to work on their own best behalf under multiple repressive conditions.

||||||||||||||||||||||||||||||||||||||||||||||||||||||||

FIVE

B AND A LEVELS

WITH BLACKOUT, ZERO, and C Level past and upward of six months at Alpha Omega House spent, women who make it to B Level are in the home stretch. Still taking part in the routine established at Zero and IOP started at C Level, residents at "B," as the women call it, are "senior girls." "Senior girls" may be called upon to escort "Blackout girls" and "Zero girls" out of the house for appointments, but more importantly, they are role models who teach their informal sisterhood and its oppositional culture.

With advancement to B, women are given more pocket change, seventy-five dollars monthly, drawn from their accounts of public-aid funds. They are also allowed to leave the house, usually in pairs or groups, for several weekend "day passes" to attend Narcotics Anonymous and Alcoholics Anonymous meetings in the community and sometimes even to shop at local stores. After about three months at B Level (sometimes longer), women advance to the final phase of stay called A Level. Sometimes their move to A Level is just as much a surprise as when they started IOP during C Level. They will only know ahead of being called to the basement offices to discuss release requirements if they happen to get a glimpse of "the board" in the monitors' office. A Level is another three-month phase, but women routinely complete it in less than one and are often released in a matter of weeks. The ticket out of A Level—graduation—is established housing. While at A Level, women are permitted a number of unescorted "home passes," and their allowance during money week is upped to one hundred dollars per month, so they can make arrangements for their final release to the community.

Having had a taste of freedom out of the house at C Level, women who make it to B and A Levels are gearing up for life on the outside. They hope to find work and a safe place to live. Three main themes mark women's experience at the final two levels: work, stigmatized labels, and housing.

Every phase of stay and the critical last months at B and A Levels are designed, according to Alpha Omega House documents, to support the central aim of "smooth and purposeful reentry" for every woman resident, yet the ante is upped for women as they near release. Many continue to feel held back by the slow pace of treatment, and they are frustrated by the idleness and passivity they feel every day. Their lack of meaningful work opportunities, new challenges in moving forward from their status as criminal woman, and their hopes for settling into community life add new pressures for them to manage as they wait for release. As their freedoms increase with each passing phase of stay, so do the women's frustrations, which they demonstrate by some of the most damaging types of resistance displayed at Alpha Omega House.

Work

Grace skips out of the building at seven-thirty in the morning, dressed in brightly colored medical scrubs dotted with flowers and white sneakers, and waits for the bus up the block. Eight hours later she returns for a search of her purse and person and then announces her return. "I'm ho-ome," she sings, smiling as she waltzes the hallway to the living room, takes a peek in, and retires to her bedroom until dinner. Today Grace returns to the living room and recounts her day at work loudly, as Mimi, Rosa, Clair, and others sit motionless before the loud television. Grace is involved in a work internship organized by Alpha Omega House and a local businessman in cooperation with community agencies. The internship, which is entirely unpaid, trains her to become a domestic maid. She "tidies up, vacuums carpet, makes beds." She has been engaged in the internship for most of the last year. She says of her achievement: "Dey say I done wit train [training]. I ain't got go train no mo. I gah new jo [job]. Dey bring me in roo [room] 'n den say I work ah nuth pla star tomorr [another place starting tomorrow] . . . Dey lie [like] me. Dey train you on stu [stuff]. Maids. How ta clea [clean], may [make] bed, tide up.

As she tells it, Grace completed her training at a nursing home and is being shifted to a hotel on the same bus route as the nursing home for more training. She enjoys the work, which, she says, makes her feel productive. She "ha fun, mee peop [meet people], work hard."

Henrietta is also doing unpaid domestic labor in the form of an internship.

She too takes the bus every day she is not at IOP for an eight-hour work shift. With virtually no work history or formal education, Henrietta would not qualify for more skilled labor. But that is not the problem for her. She doesn't mind the work, but not getting paid for her labor leaves her feeling exploited. She says: "They tryin' ta slave me workin' wit'out pay. I don't mind workin,' but I'm not gettin' paid. It not fair. I work from eight to four like I'm gettin' paid. I'm really tired, 'n I ain't gettin' paid. It make me feel sad." She even pays the eighty-three-dollar monthly bus pass that gets her to and from work. With more than three-quarters of her monthly income going to pay for her bus transportation, her donated labor is actually costing her money. She wants to quit but is worried she will be punished. She says, "I told dem I quittin,' but dey say I can't quit. How come I can't quit a job I don't get no money for?"

The volunteer housekeeping positions couched as work-training programs were sold only to Grace and Henrietta, arguably two of the least intellectually savvy women at the house. The other women will have nothing to do with the unpaid internship because they know it is unfair. Rosa will never participate because she knows the program exploits women. She says:

> I refused to do dat internship. I said I wanna work 'n get paid. I refused ta work. You think I'ma work fa free? I don't wanna work 'n not get paid. I said, I ain't doin' dat. Dey call it an internship. Dat ain't dat. Dat's dem usin' you to clean some shit, ain't no damn internship. Like cleanin' shit up— what kinda internship is dat? A internship, dat's when you learnin' somethin,' ya like learn how ta do good jobs, like college students do internships, doctors do internships, but an internship to be a janitor? I don't think so, dat dere don't even sit right wit me, nope. Dey ain't gettin' me to do dat stupid shit. I refuse. Neva. Neva.

As Rosa points out, job training should involve learning skilled work and ought to be compensated. Candy argues that the right work is that which involves skill. She rejects highly feminine work and expects help finding a job that can pay the bills and facilitate feelings of productivity and accomplishment. Candy wants "men's" work, skilled positions for which she was trained while in prison and worked when she was on the streets. She says, "I need some men's work. I can do brick mortar, plumbin,' and paintin.' I worked when I was locked up. I worked when I wasn't locked up. I've always had a job. I've always kept a job."

Women's exclusion and subordination in paid work is one of the basic structures of patriarchy that oppresses women (Walby, 1986). Even so, it is possible that gender-responsive programs for female offenders can succeed by providing them training for paying jobs that can help them to become independent. Morash (2010) reports positively on gender-responsive probation and parole job training and placement programs that can empower women and help them to move past their criminal justice status in their interaction with noncriminal co-workers in the workforce. Morash notes features of promising approaches like specialized and extensive job-training programs based in community colleges in areas like computer skills, construction and warehouse management that can help women move past stereotypically female jobs. Research by O'Brien (2001a; 2001b) similarly finds that women's determination is just part of the challenge for successfully reentry; women will benefit from job apprenticeship and need rewarding employment opportunities.

Alpha Omega House promises job-skills training as part of a comprehensive set of services to help change women's lives and facilitate their independence. But the employment programming offered to women at Alpha Omega House is nothing more than what I have described. Through training that takes the form of unpaid domestic work, Alpha Omega House rewards domesticity. This is one of the most obvious harms of a gender-responsive strategy at this reentry center. Other researchers report similar findings that employment training and job opportunities for women involved in the criminal justice system are historically limited and tend to focus on training for domestic work, like cleaning and food-service preparation.[1] Moyer (1984) argues that such programming is a function of sex-role stereotyping of female offenders. A study of vocational training in 470 state institutions concludes that women who are incarcerated are being prepared for low-paying work in jobs traditionally associated with women (Lahm, 2000). According to the study, female institutions tend to offer training in administrative and service jobs such as clerical work, food preparation, and custodial work, whereas male institutions provide training in production jobs like masonry, automobile mechanics, and construction. In fact, the study reports that female institutions are 640 percent more likely to offer women training in office-related positions such as clerical staff; 208 percent more likely to likely to provide training in service positions like food service, laundry, and cleaning; and 100 percent more likely to offer training in sewing-related jobs. Given the lack of available data, it is unclear whether other reentry centers for women are similarly deficient.

Just as they were shocked at the isolation of Blackout, made anxious by the idleness of Zero, and frustrated by the limited and slow pace of treatment intervention during C Level, women nearing the end of their stay at Alpha Omega

House face another obstacle to their reentry in the lack of meaningful services to help them get jobs. They become worried, and for good reason: inmates returning to communities from incarceration face barriers to employment, including legal restrictions in the jobs they may take, limited opportunities in the disadvantaged neighborhoods to which many reentering persons return, the stigma of the criminal label, and employer discrimination (Holzer, Raphael, and Stoll, 2003; Petersilia, 2001). According to La Vigne (2009), the single greatest worry women nearing release from prison have is that they will not be able to secure employment. One national study on reentry reports just one in five inmates have employment in place before their release (Solomon, Visher, La Vigne, and Osborne, 2006). La Vigne's 2009 study reveals even more troubling outcomes. While more than half of incarcerated women worked before their imprisonment, just 36 percent held jobs eight to ten months after release. At the same time, the post-imprisonment employment rate for their male counterparts actually increased, and men's wages were higher than wages for women.

Research establishes stable employment as a key factor to successful reintegration.[2] The role of employment in successful reentry is not newly recognized; halfway houses were founded on the philosophy that successful reintegration requires offenders to participate in the labor force (Caputo, 2004; Tonry, 1995). Normally, reentry programs establish participants in jobs in the early days of their stay and require them to maintain employment throughout their participation (La Vigne, 2003a). Every reentry center run by the Federal Bureau of Prisons requires reentry centers to offer employment opportunities for long-term employment to all participants, and the centers must also provide employment assistance in the form of job-skills training, employment job fairs, portfolio development, and related services (Federal Bureau of Prisons, 2007). Federal inmates participating in reentry centers must secure full-time employment within two weeks of their arrival and stay employed full-time as they participate in other reentry services (Federal Bureau of Prisons, nd).

In the early 1990s, an assessment of reentry programs for federal inmates reported that reentry centers were providing meaningful employment opportunities in diverse populations and that 83 percent of offenders were working in jobs and earning money (US General Accounting Office, 1991). More recently, a meta-analysis of reentry studies revealed that reentry programming for vocational training and work programs improved job skills for offenders returning from incarceration and reduced recidivism (Seiter and Kadela, 2003). While empirical data on reentry centers is scarce, a study of a Chicago halfway house for women reported favorable results as women participants received considerable help securing employment (Leverentz, 2006). However, the least educated and most disadvantaged women in the study were not assisted enough to enter the workforce without public assistance. Cases like these require active effort on the part of reentry centers to collaborate with community partnerships for employment training and job placement, but there is little if any evidence of this occurring for women at the Chicago center.

Welfare

Page 2 of Alpha Omega House's thirty-eight-page packet of rules and regulations reads, in part, "After successful completion of black-out period all residents are in the orientation phase of their process. During this thirty-day phase residents will acquire state ID, welfare benefits or social security disability evaluation."

Some of the women at Alpha Omega House have little or no aspirations of working what most people would call conventional jobs. Laurel never bought into the idea of working "nine-to-five," because, she says, "I won't earn shit. I got drugs ta sell." Just as she has for many years, Laurel plans to resume her "work" as a mid-level drug dealer. And this reluctance to join the traditional labor market is especially on display among women at Alpha Omega House like Billie, who used sex work to earn money in neighborhoods where the trade is supported or encouraged. Billie enjoys benefits of sex work and says she has no intention of quitting. She plans to supplement the daily inflow of cash from selling her sex with her first-of-the-month welfare check. Other women are content to resume their lives as welfare recipients who spend their time "chillin,'" as Rosa describes how she spent most of her days before her incarceration and what she sees of her future. Rosa lives between incarcerations with her mother and aspires to little more than to "chill 'n watch TV . . . grillin' . . . 'n sittin' in da [plastic, child-sized] pool." Rosa managed her various medications to sell some pills for cash while keeping herself functionally medicated. She was also fairly good, she says, at shoplifting for herself and for sale on the street. All of this enabled her to acquire her essentials—cigarettes, food, and money for drugs.

While welfare and Supplemental Security Income provide meaningful support, these services may also harm women, especially when work opportunities are limited and barriers to independence constrain women's ability to move past assistance. Welfare, according to some scholars, rewards domesticity and sustains women's social as well as labor subjugation. Wilson (1977) describes welfare as a set of ideas about women's proper place in society, arguing that in practice it ensures women's own participation in their economic exploitation and oppression. Given welfare's connection to the home and family and women's historical connection to those same things, welfare provisions, Wilson's arguments suggest, can represent government control of women's place in domestic life.

In a historical analysis of social welfare, argues Abramovitz (1996), welfare has always subjugated women. The welfare system supports familial patriarchy by extending the unequal division of labor to the social labor market, where women who work in devalued, low-wage jobs are rewarded. In a similar way, Sainsbury (1996) aligns social welfare with familial patriarchy by examining eligibility for welfare benefits. When states determine welfare allowances based on a woman's relationship with dependent children and male earnings in the household, Sainsbury argues, women are judged based on their domestic role and rewarded for their position within the household as wives and mothers.

This critique can be leveled against the experiences of women in this reentry center as well. Many of the women do want to work—and arguably many more would be open to working if they felt encouraged—but they are held back by the lack of employment opportunities and by the center's policy of putting every woman on welfare or ssi soon after her arrival. Victoria says the practice is intentionally destructive: "I wanna work. I've worked in an office for many years. I was never on ssi or welfare before, but they forced me to. It's like they want us to fail.

Being on welfare is not just about money and services. As Victoria sees it, keeping women dependent on social services and out of work is intended to keep women down, to subjugate and control them. And because Alpha Omega House benefits financially from the provision of welfare and ssi to its residents (taking about 20 percent of the benefit allowances from each woman), residents argue they are also economically exploited by the reentry center itself. Adeline believes keeping women on welfare and ssi and away from well-paying work not only strips them of autonomy and ability to care for themselves, it benefits the house at the women's expense:

> Why should they bother to help us get jobs? They are gettin' money from us the way it is now. Let me work in a pizza shop, let me deliver, lemme cook, I can work anywhere 'n do anything, just let me work. So I can live a normal life. Why can't ya treat me like a grown-up? Let me go out 'n get a job, work! I know what I need. I need a job. But they don't want us to work. They put us on ssi because they can take 20 percent of your money. You

probably get close to six hundred dollars a month. So they get more money, they want you on ssi.

At her admission to Alpha Omega House, Adeline was placed on ssi. Even though she qualifies, she would like to forego the benefits for work but feels kept out of the labor force, preventing her from living a "normal life." At Alpha Omega House, residents who receive ssi have mental illnesses or chronic medical problems. In the world outside of this reentry center, these women are not only oppressed because of their gender, they are exploited because of their disability. As Abberley (1987) shows, one form of oppression considers impairment the central feature of a person, thereby stereotyping people who are disabled and setting them up for discrimination. But more importantly in the case of Adeline (and Candy), who argue against their disabled status in favor of labor market participation, the oppression of people with disabilities keeps them from aligning themselves with others who are disabled. This solidarity, as Abberley and others discuss, could "normaliz[e] suffering" and lead to breaking down barriers to full employment.

Especially for those women who want to work, the reentry center enforces passivity and economic exploitation in keeping the women from jobs that can earn them independence. Years ago, Clair took welfare because she needed it. She also supplemented her drug addiction with sex work money. But she never really wanted that life of dependency. Ready to work in a conventional job, she feels held back. So too does Mimi, who sees the reentry center's use of the welfare and ssi system as backward. To Mimi, work brings more than economic freedom: it can improve a woman's emotional and social position. She says, "I didn't want welfare. I love work. I love to work. I have a job waitin.' I want to work. I love my job. I feel good about myself workin.' But they told me I have to be on welfare when I got here, so they put me on welfare. Wanting to work is not just for the money, it's social. . . . . I've had lots of jobs. I've managed places. I've managed restaurants, I've managed bars, I've managed strip clubs. I could teach other people how to do it. But here, they don't let me work."

As Mimi makes clear, participating in the labor force is about more than earning money. It is a way to be self-sufficient, to build a skills base and a reputation, to play a part in important decision making, and to experience social living. Alpha Omega House's administration and the terms of Mimi's probation prevent her from resuming her previous employment in the legal sex work industry as a manager of dancers or as a bartender in a local pub. Bars and strip clubs are officially off-limits for Mimi until she completes the two years of probation after she graduates Alpha Omega House. (Terms of parole and probation often prohibit going to or working in establishments that serve alcohol.) She says of her frustrations: "I should be workin.' I have a job waitin' for me, I should be workin.' But they said bein' in a bar is too tempting—but I don't drink! I never did." Adeline is in a similar position, having worked for years as a bartender. But that work is also prohibited.

Labels

Socially dictated labels representing primary personal, physical, or characters traits focused on gender, race, sexual orientation, and other characteristics affect our everyday interactions (Becker, 1963; Hughes, 1945). The consequence of sexist socialization, fear, and other prejudices, stigmatizing labels are often applied to girls and women when they come in contact with the criminal justice system, labels such as "delinquent girl" and "criminal woman." A Canadian study of criminal labels applied to women charged or convicted of violence offenses regardless of the circumstances of the event—the violent female offender identity—locates the label as a harm that stereotypes women and maintains their subjugation (Dell, 1999).

My argument is similar. In cases of women at Alpha Omega House, stigmatized labeling influences how women are socially presented and affects how they interact with others, how they experience the world, and how they see themselves. Candy is a lesbian who sometimes considers herself a "man" on her own continuum of femininity; she has for years been tagged an "aggressive female." At Alpha Omega House, she believes she is deliberately separated from the other women in a single bedroom at the furthest end of the hallway. She says she has never been assigned a roommate because of her sexual orientation and the threat her lack of femininity poses. Clair complains she is labeled by people inside and outside the criminal justice system a "junkie" for her drug use, and Freya has been called a "crack head" because of her addiction. Both women claim their interactions with all parts of the criminal justice system have been based on these drug-user labels. Mimi says has been called a "bad mother" by criminal justice officials, for involving her daughter in crime. Adeline believes people see her as a "weak woman" for not withstanding the violence of her partner and, subsequently, a "murderer" for taking his life to protect her own. Grace has been tagged "retarded and stupid," she says, by many people in her life, rather than seen for the kindly woman with mental illness who cannot read or write that she is. All of the women at Alpha Omega House have been tagged "felons" and now, having spent time in jail and prison, "ex-cons." Perpetuating the experience of being stigmatized, the women are reduced to "girls"—as in "Blackout girls," "Zero girls," and "new girls"—by staff and by each other, though whether "girl" originated with staff or residents is not known.

The women residents struggle to overcome these labels, but feel constrained. Freya summarizes much of the women's position on the labeling inherent in the criminal justice system:

> If the environment was a little more friendly and really helpful 'n our ideas 'n opinions were more accepted, then maybe when we leave here we won't hold animosity in our hearts and in our minds. When we leave here, of course we're gonna be resentful toward those parole officers, judges that are involved, the monitors 'n staff here, 'n others that say we're no good. We're unjustly judged, or people makin' assumptions about who we are 'n what we do just based on mistakes or things we do, like our addictions. So I'm a crack head so the rest of my life—that's all you're gonna know me as. And you're not even gonna bother to look at me as real person 'n see how honest I am, see how spiritual I am, see that I'm a good person, see that I'm not a thief, I'm not a liar, 'n all those other things that get tagged onto you when the majority says all crack heads are thieves, all drug addicts are liars, they don't have much intelligence, they are worthless. So the assumption is made and we're put in these categories 'n these little slots and it's accepted. Our mistakes shouldn't have to haunt us for the rest of our lives.

Contributing to the problem of stereotyping the women, say the residents, are practices and routines at the house that perpetuate deviant labeling. In addition to the degradation process of Blackout are practices that expose women's stereotype and subordinated status to the outside world. Rosa's and Adeline's cases serve as good examples.

Rosa is the only woman at Alpha Omega House who is participating in an educational program. She is working on a project as part of her GED class, which her IOP counselor helped to arrange. One assignment requires her to bring in an empty cereal box and submit a typewritten paper. The problem is that she has no access to an empty cereal box or to a computer or typewriter. While she has thus far been able to blend in with the other students, she feels she must now distinguish herself from the rest by outing herself as a resident in a correctional program. Rosa is biting her nails, rocking forward and back as she bobs her head like she is listening to music; she does this when very stressed or angry. She says: "I had to tell da teacher I'm in a program 'n can't type da project or use a cereal box. It's embarrassing as shit. I hope she doesn't kick me out 'cause I'm from jail or think I'm court-ordered 'n just don't give a fuck, 'cause it was my idea to do this."

More systematic problems for the women stem from the required use of correctional identification in place of IDs ordinarily carried by citizens. Upon their admission to the Alpha Omega House, women relinquish all common forms of identification and are issued Alpha Omega House ID cards. To what extent this practice is the norm for prisoner reentry centers is not known, but it is common in jails and prisons, where it is seen as a matter of institutional security. Adeline's narrative of two encounters in the world illustrates how the practice is problematic. The first describes an initial appointment with a physician and clinic staff that had become acquainted with her by way of her only form of identification, a booking photo and her release papers naming her as prisoner 94177. Realizing that she would be identified as a former inmate, Adeline was feeling vulnerable. What actually occurred was much more troubling than she expected.

> When I went to the clinic, the first time bein' out the door, I automatically felt that everyone is givin' me this look, they must know I just got outta jail. Goin' to the doctor—I had to go there; I didn't have no identification yet—they [Alpha Omega House staff] had to print out and give the doctor the copy of my release papers, which was my mug shot—the mug shot of that night when I got locked up was my identification. And when they pull out the picture of that night, it is remindin' me of that night, like I can't get away from it. I seen the picture with the big bruise under my eye 'n they just seen that, 'n now I look like a complete lunatic 'n they found out I just got out of prison. And then, they always ask you to tell 'em about it, why you're there, how long. It's embarrassin' 'cause now more people know... to society I'm a felon, that's all I am.

Harmed by her felony label, Adeline feels shunned. She says, "Society says you're not one of us anymore." In Garfinkel's words (1956, p. 420), degradation like this carries the message "I call upon all men to bear witness that he is not as he appears but is otherwise and in essence 'of a lower species.'"

Adeline's experience is repeated at the welfare office. She likens the labeling to an enduring bad relationship that constantly repeats itself:

> Once again, they pulled out the mug shot 'cause they need two forms of ID. And the paperwork, now I have to check off that box, the felony. I ask myself, What are they thinkin'? Here comes another one, jailbird, wants somethin' for nuthin.' Not only are you put in this category of being a murderer, a criminal, I'm constantly reminded of it. It's like when you're in relationships, people always bring up the past 'n throw your faults from the past in your face. That's kinda like the same thing, in that you're just gettin' whipped over 'n over again with the same thing. I'm just getting labeled again.

Not only is she perceived as a felon and murderer, Adeline assumes others define her as irresponsible and lazy. Tired of being known as a murderous woman, she faces continued stress as she works to manage her interactions and self-image. She desperately wants to find work so that she can take care for herself, but she knows the road ahead will be hard. She puts it simply: "I'm a felon. I'm a murderer; who wants to hire a murderer?" Candy finds this to be true as well. She said, "I filled out an application ta get a job at this place. I got the experience ta work unloadin' da trucks. I ask 'em, What's up? Am I hired? Nuthin.' It's bullshit. Nobody wants to hire an ex-con." Other women share similar stories of continued stigmatized labeling. The past is the past, argues Billie, and the other women agree that their move toward reintegration means past actions should not continue to haunt them. Billie says, "Dey 'posta keep our past in our past. Dey not 'posta put our past in front of us. That's some sick stuff. Once we did our past, our past is our past. Why we gotta every time we go somewhere, we gotta bring up our past? I had to deal wit it a year in jail, 'n here again, 'n every time I go out. I think it sucks. I ain't bad. I just went 'n sold my ass on da block. I wanna be able to accomplish sumthin.'"

Yet Billie, like many of the other women, continues to feel the heavy weight of past actions.

Housing

After ten months, Laurel finally reaches A Level and has a release date set for less than a month away. It has been three years since she lived alongside other citizens, and she is worried because she has not been able to find suitable housing.

She has two home passes remaining and hopes those outing will be more productive than today's. She was given a pass this Saturday at 8 a.m. to make housing arrangements, but she hopped a bus to see her "baby daddy." Laurel wants to live with her son and Clive, who has custody of the child. But house staff and Laurel's probation officer prohibit her, she says, because Clive is on probation for a drug crime and the pair has a violent history.

Laurel spent her second home pass the following Saturday visiting her grandmother and sister who live locally in a drug- and crime-ridden area. She would stay with either of them, she says, but those plans might be difficult too. Both her grandmother and sister are drug dealers who smoke a lot of marijuana, and Laurel can be a moment away from jail if she violates probation. She says, "I am an alcoholic 'n I can't smoke blunts when I'm on probation. Don't have dat shit aroun' me. I can't be around it. But at my grandmom 'n sista—up in there smoking 'n shit. I can't stay there, 'cause I ain't goin' da fuck back ta jail."

With time running out, Laurel quickly puts together a list of potential rooms to rent by searching local listings on a computer she secretly uses at a library when she is traveling to and from IOP. One is an apartment by a river "with ducks 'n shit 'n guys fishing 'n the weed smokers over dere 'n da paddle boats." Another is a second-floor room in a seedy hotel, and the third is a boarding room in a row home broken up into apartments. The first is too expensive and the second is already rented by the time she checks it out. She figures she could get the third for about $450 a month. Even without a job she can pay for rent with her welfare check, but that does not leave her much for other expenses. In the end, she broke the verbal agreement she had with the boarding house because she could instead provide a fraudulent lease to Alpha Omega House staff (a condition of release) and save money by staying with her boyfriend.

Like many women returning from incarceration, Rosa and some of the others have family they can live with, but many women simply have nowhere to go (Mallik-Kane and Visher, 2008). Adeline has no home waiting, and neither do Candy, Victoria, or Grace. Grace's case is particularly problematic because it seems as though she may need a group home or other structured environment. If Grace returns to the dangerous streets of her neighborhood in a room for rent, she will be as vulnerable to victimization as she has been throughout her life. Phoebe does not want to return to her dysfunctional family environment and would rather have her own apartment, but with no job or source of income beyond welfare, she has little choice. Mimi is on A Level with two weeks to find a place to live before her release date. She does not own a home, and her family no longer lives locally. Like Laurel, Mimi searches for housing when she is out to attend IOP treatment. The only place she can find, she says, is a room in one of the most dangerous parts of the city where drugs are sold openly on the streets. But the rent is too high, so she plans to stay in a local hotel with her boyfriend until she can save up some money. She will tell probation and house staff about the hotel and room plan, but she is keeping quiet about the part that involves her boyfriend, who was convicted at the same time she was and is recently released from prison.

Housing assistance is especially important for female correctional populations who more often than males live in unstable housing arrangements or are homeless before incarceration and who often have few financial resources.[3] A study of 1,100 prisoners returning to communities reports that stability in housing arrangements after release was more problematic for women, with 59 percent reporting at least one change in residence eight to ten months after release, compared to 40 percent of males who changed residences (Mallik-Kane and Visher, 2008). So too was homelessness a problem for women. While most women arranged to stay with family at release, 7 percent of women reported being homeless their first night out of prison and through the first three months of release; this number jumped to 13 percent eight to ten months post release, compared to 5 percent of men. According to Mallik-Kane and Visher, the problems of housing and homelessness appear to affect some women more than others. Women with mental illness and substance-abuse issues are more likely to experience homeless after release than other women. With few resources, many returning prisoners live in housing arrangements that are potential damaging to their reentry (Leverentz, 2006), as they may involve people active in crime and substance abuse (La Vigne, 2009).

Once they are moved to A Level, the women at Alpha Omega know their release is near, and they learn from their predecessors that this phase brings them closer to the struggles of everyday life outside the reentry-center gates. In addition to the difficulty of finding housing, what makes the last phase of their stay even more challenging is that they are jobless and will carry debt from court costs and fines owed for their criminal offending. In addition to rental costs, they will have to pay for food and transportation as well as supervision fees to offset the cost of their probation or parole supervision. Without jobs, the women rely on welfare or SSI. In short, without housing and jobs, they are set up to fail.

It has been my experience observing women at Alpha Omega House that while the center promises women housing assistance, they are actually given little if any help by reentry center staff to locate safe and stable housing before release. They have no computer access or newspapers at the center to assist their search efforts, and they are banned from using the telephones during the daytime, which makes their task that much more cumbersome. Instead, they rely on the assistance of friends and family to help them find suitable living arrangements as they approach release. When they are released, they might stay in rooming houses, hotels, or low-rent apartments in areas of this city that might not be safe for them, and most of them anticipate being transient for some time. Those who plan to live with family and friends might not be much better off because they too are without money and work. Most of the women will return to the very same neighborhoods that precipitated and fueled their involvement in crime and drugs.

Resistance

It is 10:30 a.m. and the morning rituals are completed. Some of the women leave for treatment at IOP, others for medical appointments, court hearings, or visits with probation and parole officers. But with no treatment or services planned for their day, no job, no class to attend, and no outdoor leisure, the majority of women stay behind. Despite promises of opportunities for women to practice social and economic independence, the rules and everyday practices of Alpha Omega House actually reinforce the stigma of dependent women. As the women see it, these last phases of stay transfer a criminal labeling process from the punitive criminal justice setting to civic life, hinder financial and social independence, and limit access to satisfactory work and housing.

The women's focus now is to hold out just a few months more, and, as Laurel says, "have the system off our backs." Not a single woman in this study voluntary left Alpha Omega House during her stay at B or A Levels. Resistance strategies used in this last part of women's stay can be as simple as withholding information, but with mounting tensions and frustrations, other forms of the women's resistance come into play. Some of these are harmful, as is demonstrated in incidents of horizontal violence; others are deeply counterproductive—for example, when the women demonstrate agency by taking advantage of unsurveilled and unescorted time outside of the house on weekends during day passes and home passes.

WITHHOLDING KNOWLEDGE

Women at Alpha Omega House routinely protect one another and their own interests by withholding and restricting information requested by monitors and administrative staff. Laurel would never "rat" on Mimi, Phoebe, or Adeline unless her liberty was at stake. Henrietta would never inform on Rosa and vice versa. Grace keeps the gambling games of Henrietta and Rosa secret, because she relies on Rosa for emotional support. Preserving such loyalties enables the women to maintain a symbolic distance from the staff and build a wall of silence that benefits them individually and as a cultural group insofar as it helps to support the oppositional sisterhood within the house. Studies on withholding and restricting information reported elsewhere as strategies of resistance to oppression note everyday actions of "willful ignorance" about seemingly mundane subjects—such as who is on a smoke break, what woman is doing her laundry at present, or what staff member was working over a weekend (Collinson, 2000; Gilson, 2011, p. 321). Silence, also reported elsewhere as a resistance strategy (Alsop, 2012; Clair, 1998), is used effectively when residents maintain vital confidences, such as women deviating from rules and regulations when out for IOP or other appointments, acts that risk immediate discharge or, worse, a return trip to prison.

One example of the cultural wall of silence at Alpha Omega involves a cell phone Adeline smuggled into the house. She used it to keep in contact with her mother and daughter and save money she would otherwise have spent on the payphones. When asked whether they knew about a cell phone in the house, Mimi and Phoebe withheld knowledge and protected their friend. Adeline was eventually caught with the phone and placed on a one-week restriction during which she was confined to her room and given additional chores. But Adeline reciprocated when asked if she was aware of Phoebe's alcohol use at the house. Such group resistance was an integral part of the women's culture, and in most cases, they protected one another because it was the ethical thing to do from the perspective of subjugated women. Residents also restricted or withheld information to benefit themselves directly. Candy, a known snitch, withheld confidential information when questioned about her once in-house girlfriend, Charisse, who got high on marijuana when out for IOP. This silence protected her own interests—having a sex partner. On another occasion, Clair knew that Billie had had sex in the bushes with a trick after IOP, but she never revealed this information to staff. When approached by staff about Billie's whereabouts, Clair revealed only very basic details—not because she was necessarily concerned about Billie's welfare, but because the favor might someday be returned.

Unlike other forms of resistance like jumping and confrontation, which usually met with strong counter-resistance, withholding knowledge by restricting information or maintaining silence produced little if any negative consequence, making it a preferred resistance strategy throughout the women's stay. When used effectively, withholding knowledge also benefited women who employed the more risky resistance strategies.

CONTRABAND

As B Level and A Level residents, Phoebe and Mimi are permitted to leave the house unescorted for a Saturday Narcotics Anonymous meeting on a cool fall day. Phoebe is dressed in a hooded sweatshirt and jeans. Mimi is wearing a short jacket with boots over her jeans and carrying a large purse. Unlike IOP attendance, women's participation in such meetings is not tracked, making it easy for them to skip out on their appointments. Phoebe and Mimi never attend the NA meeting and instead "deviate" so Phoebe can see her family and Mimi can look at an apartment for herself and her boyfriend. The pair returns together several hours later. Knowing staffing is lightest on weekends and administrative staff is off work, Saturdays and Sundays are also the preferred days to carry in contraband. Having stepped in the front door, Phoebe is met by the monitor for a search. Phoebe unzips her sweatshirt and lifts her shirt to show that her bra is not concealing contraband. She shakes her jeans at her shoes to cause anything hidden there to fall out. Mimi takes off her jacket and unzips her bag for a close look by the monitor. She takes off her shoes and shakes the legs of her jeans. "Okay," says the monitor and allows the pair to pass. Relieved, they quickly walk the hallway and shout "Going up!" when they reach the stairway.

Phoebe and Mimi both slipped contraband through the search. Phoebe says, "They wouldn't let me get my mother's drop-off last weekend, so me 'n Mimi met her. I layered my clothes 'n whatnot. I had on like three layers 'n put a pair of jeans in my hoodie." Mimi stuffed two new bras in one boot, a scarf in the other, and hid perfume in a side pocket of her purse. "Drop-offs"—care packages delivered to the house for a particular resident—are not allowed on weekends, so Phoebe's mother had been sent away the weekend before, without leaving a package of clothing and toiletries. Phoebe rationalizes her behavior as a productive response to injustice, breaking rules to get what she needs. She points to the irony of being deviant in an environment of criminal reintegration: "It's sad we're supposed to be in recovery 'n have to do this shit to survive, be dishonest and lie."

Anything prohibited at the reentry center—not only cellphones and computers, drugs and alcohol, playing cards, and any money that is not distributed during "money week" but also personal items such as writing and notebook supplies, toiletries, and clothing not first inspected and approved by staff—is considered contraband. Just like prison, personal property is strictly controlled, and items that are not "issued" by the organization or approved by staff are subject to confiscation (Owen, 1998). Food items not distributed by monitors or purchased from the vending machine in the evenings are also prohibited; women are not permitted to bring any food into the house. Anything a woman purchases while outside of the house, such as nail polish or other personal items, must pass inspection by monitors before the women are permitted to bring the items inside. Alcohol and drug use is strictly prohibited.

To prevent contraband in the house, women are inspected by a pat-down search when they return from outings. But as the forgoing example illustrates, women find ways to pass contraband by the monitors. Common contraband inside the house includes items women use to improve their living conditions, such as clothing, food, toiletries, or "personals" given to them by friends and family, purchased by the women, or shoplifted from local stores. Rosa brought in a deck of playing cards that she hides in her room so that she and Henrietta can covertly play together. Grace likes to bring in candy that she hides under her pillow. Cigarettes are a common contraband, tightly controlled by monitors. As described earlier, cigarettes are kept locked away in the monitors' office and given to women only during the two daily smoke breaks and when a woman leaves the house. But if a woman is able to have a pack of cigarettes within her control, she might be lucky enough to sneak a smoke out the window at night. Sometimes women also hide condoms so that they are better prepared for safe sex when they are able to meet up with their partners or sex-work customers.

Personals and clothing are only permitted after being inspected by monitors and approved by staff. Such items normally include the possessions women carry in with them from jail and prison, items they acquire in drop-offs from friends and family, and items they purchase during the occasional house-approved trip to a local Wal-Mart. Whatever a woman purchases outside the house must be accompanied by a sales receipt so she can account for the funds she brings back, or "get square," as the women say. Rosa says, "Dey check our money every day even when we go to IOP. Dey keep track of it. We can't come in wit a dime more or less dan what we left wit, 'n dey check our receipts to see if it matches up." When women do not have receipts for purchases or when they are given items by others on the outside, they must come up with the money to get square or conceal the contraband and hope to pass through searches undetected.

Money is thus one of the most common types of contraband at Alpha Omega House. Only that money distributed to women during money week is permitted, but women find ways of carrying in other funds that are usually provided by friends or family and sometimes earned through sex work. Rather than account for every purchase on the outside with receipts, women often keep "money-week money" in one pocket and spend contraband money instead. Having extra cash is always helpful when a woman wishes to buy things like cigarettes, the occasional beer, a prescription pill, or other items prohibited at the house.

Concealing and consuming contraband is a form of covert resistance intended by women to mitigate the hardships of living at the reentry center. Like the sneak trips and self-reliance strategies the women used at C Level, contraband involves subverting rules, or "deviating," as the women say, to meet personal needs. Passed on to "new girls" and supported by the resident sisterhood, tactics for concealing contraband are used by virtually all of the residents once they're eligible to go outside the house. While most of the goods they bring back are minor forms of contraband—candy, cigarettes, snacks, and clothing—sometimes the women also smuggle in alcohol and drugs.

DRUGS AND ALCOHOL

> Being locked up, actually I look at it as it saved my life. It really saved my life 'cause if I didn't get locked up I probably would be six feet under. I was doing two bundles of dope a day 'n about twenty bags of coke a day 'n whatnot. And mixin' coke 'n dope together is a death wish. And I was doing a lot a day, like so the system saved my life. It really did, yeah. It gave me the push to get clean, 'n now that I'm clean I'm stayin' clean.—Phoebe

Eight months after this declaration, Phoebe is confined to her room for the second of five days. She is permitted to use the bathroom, but cannot stray from those ten steps down the hall and back. No resident is allowed to interact with her. She cannot attend Narcotics Anonymous and Alcoholics Anonymous meetings or any IOP. Her meals are also taken in her room. Phoebe had been set to graduate in two days, but instead she was dropped back down to C Level, adding at least ninety days to her sentence. Phoebe's room is different than it had been the day before. The bed across from hers is stripped to the bare mattress. The dresser top is half empty, as is half the closet. The magazine pictures of dogs on the wall above the stripped bed have been removed. In fact, all traces of her roommate, Mimi, are gone as if she were never there. All of this is punishment for drug use. Phoebe accepts the extended stay at Alpha Omega House because she knows it is deserved. What makes being locked in her room on restriction so hard to handle is not the terrible heat or the isolation. It is the torture of her mind. She says, "Bein' here means I'm just in my head more. I'm goin' crazy." The guilt is gnawing at her too; she disappointed her confidant, Mimi. And because of her violation, which she admitted, all weekend trips including day passes, home passes, and NA and AA meetings are cancelled for two weeks for every resident, who will also be subjected to unannounced drug and alcohol testing during this time.

Phoebe's hand shakes as she sits on her bed. Despite her guilt, she grins, "It was worth it. It was goood," as she shows the still-fresh needle mark in her arm from her heroin use. Partly, she reasons, the environment here is "so negative" and reentry programming so limited that she wanted to rebel. "You will fail, you can't do it," she remembers a volunteer teaching a new class on prisoner reentry telling her days earlier. Part of Phoebe's vulnerability comes from her troubled family situation and concern for her loved ones. Her mother and sister, both heroin users, were "so high, nodding off" when she visited them the day she deviated from the scheduled NA meeting. She cannot bear to "cut ties with her family," but she now reasons doing so is the only way she can survive abstinence. Phoebe is an untreated drug addict and alcoholic who needed barely a nudge to "go and cop" the drugs she craves.

Phoebe had been using drugs and alcohol over a three-week period. It started when she made a sneak trip, leaving early from IOP to take prescription pills she pulled from her mother's house. Leaning across her bed, she says sheepishly, "I took six Ativans 'n chugged vodka." The vodka she concealed in her jeans and drank straight from the bottle that night in her room, throwing the empty bottle out of the bathroom window to the overgrown lot below. Mimi tried at first to reason with her, but then she too drank from the bottle. The next day Phoebe smuggled in another bottle and consumed it that night. A week later Phoebe skipped IOP and traded sex for heroin from her drug-dealer. While on the street she mixed two bags of heroin with water in a soda cap and "shot up," then "just drifted away."

As it happened Phoebe returned to the house when an NA meeting was being held in the living room. "She was noddin' off. I knew she was fucked up," says

Violet. "Baywatch [Candy's name for Phoebe, who resembles a busty lifeguard] turned blue," jokes Candy. Adeline adds, "Oh my God, it was so scary. She fell out of the chair 'n smacked her face on the ground." Phoebe says, "They said my eyes were rolling in my head 'n whatnot, and my lips turned blue." Accompanied by Mimi, Phoebe was taken by taxi to a local hospital. "I ditched my jammer [needle], ha ha ha, 'n the other bag [of heroin]" in the waiting room, she says. She did not admit the heroin use to the doctors, but they knew. She was treated for dehydration and sent back to the house with a portable intravenous bag so she could continue getting necessary fluids. Phoebe admitted to staff that she used drugs, a major infraction that could have returned her to prison.

Phoebe's overt use of hard drugs is exceptional at Alpha Omega House, but other women say they sometimes drink alcohol and use drugs when they are on day trips or that they smuggle inside. On one occasion, Clair and Violet slipped from a group shopping outing and "got really drunk" on "tequila shots 'n some beers" on the tab of male patrons at a corner bar up the street from the house. Obviously intoxicated, they were discovered by monitors upon return, restricted to their rooms, and given extra chores for the week. Adeline's use of alcohol was primarily a form of defiance. She managed to get a quick drink when she attended church for the first time with Grace and Henrietta on Easter Sunday. She exclaimed, "I scored! I drank wine at church on Easter. I took the goblet 'n chugged it. This old little lady was tryin' to pull it back, but I kept on drinkin.' She was pullin' the bottom 'n I was holdin' onto the top. It was great!" Even if she drank only a little, the act of defiance was enough for her to feel relief.

Whether they smuggle in pills or alcohol to consume at the house or they use drugs or drink alcohol on the outside during day passes, home visits, appointments, or IOP, residents say they do it to "have some fun" or to "get away from this place." It is not a resistance strategy that changes the conditions under which the women live, but rather an escape from the oppression they experience. For some of the women, such as Phoebe, this resistance strategy provides an obvious example of how women's agency through resistance can sometimes work against their own best interests.

INTERGROUP VIOLENCE

As women oppressed in various spheres of their everyday lives at Alpha Omega House, residents often engage in intergroup violence of varying seriousness. The women normally call these conflicts "beefs," and they may be compared to bullying, which is often interpreted as oppressed group behavior (Duffy, 1995), or to horizontal violence, a term used commonly in nursing research to describe conflict among people who share a subjugated status.[4] According to Leap (1997, p. 689), horizontal violence is a type of resistance in which individuals "direct their frustrations and dissatisfactions towards each other as a response to a system that has excluded them from power"—a definition that accurately describes interpersonal violence at Alpha Omega House. Conflict among the women at the reentry center, like bullying among oppressed nurses (Purpora and Blegen, 2012), takes the form of sarcasm and mocking, nonverbal aggression, and physical altercations.

Beefs often involve put-downs, attacks on a woman's character, challenges, and exchanges of angry words. On one occasion, an encounter between Candy and Phoebe nearly got out of hand. It started with a remark from Candy, who had grown tired of Raquel's delusional and angry outbursts. Everyone knows that Raquel is a seriously mentally ill woman who routinely displays paranoid behavior through verbal attacks, and most of the time women leave her alone. But on one occasion Candy is especially irritated with her behavior and says to Raquel, "You a racist, always hatin' on us blacks." The living room grows silent. Phoebe intervenes, asking Candy, "How can she be racist when her husband is black?" Candy fires back: "Nobody askin' you, bitch." Had Candy chosen any other word, the situation might have evolved differently, but "bitch" is a particularly derogatory fighting word among the women and usually incites violence. Yet Phoebe, perhaps acutely aware of Candy's violent tendencies replies, "Just be quiet. Nobody wants ta hear you." Candy escalates the situation, this time yelling as she crosses the room toward a sitting Phoebe: "You stay outa it, ya bitch, fucking junkie!" Phoebe is tired of the label "junkie." In defense, Phoebe shouts back: "Yeah, I use needles, but I'm no junkie so shut up, nobody wants to hear you!" Now Candy jumps directly in front of Phoebe, leans close, and challenges: "Make me shut up, make me shut up, bitch, make me shut up." Before Phoebe gets fully to her feet, a monitor rushes into the room and pulls Candy aside. Candy curses as she is led away. The room remains silent. Candy returns moments later to take a seat while she watches Phoebe. No words are spoken. The confrontation is over.

Sometimes tensions from a beef linger, triggering further conflict without much warning. An example of this sort of outburst occurs while Henrietta and Rosa play a board game together in the dining room. Candy walks past the pair to the water cooler, giving Rosa a long sneer before slowly walking out of the room. Rosa exhales, saying, "My fuckin' day's ruined now. Dat bitch is still fuckin' here. I wish she'd get da fuck outta here. I hate her." Henrietta adds: "I hate dat bitch." This particular beef is fueled by some of the residents suspecting that Candy is the "snitch" who informed staff that a resident was hiding drugs, prompting "strip searches" of all residents down to their undergarments. Laurel enters the dining room moments after saying to Rosa, "Somebody tellin' there was drugs in here last night. It probably dat black bitch." Rosa agrees: "I bet it dat bitch. I see her on da streets, she gonna get popped." Rosa and Laurel continue to discuss Candy's suspected snitch relationship with the staff and how this is a source of trouble and a major trust violation. Rosa says, "She makin' shit up to get everyone else in trouble." At this, Candy reappears in the hallway where Rosa takes the opportunity to provoke her, but Candy walks away, mumbling under her breath. Rosa shouts, "Ya fuckin' snitch!" as Candy disappears down the hall. Then Rosa turns to Henrietta and Laurel, promising, "I'ma roll dat bitch. But not in here, when we out on da streets I'ma roll." Rosa and Laurel continue, this time in Spanish, about how Candy is a snitch who needs to be taught a lesson.

Short-lived arguments or minor disputes like these are commonplace at this residence of women stressed by their confinement and anxious about their impending release. But when a beef escalates, women "roll" or "rumble." An anecdote illustrates this intergroup violence when it takes physical form.

It is a summer afternoon and the women's irritabilities are as steaming as the temperature inside the living room. The heat of the bright florescent lights above, the deafening television, the drone of a floor fan, and women's idleness contribute to the bad mood. Keira is sunk in the sofa across from Victoria, who is on the edge of a wooden chair with her always-present books and manila folder of rules in hand. Victoria reaches to her left and turns a floor fan away from her legs, unknowingly pointing it directly toward Keira. Keira looks toward Victoria and asks, "Can you please turn that back? I don't want it blowin' on me." Victoria responds, barely audibly: "Well, move." Keira retorts, "Ya don't gotta be nasty." Before Keira can take a breath, Victoria pops up from the chair and lunges across the room, winds her arm up, and punches Keira squarely in the face, knocking to the floor Keira's prison-issued black glasses as she yells, "Bitch, whadda want!?" Keira struggles to her feet, swearing and clawing at Victoria's face with one hand and clutching what she can grab of Victoria's short hair with the other. They are "goin' at it!" shouts an amused Candy who pops her head into the room from the hallway. Adeline and Mimi rush to break up the fight as two monitors appear to drag Victoria away to the downstairs offices. Keira is sent to her room.

Victoria and Keira had no real beef between them before their fight. As Victoria later explains, she was lashing out at the oppression she felt mounting against her as a resident, and Keira happened to be the target of her frustration. Physical violence like this rarely occurs because the women know the consequences are too great to risk. Clair explains that despite her readiness and willingness to fight, she works to channel her frustrations rather than ignite intergroup violence: "I was born 'n raised in Southville. Growing up, you'd get your ass kicked if you weren't tough. I grew up out on those streets, I know what to expect. I know how ta fight. You gotta fight your way around. You're in so many situations all day long, there's danger all around, so you got it instilled in your head when you're young—get out there 'n fight. But, here I don't do it, 'cause I'd go back to jail. I just find other ways to deal with it all."

Even when Billie ratted out Clair to staff when she had promised to keep secret Clair's sex work when the two women were returning from IOP, Clair resisted the urge to beat Billie up. She chose not to fight, she explains, because she has too much to lose. Physical fights strain women individually, are not tolerated by staff, and disrupt the women's sisterhood and the solidarity in resistance that it supports. At this reentry center, that the women who have made it through Blackout and the long months that followed can hold back from lashing out against their peers in frustration over what has been promised but not delivered demonstrates the power of women's agency. When it does occur, intergroup violence brought on by the stressors of living in a repressive environment can be misdirected resistance that creates harm in new, yet all too familiar forms of domination.

But sometimes, intergroup violence happens without warning, and women have little time to decide how to react. Such violence between Candy and Adeline happened suddenly. Candy and Adeline had been getting along like pals, living harmoniously over the last eight months. Candy had previously told me she could relate to Adeline more than the others as a result of their violent crimes and prison time, as well as the troubles they shared finding employment because of the stigma of their crimes. But it also seems that Candy may have misinterpreted their camaraderie, reading more into their relationship than Adeline intended. As the women tell it, and as Candy revealed privately to me, she felt a sexual attraction to Adeline and fantasized about having sex with her. Henrietta said of Candy's desire for Adeline, "She wanna tap dat pussy." When Adeline began to spend less time with Candy and began buddying up with Violet during down time in the living room, at meals, and during chore time, Candy was pushed to the boiling point. "She jealous dey spendin' time," said Henrietta after Candy shouted a sarcastic comment at Adeline in the presence of others in the living room. In retrospect, Candy was seen to be monitoring the pair during chore time and when the house was "open" at the end of the day, and she even tried to gather information about their goings-on while Adeline and Violet attended treatment at IOP. Candy was also having a hard time with the emotional disconnection she felt from her wife, Valencia. She stopped taking her medications for two weeks, hiding the pills in her cheeks when dispensed medications by monitors at lockdown and in the morning. On a Wednesday afternoon she said to me, "It's been eight years since I hit a bitch—I'ma get a bitch." Adeline would be that bitch.

Annoyed by the constant negative attention shown to her, Adeline asked Candy to "take it easy 'n leave us alone," but this prompted an immediate and hostile response. Candy shouted back to Adeline in the hallway outside the living room: "I hope you kill youself like you said if you neva get your daughter back, 'cause you ain't ever gettin' her back. You're not gonna be able to take it." Shocked, Adeline walked closer to listen, as she is deaf in one ear from prior intimate partner abuse. Apparently interpreting this as a hostile turn, Candy lunged at Adeline and began punching her repeatedly in the face with both fists. Adeline punched back in defense, but not before being bloodied from the first shot to the face. Her lower teeth protruded through her lower lip, and the left side of her face swelled and grew red. Mimi, Rosa, and Clair jumped into action to pull the pair apart. Candy was swept away by administrative staff entering from the floor below. Adeline was taken to the monitors' office. Both women suffered major consequences. Despite her provocation, Candy remained at the house for another two days before being transferred to a less restrictive reentry center. Adeline was returned to prison.

EPILOGUE

EVERY WOMAN WHO participated in this research departed Alpha Omega House. Most graduated the program, meaning they had "successfully" completed it. Others received what the women call a "dishonorable discharge"—they were transferred out of the program to another community-based intervention or returned to imprisonment. This final chapter describes departure from the house, what happened to some of the women following release, and the further need for sober, unflinching research into the real-life consequences of reentry programs intended to empower women.

Release

I can't even be excited about leaving this place, it's so sad. When I came, monitors and them downstairs barely said hello. I never felt so helpless in my life. And now, they don't care where I'm goin.'—Mimi

ROSA

It is Rosa's graduation. At 8:15 a.m., women of the house gather in the dining room for a special graduation breakfast—scrambled eggs, grits, bacon, sausages, juice drink, and milk. Entering the room together, the executive director and another administrative staff member quickly begin the ceremony. A smiling Rosa stands as she is presented with her Certificate of Completion and a butterfly necklace. "You are now," says the director, "a member of the sisterhood of Alpha Omega, the beginning and the end." "You are," continues the director, "like a butterfly, a woman reborn and renewed."

Other women of the house sit silently at the tables eating breakfast. The director tells the women that the house "is about helping women and giving them everything they need for a good life." She then leads the women in rehearsing the pledge for this sorority that all of them learned in Blackout. It is 8:20 a.m. and the ceremony has concluded.

Rosa anxiously waits for her discharge as she sits with the other residents in the living room before the booming television. This ceremony is like any other graduation here—short, rote, mechanical. Adeline's sentiment captures the mood. She says, "It is just to say it was done, that something was done for the cameras that weren't here."

Graduation occurs at Alpha Omega when a woman successfully completes the house's phases of stay and has secured housing. It is a ritual of rebirth in ceremonious form just as convent departure was for the nuns who lived here before. And like those nuns transformed toward spiritual awakening with new identities (van Doorn-Harder, 1995), reentry center graduates are said to be transformed as they are presented the butterfly necklace and the certificate of membership into a sorority of women resocialized for productive community life.

The intercom sounds: "Rosa, report to the monitors' office." As Rosa rises from the sofa to leave, the mood is quite somber. She and the others have bonded, but they know their relationships have come to an end. When women leave, they want nothing to do with this reentry center. Rosa says of disconnecting with Henrietta, "It's betta' to forget about it, to put it out your head 'n see her when she get out." Even while the women's connections are strong and essential, the relationships are typically "only for a minute." When they leave the house, rarely do they ever look back; most relationships move into history, and the women are once again on their own.

Rosa gives Henrietta a long embrace and hugs Mimi and Phoebe. She returns to Henrietta, who is crying aloud, and says, "I love you, Hen." With two white, kitchen-sized plastic bags filled with her clothing and other personals, Rosa stops at the entrance to the monitors' office, where she collects her bank ATM card and state identification card (kept by the house during her stay), all of her medications, and a partial payout of the money left on her books. She says not a word to staff, turns, and waves to the other women standing in the narrow hallway to see her off. Rosa has been discharged. Like other women graduating the reentry center, she will be supervised by probation or parole for the length of time she owes the criminal justice system that she did not serve in confinement or at Alpha Omega House. She owes five years.

Rosa lights a cigarette as the reentry center door shuts behind her and says, "I'm out. I'll neva come back to dis mothafucka." She tosses her Alpha Omega ID to the ground. There are no family members at the gate, no flowers or balloons, no smiles, no open arms for her to run to. Rosa acts tough, but as Candy surmises later, she is "scared as shit inside." Before she hits the gate, Rosa rips the necklace off and says: "Dis shit don't mean nuthin' to me. Dat sisterhood is bullshit. Dey put me out on da street. Dey just throwing me out, dey don't care. It's all about control."

As she steps onto the city sidewalk, Rosa inspects the two gallon-sized Ziplock bags of medication bottles given to her by staff. She counts each bottle, dividing up what she will keep and what she will sell; the sleeping pills and bipolar meds are quick sales. Graduation is like hitting the play button after a year on pause. Rosa is not reintegrated. The pressures and crises of everyday life, the pulls of fast money on the block are dangerous. One of the administrators at the graduation says of Rosa: "She'll fail within three months at the latest. She not ready. She hasn't learned to live outside her emotions. She not been able to take responsibility." But as Rosa walks the sidewalk to the bus, she says as if making promises to herself: "Dis time, I'm not gonna do dat. I'm not goin' down dat road again. I'm not gettin' high no more. I'm not gonna let my family down, again. I don't wanna smoke wet no more. I don't wanna wake up 'n say what am I gonna do today fo money to get high. A blunt is not dat importan' to me. I'm on paper fo five years, so I get high I'm facin' five up in Copley. Dat ain't gonna happen."

As she arrives to her neighborhood appropriately called "mean street," Rosa nods a hello to familiar drug dealers on her street corner as she makes her way down the narrow litter-strewn block of small indistinguishable row homes covered with graffiti, past neighbors drinking from paper bags and smoking blunts on their porches. As she reaches home and steps through the locked gate onto the porch, which from ceiling to floor is entirely enclosed in an iron barrier resembling prison bars, she turns and says: "I'm free. I'm free at last."

Two months later Rosa cries to me on the telephone: "It's ROLA. I hate ROLA. I want Rosa back. I'm so messed up. I relapsed 'n been doin' some fucked-up shit. I hate myself. I lost so much weight from da wet. I just wanna die. I'ma piece a' shit. I been pushin' all dat abuse shit down for so long, it's a devil on my back. I just been gettin' high like my life ain't worth shit, 'n I know I'ma do somethin' crazy. I caught another fuckin' case . . . Bring me back to da psych jawn."

Despite her pledge to stay clean, Rosa is back to smoking the wet weed that leads her to violence and self-destruction. Once her SSI is spent on drugs, which happens within a day, Rosa steals from her mother and dying grandmother, shoplifts to resell goods, and hustles her psychiatric medications on the streets. She attended her GED program just one week before quitting; school was keeping her distracted from the real life about her.

At her request, I drive Rosa to a hospital for mental-health inpatient services —the psych jawn, as she calls it—but not before she "copped" some wet weed and smoked "da last one." She had left this "psych jawn" two days before, but wants to give it another shot. It is the only place she could think for some relief from the torment of mental illness and the pulls of her drug addiction.

Within a day Rosa checks herself out of the hospital and flees back to the streets of her neighborhood, seeking drugs and shoplifting to pay for them. Within a week, she is in new trouble with the law. She is arrested for felony retail theft and possession of drugs and ordered to surrender to Alpha Omega House for violation of probation.

Rosa will successfully complete the program for the second time, again graduating with ceremony. Back down the block and onto the fenced porch, Rosa will be in the community for just one month before the cycle of drug use and crime becomes a daily routine. My phone rings, and Rosa says, "I caught another fuckin' case 'n dey sendin' me back ta Alpha Omega House." After just weeks in her third try at Alpha Omega House, she is unexpectedly released. She recalls staff saying, "There's nothin' we can do for you." Rosa rings my phone. She is speaking rapidly and loudly with slurred words barely understandable. She says, "I bounced. I don't gotta stay in dat fucked-up place. Fuck dem muthafuckas. Ha ha! I'm out. I'm back in da 'hood where I belong."

Instead of placement at Alpha Omega House, Rosa will be shuffled by the criminal justice system to an IOP where she is slated for group therapy and individual counseling while she lives with her mother and grandmother. But what Rosa deserves and desperately needs is a long-term inpatient program where she can learn to live without drugs, manage her mental illness, and get services she needs so that she can aspire to more than this life of welfare dependency, drugs, and crime. Just one month after this new release to the community and her required participation at IOP, Rosa is returned to custody in the county jail before being sent to state prison.

LAUREL

Grabbing my phone, Laurel posts a quick message to her Facebook page as she steps outside the doors of Alpha Omega House on the day of her release: "Hey fam n friends I'm free to be me need support lots of it pray for me love you all going to do da right thing." Wishing to do the right thing, Laurel is nevertheless heading directly to trouble. She is afraid of the destruction she is capable of and disgusted at her life. "I destroyed my life. I'm all fucked up," she says as she looks toward the street.

Laurel had a ceremony similar to Rosa's, complete with the butterfly necklace, the certificate of completion, and the sorority pledge weakly spoken in unison by the women she leaves behind. And she too would make her way through the women in a procession of tearful goodbyes before collecting her medications, identification, winter coat, and money. And like every other woman who departs the Alpha Omega House, she turns to a wave at her sisters as she walks out of the doors without a word to staff.

Laurel graduated with a bitter disdain toward the reentry center organization and the larger criminal justice system. As she walks the short path from the front door to the iron gate, she turns and throws a quick middle finger to the building. "I'm outside of dis jail. I'm gonna walk right da fuck out da gate. Everythin' I've done 'n seen I take wit me. The pain, the degradation, the rage." Her entire reentry experience was, in her words, "unsuccessful," and Laurel walks away just as defiant as the day she entered.

She never did rent a room, as she made staff believe. She hopes to stay with her ex-boyfriend despite his apparent reluctance, his violent behavior, his ongoing drug addiction, and her probation officer's warning not to take up residence with him. But rules were never important to Laurel. As she tells me in a drunken phone call late the following night, she strode directly to a liquor store "to chug a Yak," that is, to get booze. By the end of that night, Clive would send her packing from his apartment, and she would return to "da block," trading her body to two strange men for more drink and drugs and setting off a weeklong drug and alcohol binge.

Having immediately resumed her drinking and drug activity nearly to pre-incarceration levels, Laurel was on a fast track to trouble. Just days after graduation, she returned to Alpha Omega House seeking help and money but was turned away by staff. Of Laurel's appearance that day, Candy says she was probably smoking crack: "She all da fuck snorted up. She looked real bad, hair crazy, smellin' like booze." By the end of her second week of freedom, the physical markers of addiction were showing in weight loss, jitteriness, and a deteriorated and disheveled physical appearance. She had been sleeping on couches and on porches, working her smile to get one last favor from the few friends and family that would help. She is, in her words, "runnin' in circles."

Laurel has no intention of living a conventional life. She says, "Don't get it fucked up. I'll be doin' some shit. My niggas got my setup waitin.'" While she is subject to supervision in the community as a probationer and required to check in with her probation officer, Laurel plans to resume her drug dealing and has the support of extended family members who regularly deal drugs. Just as she managed to dodge the system with an active warrant for ten years "bein' ghost," as Candy says, Laurel had some time on her side. But one year after her release she would be arrested and jailed for several crimes, including felony burglary, robbery, and assault. As of this writing, Laurel is serving a sentence for those crimes at Copley prison.

ADELINE

With just a few weeks remaining before graduation, Adeline was reincarcerated after the fight with Candy. She was victim and did not precipitate the aggression. Had she been convicted of a minor crime, Adeline might have received no punishment at all. But because she is a violent felon in the eyes of the criminal justice system, any hint of recurring violence suggests she is not ready for community life. "They done me dirty," she says of the criminal justice system's response to her physical beating by Candy. For her role in the fight, Adeline was remanded to county jail where she stayed for forty-four days before a judge presiding over her probation revocation hearing ordered her back to Alpha Omega House to start anew.

A year later Adeline would finally graduate. Jobless, she took a less-than-desirable rented room in one of the neighborhood's most dangerous sections. She worries about her safety; the family of her deceased boyfriend has been notified of her release to the community via services to crime victims. She is also concerned about being thrown back in jail for even the slightest infraction. She says, "I have five years probation comin' up. You know how hard that is? You really gotta be careful. I can't even jaywalk. You're goin' down. You have to have ID, and if you don't have ID, you're goin' to jail. Bam! That's VOP [violation of probation] right there. I'm done."

Ten months after graduating the halfway house, Adeline is struggling to stay positive. "The world is hard," she says. She cannot find work, she says, because "who wants to hire a murderer?" With the cost of bus transportation, normal living expenses, probation supervision fees, and fines levied by the court, Adeline is in a rough spot. Welfare is not enough to keep her afloat. She left the rented room to stay with a friend of a friend, where she pays a little less each month for a bed.

With letters of support from her probation officer and judge, she was accepted
into a training program for woman abuse counseling. She attended that program
for weeks, traveling almost two hours each way by bus to attend classes. But once
she revealed details of her own victimization experience and criminal case during
class, she says she was immediately dismissed and told not to return, because "we
have concerns for the safety of the others here."

Adeline continues to experience the negative effects of living with a felonious
label and realizes her choices will always be limited. "The system stinks," she says.
She continues:

> I learned a lot of the other side of the [criminal justice] system from the
> inside. I got more issues and problems from bein' in jail and the halfway
> house than the night of the murder . . . Now that I experienced the system
> and what they do to us, I think a lot of other people woulda broke down.
> I never wanted to kill myself until they threw me in jail. If I gotta live like
> this, if this is how it's gonna be, suicide watch, I'm out. And the halfway
> house wasn't no better. It didn't do shit for me. And the system's still doin'
> it to me.

But Adeline still hopes to one day open the doors of a reentry center to victims
of woman abuse that would meet the needs of women returning to community
life. She'll call it "Adeline's Angels." Her plans are put to work; she is fundraising
and spreading the word.

BILLIE

Billie entered Alpha Omega House on her thirty-fourth birthday. As she prepared for her new round of correctional rehabilitation that first night of Blackout, she cried: "I wanna do something wit my life. I wanna be able to talk to
somebody witout sayin'—hey, ya want a hit? I wanna be able ta talk to somebody
wit'out sayin'—hey, come wit me, I can suck your dick. I wanna be somebody."
She hoped to become successful at something, to become someone who would
live in society without prostituting or using drugs.

Soon after feeling some advancement through IOP, Billie is surprised at the
notice of her immediate release from Alpha Omega House because she is still on
C Level. Just four months into her stay, the release, she says, is punishment for
an argument with the executive director days earlier. Immediate release means
she will be discharged without ceremony and good wishes. Her housing plan is
to live with the man she calls her husband in a rented room where she used drugs

and prostituted for many years. According to the terms of her discharge, Billie says, she will be supervised by county probation for the next couple of years. She must attend the IOP she started at the halfway house and remain drug free or risk incarceration for violating her probation.

On her last day, Billie's change in appearance matches her mood. She is no longer dressed in one of the donated business suits she liked to wear. Her hair is no longer neatly combed to the side, and she is free of bright makeup. Her high-heeled shoes are replaced by prison-issued plastic orange flip-flops. She wears a wrinkled white men's T-shirt spotted with stains at the belly and heavy black sweatpants billowing at the knees, just as she did the day she entered. As she gathers her belongings in a single black trash bag and laments about time she feels has been wasted at Alpha Omega House, Billie cries: "I had all bad experience here, all bad experience 'n I don't like it at all. I would never send nobody here 'cause dey take your life in they hands. Dey try to put you back not put you forward."

This bad experience and backward motion would continue after Billie's release. She attended her required IOP treatment, says Clair who also attends, just three times during the first two weeks of her release. She also looked jumpy and thinner. By the fourth week, Billie is a no-show at IOP. In less than three months' time, Billie would return to incarceration for violation of probation and new crimes related to crack addiction and prostitution. In classic revolving-door fashion, Billie would then be released, arrested, and returned to jail three more times over the next seven months.

CLAIR

No one thought Clair would ever make it out of Blackout. Her long criminal history of prostitution and seemingly helpless drug addiction made her appear a lost soul. But over the course of a hard year, Clair toughed her way through every phase to A Level and then graduation. On the day of graduation, with the butterfly necklace hanging over the neck of her sweater, Clair tucks the certificate of completion inside a garbage bag filled with her personals and clothing. From a monitor she retrieves money remaining on her books, identification she brought in with her, and the gallon Ziploc of medications. Then like every other woman who leaves, Clair bids farewell to her fellow house sisters and walks directly out the door without any nod to staff. She has no job waiting, but she does have a stable residence in the home she and her husband share on the outskirts of this city.

One year after her release, Clair says she is doing well. She found work in telemarketing and started an online GED program. While she has not regained custody of her children, she visits them regularly. Clair is a success; she continues to live within the constraints of probation supervision and remains drug free.

FREYA

Freya was dismissed from Alpha Omega House with a "dishonorable discharge" as the women call it, days after moving to B Level. She was transferred into another reentry center for getting into a heated shouting match with the executive director and failing a drug test with a "hot urine" for crack (she claims a false positive). While at the other reentry center, Freya is required to abide by probation conditions and attend the IOP she started while at Alpha Omega House. Because she was not reincarcerated for failing Alpha Omega House but transferred to an alternative program to complete her reentry, she will not face her "back time" in prison; Alpha Omega House also benefits if this type of discharge—a transfer to an alternative program—does not count in its official completion rates.

As she prepared her belongings for discharge, Freya reflects on what could have been a positive transition: "This is supposed to be rehabilitation. However, the environments they force us into with the threat of more jail time is basically the only reason we stay here. It's a negative environment and we want to act out against. So it's not really helping. I believe some things need to be changed in order to prevent the revolving door."

I run into Freya at a bus stop a few days after her transfer. She says she enjoys the reentry program and is glad to be out of Alpha Omega House; as a new girl in that program, she has already begun a regiment of treatment and has more freedoms than she ever had at Alpha Omega House. She appreciates that she may carry a cell phone and hold her own money, which makes her feel "more normal and responsible."

Three weeks later, I bump into Freya again. She is walking quickly past the building housing her IOP treatment program and is smoking a blunt with two men. Her speech is slurred and much quicker than normal, her body twitches as if controlled by drugs, and her breath reeks of booze. She is thinner and appears disheveled. Four months later, Freya is ordered back to court for violating terms of her probation.

MIMI

Mimi successfully completed all phases of stay and graduated with ceremony, but had no intention of moving forward with the housing plan approved by house staff; that was just a way to earn her freedom from the program. Instead, she moves into a rented room on the third floor of a large run-down duplex on a dilapidated and litter-ridden street in an area of this city known for high crime and open-air drug selling. She'll be working to pay the $170 weekly rent for herself and her boyfriend, recently released from prison. As she carries the last of her belongings to her new room, Mimi stops and looks around at the children playing in the water from the opened fire hydrant, women sitting on their stoops, and men smoking blunts on the sidewalk. "This'll do," she says. "It's not that bad." Mimi would spend some private time with her boyfriend before returning that very night to bartending at the corner bar where she worked before her incarceration.

A week later, Mimi feels a bit out of sync, she says, as if she is being watched. But she is thrilled to be out of Alpha Omega House and moving on with life. She'll avoid drinking and smoking pot, she says, until her probation ends in three months. Mimi earned six hundred dollars cash working at the bar over the course of that week and expects the same tax-free cash payment every week. House staff prohibited her from working at the bar while she resided there even though she had the job waiting—and even though she actually started work at the bar two weekends before she graduated, socking away some hard-earned cash to help her get settled with a cell phone, bus passes, and food. Of her victory over the suppressive house staff, she had said: "They think I'm not workin,' but this is the ultimate fuck you."

Mimi's goal is to save enough money to get her own apartment outside of the city with a yard big enough for a couple of pit bulls. A year after her release, she had left her boyfriend and kept up the rent in the third-floor walkup, working many hours at the bartending job. She was "partying" a bit, smoking marijuana, and as some of the other women who maintaineded contact with her said, using cocaine. Sadly, Mimi was once again arrested and after a probation revocation hearing served a short term of jail confinement followed by an extended term on probation for possession of drugs and driving under the influence of drugs.

GRACE

Grace is finally graduating after more than two years at Alpha Omega House. She does not know why she stayed that long when most women leave before a year is up, but she has felt safe there and even called it home. From the little details she is able to give, it appears she will be moving into a room funded by a local social service agency. She says excitedly, "Dey get you roo, che [check] up on you, sit wit you, taw bout thin,' ha fun, yeah, taw bout fam [family], wha ba [bothering] you lot, yeah." She is "happy" to be moving, she says, but will miss her room at the house, some of the other women, and especially the house cat, Oscar.

Grace plans to continue working in the volunteer domestic-labor internship she started more than a year ago because it makes her feel productive and she likes to ride the bus. She has been seeing a man she works with, first calling him her boyfriend and then fiancé. She says, "My boyfren' go dere, bring me box choc-at, ted bear." It is his birthday, and she wants to give him a card but cannot read or write. She presents me with a birthday card and asks me to read it to her and then write a note inside. She selected this particular card at the dollar store on her way to the halfway house because it is "pretty." She says: "I nev wrote a lett, I don' know, jus' wri wha you wan." I ask her what she would say to him if he were standing before her. She replies, "Happ bir-day." Then she says, "I don' know more." I ask what she would want someone to tell her in a birthday card, and she replies "I love you, I love you for ev. I wan' to squee you for ev. I ho you ha nih day. You my ted bear." And we close the letter with the words "Love, Grace" with a heart next to her name. Smiling, she takes the card and skips away. This man is an alcoholic and has a drug problem, Grace says, but she says she loves him and enjoys his company. The pair likes to have sex, she says, but she is not concerned about getting pregnant.

I ask Grace what she is thinking about the future and what might be challenging or different for her when she is outside the halfway house doors. She replies simply, "I gah no guh slee [good sleep] he [here], fore I slee cah [calm], buh he I geh no guh slee. Buh den I geh guh slee." Looking forward to restful nights, Grace seems to have a limited awareness of the challenges ahead for a woman returning to community life after years in total institutions.

After a graduation with ceremony, Grace would return to Alpha Omega House just days after her release, wearing medical scrubs and her butterfly necklace. She had not commited a new crime or violated her terms of probation. Rather, she returned to volunteer. Logging into the binder next to the front door as visitor, Grace volunteers to "help out, file pap [papers], and clean." She is having a difficult time on the outside; she says it is "hard ow dare," and finds comfort in the familiar routine of Alpha Omega House. One year later Grace is returned to custody.

CANDY

For her vicious attack on Adeline in the hallway of Alpha Omega House, Candy was neither returned to court for a new offense nor reincarcerated. Instead, she was transferred to a different reentry center nearby. Out of all of women in this study, Candy is the most highly institutionalized, having lived more years behind bars in her adult life than she has spent in society. She has difficulty interacting outside of a controlled setting; an interaction with a man at the local Chinese restaurant not long before her transfer helps to illustrate this point. Having been sent up the block to place a food order for monitors, Candy hands the man, who stands behind a Plexiglas barrier that resembles a bank teller's window, a food order written on a scrap of office paper. The man reads the order back and asks Candy to clarify which of the barbeque pork dishes should have the onion rings. She seems stumped by his question and points repeatedly to the piece of paper, saying "read it." As the man continues to ask for clarification, Candy raises her arms in frustration and shouts, "It written da fuck right dere!" and pushes the paper through the Plexiglas opening in aggravation. She shouts, "Fuck!" as she walks out to the street for another cigarette before she returns to tell the man to put the order together "howeva da fuck ya want."

When she was in Blackout, Candy hoped to learn how to live in society "like everybody else" and without the violence upon which she has relied through-out her life. But to "live outside the box," as she puts it, will be difficult for her. While she has received substance-abuse counseling at IOP treatment and coun-seling for her violent temper, her inability to handle an everyday interaction with a stranger, not to mention the fight with Adeline, suggests she has a long way to go before she can properly handle her emotions. She says of others who have left before her, "Everybody throwin' up a facade dat dey happy ta leave, but dey know from getting' abused dat dey put on dat mask in fronta otha people to make it seem like, I'm 'ite. Like dey not scareda nuthin' no more, like I got this, I can do this. But all along, dey scared." Candy knows that living in free society will not be easy for her and despite her outward toughness, she too is frightened at the prospect of managing every part of her life entirely on her own.

Eight months after her transfer out of Alpha Omega House, Candy would be sent back to the same prison she had lived in with her wife for many years.

PHOEBE

Despite her heroin relapse and near overdose, Phoebe successfully completed Alpha Omega House. That rule violation cost her a setback in phase of stay and an additional two months at the house, but she would graduate nonetheless after a hearty breakfast and ceremonious speech by administrative staff. Like all the others before her, Phoebe receives the certificate of completion and butterfly necklace signifying her rebirth from criminally involved to renewed woman. And like most others, she exits without forward advancement. As she steps outside the convent gates, Phoebe has no job and returns to live in her destructive home environment with her substance-abusing mother, her abusive and drug-dealing stepfather, and her heroin-addicted siblings. Her plan upon release, she says, is to finally touch her new boyfriend, a prison inmate with whom she secretly corresponded as "pen pal." Her hope is simply to stay off drugs, she says. "My accomplishment would be staying clean." But two weeks after her release, Phoebe was spotted on the street "all wild and fucked up," says Mimi, apparently hooked back on heroin and cocaine.

HENRIETTA

Henrietta graduated in springtime and returned to the graffiti-tagged city row home she rented for many years with her abusive husband. As a woman close to retirement age who has lived a rather simple life, Henrietta does not aspire to work in any job, criminal or otherwise. Content with the monthly welfare check, she plans to relax, play dominoes, and drink beer with her wife, Jo-Jo, whom she missed during her yearlong stay at Alpha Omega House. She looks forward to "bein' happy" and loving her "grandbabies." Henrietta will be on probation for the next five years and must avoid drinking to maintain compliance with probation rules, which she says will be her toughest challenge. One year after her release, Henrietta seems to be living her plans and should fair well if she can keep her assaultive temper under control and avoid any contact with the police.

VICTORIA

Victoria was discharged from the house for fighting. While she only made it to C Level, she had already served the remaining portion of her jail sentence at the house. Thus having paid her debt to society, her discharge carries no criminal justice repercussions, and she leaves without community supervision by probation or parole authorities. She also exits without employment and plans to live with a relative until she can get back on her feet. But Victoria is not a high risk for re-offending. She has no criminal history other than the altercation on the city bus that landed her in jail and Alpha Omega House. She also has no drug or alcohol addiction and lived independently, working steadily for many years. Her biggest challenge will be to reestablish ties to conventional society while returning with a felony record.

VIOLET

Violet is the only woman in this study who left Alpha Omega House with a paying job approved by house staff. She was hired to work with the volunteer bicycling group that led bicycle rides for some of the women at the house. This is quite an accomplishment for a young woman who was homeless just two years earlier and selling her body for crack. At the start of her one-year stay at the house, Violet reflected on her past attempts at getting clean and her doubts about renewal: "I thought I was done the last time I was at a program. I thought I had it the last time and I went and messed it up. What makes me think I got it this time and ain't gonna mess up? Ain't nuthin' much out there for us ladies."

Violet graduated to live with her parents and siblings on the outskirts of the city and by all measures seemed to be fairing well. But just one month after her release, she was smoking crack and drinking and had lost the paid job, says Adeline, who kept in close contact with her. Just two months post-release, Violet was arrested for drug possession and prostitution and remanded to jail. She pled guilty and was sentenced to six months' probation. Eight months after that conviction, she would try yet again to quit drugs, moving to a rural part of the state in an inpatient drug and alcohol program.

Damage

> For a place dats supposta prepare you for a society, dey damage you. Dey bring you down 'n dey damage you. If you let dem damage you dey will damage you. Dey wouldn't dare treat a man da way dey treat women in here.—Billie

The women in this study faced obstacles in virtually every sphere of their lives that most people could not imagine. From childhood traumas to sexism in the world of crime, substance abuse and corresponding homelessness and poor health, neglect by the criminal justice system and abuse at the hands of treatment providers, they have experienced continued oppression that has limited their true potential and caused great harm to them and to others. They are tough-skinned from years of enduring so much, and most are strong-willed as they continue to resist various forms of coercion and control to exert their independence and manage their own lives.

As a middle ground between the highly punitive confines of incarceration and the independence of civic life, the reentry center I call Alpha Omega House advertises structured and supportive intervention to help women rebuild their lives after incarceration. It promises to "empower" ex-offenders and to help such women to become independent and confident citizens. Sadly, this study reveals evidence to the contrary. The house does not facilitate reentry into productive community life, but rather reentry to incarceration for some, and for others reentry to familiar social, personal, and economic circumstances of hurt, exclusion, and domination.

The damage Billie refers to when she says "dey bring you down 'n dey damage you" is the consequence of patriarchal oppression that pervades virtually every part of the reentry experience. From Alpha Omega's architectural style and organizational structure to its gendered chores and absence of work and other opportunity, the reentry experience at the house harms women. Oppression and domination are also meted out through rules and regulations, staff supervisory styles, exclusion from the outside world, unmet treatment needs and medical care, disconnected relationships, and many other ways. What was promised to the women as reformation, renewal, change, and empowerment in a therapeutic environment was not delivered. Instead, the intimidation, coercion, abuse, marginalizing, and exclusion observed in this study reproduce social-order inequities the women as a group have experienced throughout their lives and which precipitated many of their involvement in criminality and substance abuse. Like Billie, many of the women recognize their placement at the reentry center as another exercise in a lifelong struggle for independence and self-actualization in a broken criminal justice system and a society that rejects them.

Resistance is a prominent and pervasive feature of the halfway-house experience, as the women demonstrate agency in action, speech, posture, and routine. Varying with situational and temporal opportunities, women put to work a range of oppositional strategies to maintain dignity, show disapproval, and care for themselves and others. As they experience the phases of stay from the darkest days of Blackout through the ceremony of graduation, the women continuously seek to mitigate oppression, but their resistance does not always bring relief. Sometimes it can be as destructive as the forces it challenges. Nonetheless, what remains steady in the lives of these women is their resilience and response to domination and control despite limits of agency and the uncertain results of resistance.

Though many of the women whose voices are gathered here have returned to crime, drugs, or what many would consider deviant or unproductive ways of life, I do not consider them failures because they acted and, I suspect, continue to act against repression. These women and no doubt many others like them are not beyond hope. A long-term solution to the problems faced by the women in this research before, during, and after their participation in the reentry center must involve the end of patriarchy and other forms of oppression. In the short term, more effective reentry programming in a "seamless system of care" (Taxman, 1998) is needed at all phases of the criminal justice process, not just at the back-end in community-based reentry centers like Alpha Omega House. Empirical research on reentry continues to advance programming both inside and outside of correctional institutions, but more research on programming for women is needed. My research shows that reintegration programming for the women at the reentry center described as gender specific was, at the very least, poorly conceptualized, inadequate, and badly implemented. These failures certainly played a role in women's efforts of resistance, including their deviance, and how quickly they returned to drug use or were arrested and reincarcerated after departing the reentry center. How Alpha Omega House compares to other reentry efforts for women is simply not known. More qualitative research is badly needed on how reentry centers actually operate in practice and how participants are affected.

While important questions remain about how gender-specific treatment models actually affect women who participate and to what extent women benefit, scholars have already advanced proposals for progressive gender-responsive strategies. There are, no doubt, programs based on these models that are working for women. Other researchers have worked to design assessment tools for practitioners to identify needs of women offenders most in need of treatment response, which will assist in the delivery of those gender-specific treatment models. One of the many failures of Alpha Omega House, and a criticism raised of gender-responsive strategies by other scholars, is that a focus on particular needs of women at the expense of needs shared by men and women alike is a mistake and may reproduce women's subordination and dependence. Further, when treatment needs are met in ways that increase the control and punishment of women, gender-responsive strategies harm women in other ways.

The challenge is figuring out what treatments and services work best, how they should be delivered, and how corresponding supervision can best be organized to empower and benefit women. Designing effective gender-responsive strategies is not as simple as offering treatment and services in the areas of need suggested by empirical research. It requires continued assessment and refinement from analyses of how treatments and services actually function in practice. Empirical research is needed that considers not just the impacts of programming in outcome evaluations but more immediately in ongoing process evaluation to ensure that strategies are delivered as designed by trained staff in environments of support and care. New theoretical, empirical, and policy research that focus on the development, implementation, and evaluation of gender-responsive strategies will prove useful for women offenders in the future. Especially as community reentry centers are highly privatized and reintegration involves a host of agencies and organizations, ongoing oversight and accountability is absolutely necessary. While organizations like Alpha Omega House and the larger criminal justice system cannot solve problems of patriarchy and other oppression in the lives of women offenders, they must not be complicit in perpetuating harm.

As to future theoretical research, this study reveals that patriarchal oppression and other forms of domination occur in settings many people would believe are safe and progressive. The same may be true in other environments used to assist, empower, shelter, and reform vulnerable populations. In addition to demonstrating that oppression is reproduced, my findings show that women participate in the oppression of other women even when they are themselves victimized. In the hierarchal chain of command in this reentry center, women monitors are subordinate to higher-level workers but exercise power and coercion over residents. Women residents also sometimes oppress other residents violently when they challenge oppression through resistance. New research could consider how oppression and resistance interact and evolve over time and space.

Though their placement at Alpha Omega House is intended to help facilitate women's reentry to society, the group of women in this study return to their communities with the stigma of a felony label, poorly treated substance abuse, mental and physical illness, weakened relationships of importance, and disconnection from mainstream opportunities. Like Carlen's argument (1983) that female imprisonment cultivates domesticity, my findings show that the reentry center for women reinforces a highly stigmatized image of the female offender as outsider, unproductive, and dependent. And just as Wacquant (2010, p. 616) argues that reentry programs extend "punitive containment," my research similarly reveals oppression and domination in the name of reintegration and reformation. The renewal symbolized by the butterfly in this reentry center's Alpha Omega pledge did not occur for women in this study. The women have not transformed, and they have not reintegrated into their home communities. In fact, the symbolism of the name Alpha Omega has revealed itself as unintentionally, and heartbreakingly, ironic. The women at the end of their stay at this house are much like they were at the beginning.

NOTES

PREFACE

1. The name Alpha Omega House is a pseudonym for the reentry center that advertises its own sorority of women residents, called Alpha Omega, along with a pledge by the same name.

INTRODUCTION

1. Jails are local correctional institutions housing defendants awaiting trial or sentencing and those incarcerated for offenses that carry short periods of imprisonment (normally less than one year). Prisons are normally reserved for offenders convicted of serious crimes and those serving sentences of more than one year.

2. For more on prisoner reentry, see Chesney-Lind and Mauer, 2011; Lattimore, Steffey, and Visher, 2010; Lynch and Sabol, 2001; Petersilia, 2001; Petersilia, 2004; Petersilia, 2009; Richie, 2001; Seiter and Kadela, 2003; Solomon, Visher, La Vigne, and Osborne, 2006; Travis, 2002; Travis, 2005; Travis, Keegan, and Cadora, 2003; Travis and Petersilia, 2001; Travis, Solomon, and Waul, 2001; Visher and Travis, 2003.

3. See De Leon, 1989; De Leon, 1995; De Leon, 1997; De Leon and Wexler, 2009; Inciardi, Martin, and Butzin, 2004; Chesney-Lind and Mauer, 2011; Dodge and Pogrebin, 2001.

4. See Condelli and Hubbard, 1994; Gerstein and Lewin, 1990; Inciardi, Martin, and Surratt, 2001; Inciardi, Martin, and Butzin, 2004; Knight, Dwayne, Chatham, and Camacho, 1997; Sullivan, Sullivan, McKendrick, Sacks, and Banks, 2007; Sacks, Sacks, McKendrick, Banks, and Stommel, 2004; Wexler, Falkin, and Lipton, 1990; Wexler, Falkin, Lipton, and Rosenblum, 1992.

5. For more, see Belknap, 2007; Belknap and Holsinger, 1998; Belknap and Holsinger, 2006; Blanchette and Brown, 2006; Blitz, Wolff, Pan, and Pogorzelski, 2005; Bloom, 1999; Bloom, Owen, and Covington, 2002; Bloom, Owen, Deschenes, and Rosenbaum, 2002; Bloom, Owen, and Covington, 2003; Bloom, Owen, and Covington, 2005; Caputo, 2008; Carson and Sabol, 2012; Chesney-Lind and Rodriguez, 1983; Chesney-Lind and Shelden, 2004; Covington, 1998; Covington, 2004; Covington and Bloom, 2007; Daly, 1992; Dodge and Pogrebin, 2001; Guerino, Harrison, and Sabol, 2011; Harm and Phillips, 2000; Hartwell, 2001; Henriques and Manatu-Rupert, 2001; Kassebaum, 1999; Maher, 1997; Messina and Grella, 2006; Morash, 2010; Owen, 1998; Owen and Bloom, 1995; Peugh and Belenko, 1999; Sokoloff, 2005; Van Voorhis, Wright, Salisbury, and Bauman, 2010; Van Wormer, 2010.

6. See Bloom and Covington, 1998; Bloom, 1999; Bloom, Owen, and Covington, 2002; Bloom, Owen, and Covington, 2003; Bloom, Owen, and Covington, 2005; Covington and Bloom, 2007.

7. See Davidson and Chesney-Lind, 2009; Hardyman and Van Voorhis, 2004; Holtfreter and Morash, 2003; Salisbury, Van Voorhis, and Spiropoulos, 2009; Van Voorhis, Salisbury, Wright, and Bauman, 2008; Van Voorhis, Wright, Salisbury, and Bauman, 2010.

8. See Andrews, 1994; Andrews et al., 1990; Andrews, Dowden, and Gendreau, 1999; Gendreau, 1996; Gendreau and Goggin, 1996; Van Voorhis, 2012.

9. See Bloom and Covington, 1998; Bloom, Owen, and Covington, 2003; Hannah-Moffat, 2009; Hardyman and Van Voorhis, 2004; Salisbury, Van Voorhis, and Spiropoulos, 2009; Spjeldnes and Goodkind, 2009; Van Voorhis, 2012; Van Voorhis, Wright, Salisbury, and Bauman, 2010.

10. See Gehring, Van Voorhis, and Bell, 2010; Kelley, 2003; Messina, Grella, Cartier, and Torres, 2010; Messina, Calhoun, and Warda, 2012; Prendergast, Messina, Hall, and Warda, 2011.

11. See Bouffard and Taxman, 2000; Feinman, 1983; Morash, Haarr, and Rucker, 1994; Pollock, 2002.

12. See Britton, 1999; Britton, 2000; McCorkel, 2003; Ridgeway, 1997.

13. See Barak, Leighton, and Flavin, 2010; Burgess-Proctor, 2006; Chesney-Lind, 2006; Crenshaw, 1989; Crenshaw, 1991; Davis, 2008; DeKeseredy and Dragiewicz, 2012; Dragiewicz, 2011; Hancock, 2007; Renzetti, 2013; Richie, 1996; Yuval-Davis, 2006.

14. See Chesler and Goodman, 1976; hooks, 1984; Lerner, 1986; Pleck, 1984; Ramazanoglu, 2012; Ramdas, Manan, and Sabapathy, 2010; Sacks, 1989; Wolf, 1972.

15. See Firestone, 2003, for patriarchy's roots in biological production. See Delphy, 1988; Lim, 1983; Walby, 1997; Witz, 2003 for the roots in work and the division of labor. See Rich, 1980, for roots in compulsory heterosexuality; Roberts, 1993, for roots in mothering; Scraton, 2001, for roots in sports; and Brown and Bohn, 1989, and Condren, 1989, for roots in religion.

16. See Acoca, 1999; Acoca and Dedel, 1998; DeKeseredy, 2003; DeKeseredy and Schwartz, 2009; Dobash and Dobash, 1979; Dragiewicz, 2011; Johnson, 1995; Flowers, 2001; Gavazzi, Yarcheck, and Chesney-Lind, 2006; Golden, 1992; Owen, 1998; Radford and Stanko, 1991; Renzetti, 1992; Schwartz and DeKeseredy, 1997.

17. See Anderson, 2005; Bourgois and Dunlap, 1993; Caputo, 2008; Inciardi and Surratt, 2001; Maher, 1997; Miller, 1987; Steffensmeier and Terry, 1986.

18. See Chesney-Lind, 1997; Fletcher, Shaver, Moon, and Billy, 1993; Freedman, 1984; Girshick, 1999; Owen, 1998; Richie, 2001; Ross, 1998.

19. See Abramovitz, 1996; Barrett, 1980; DeKeseredy, 2003; DeKeseredy and Schwartz, 2009; Eisenstein and Bengelsdorf, 1979; Hunnicutt, 2009; Millett, 1970; Smith, 1990; Ursel, 1986.

20. See Barrett and McIntosh, 1998; Bowker, 1983; DeKeseredy and Kelly, 1993; DeKeseredy and Schwartz, 1998; Dobash and Dobash, 1979; Harman, 1989; Pateman, 1988.

21. See Britton, 2003; Hodson, 1995; Jermier, Knights, and Nord, 1994; Johnson, 2010; Jurik, Cavender, and Cowgill, 2009; McColgan, 2005; Sen, 1999b.

22. See Bosworth, 1999; Bosworth and Carrabine, 2001; Gilligan, Rogers, and Tolman, 1991; Hollander, 2002; Kelly, 1988; Lewis, 1990; Lykes, 1983; Profitt, 1996; Shorter-Gooden, 2004.

23. See Burstow, 1992; Collinson, 2000; Handler, 1992; Jurik, Cavender, and Cowgill, 2009; McColgan, 2005; Prasad and Prasad, 2000; Sarat, 1990; Ullman and Knight, 1993.

24. See Bosworth, 1999; Bosworth and Carrabine, 2001, for challenges to diet and dress. See Trethewey, 1997, for general discussion of resistance as more than action and talk; Riessman, 2000, on thoughts; Paules, 1991; Pitts, 1998; St Martin and Gavey, 1996; Weitz, 2001, on women's bodies as sites of resistance; Leblanc, 2000; Katila and Meriläinen, 2002; Trethewey, 1997, on personal identities.

25. See Crewe, 2007; Gerami and Lehnerer, 2001; Jurik, Cavender, and Cowgill, 2009; Sotirin and Gottfried, 1999

26. See Armstrong and Murphy, 2012; Bibars, 2001; Broman, 1996; Jurik, Cavender, and Cowgill, 2009; Kandiyoti, 1988; Scott, 1990; Scott, 1985; Shorter-Gooden, 2004; Wade, 1997.

27. See Brock, 2010; Hollander and Einwohner, 2004; hooks, 1984; Scott, 1985; Sen, 1999a.

ONE | RESIDENTS

1. See Acoca and Dedel, 1998; Belknap and Holsinger, 2006; Bloom, 1995; Bloom, Owen, Rosenbaum, and Deschenes, 2003; Bloom, Owen, and Covington, 2004; Caputo, 2008; Chandy, Blum, and Resnick, 1996; Chesney-Lind and Rodriguez, 1983; Dalla, Xia, and Kennedy, 2003; Fergusson, John Horwood, and Ridder, 2005; Finkelhor, 1993; Finkelhor, 1994; Fullilove, Lown, and Fullilove, 1992; Gilfus, 2002; Harlow, 2003; James and Glaze, 2006; Kenning, Merchant, and Tomkins, 1991; Kilpatrick et al., 2000; Owen and Bloom, 1995; Sokoloff, 2005; Wilsnack, Vogeltanz, Klassen, and Harris, 1997.

TWO | BLACKOUT

1. With the emergence of the Second Vatican Council over the last half century the Catholic Church and its convents moved away from the traditionally rigid convent style in favor of a more modern structure including contemporary lifestyles and routines for nuns outside of the convent. The comparisons I make to the convent and Church are not tied to any particular religious order or period in church history, but rather to the traditional convent experience of cloister, solemn vows, and prayer. For more on the history of the church and women, see Katzenstein, 1995; Koehlinger, 2007; Mills and Ryan, 2010.

2. Rafaeli, Dutton, Harquail, and Mackie-Lewis (1997) address the relationship between dress and credibility and status; Ebaugh (1977) addresses social control; and Crockett and Wallendorf (1998) addresses discipline.

3. See Eberhardt, Goff, Purdie, and Davies, 2004; Russell, Wilson, and Hall, 2011; Russell-Brown, 1998.

4. For example, see Hannah-Moffat, 2009; Reisig, Holtfreter, and Morash, 2006; Van Voorhis, Wright, Salisbury, and Bauman, 2010.

5. See Buzzanell, 1994; Dow and Wood, 2006; Ferguson, 1985; Fletcher, 2001; Walby, 1990.

6. See Chesler and Goodman, 1976; Hackman, Furniss, Hills, and Paterson, 1992; Hearn and Parkin, 1986.

7. See DeKeseredy and Schwartz, 1998; Kandiyoti, 1988; Lerner, 1986; Walby, 1990.

8. See Brown, Sanchez, Zweben, and Aly, 1996; De Leon, 1989; Welsh, 2007.

9. See Lussier, Heil, Mongeon, Badger, and Higgins, 2006; Prendergast, Podus, Finney, Greenwell, and Roll, 2006; Prendergast, 2009.

10. See the following works: Hollander, 2009, and Ullman and Knight, 1992, on fighting back against sexual assault; Berman, 2006, and Griffin, 1996, on nuns escaping the church; McColgan, 2005, on senior citizens escaping nursing homes; and Lutgen-Sandvik, 2006, on workers escaping workplace bullying.

THREE | ZERO

1. For links between smoking and women's adult and childhood victimization, see Anda et al., 1999; Koss, Koss, and Woodruff, 1991; Walker et al., 1999; for links between women's smoking and substance abuse, see Burling and Ziff, 1988; and Sullivan, 2002.

2. See Barrett, 1980; Blair, 1980; Boydston, 1990; Brenner and Laslett, 1986; Delphy and Leonard, 1984; Epstein, 1981; Glenn, 1992; Lorber, 1994; Mies, 1998; Shelton and John, 1996.

3. See Glenn, 1992; Blackwelder, 1978; Lorber, 1994; Rollins, 1987.

4. See Duffy, 2005; Nakano Glenn, 1985; Romero, 2002.

5. See Bianchi, Milkie, Sayer, and Robinson, 2000; Kennedy and Davis, 1993.

6. See Acoca, 1998; Anderson, 2003; Barry, 2001; Freudenberg, 2002.

7. See Dallaire, 2007; Miller, 2006; Siegel, 2011; Tuerk and Loper, 2006.

8. See Gilligan, 1982; Gilligan, Ward, McLean Taylor, & Bardige, 1988.

9. See Austin, 2001; Batchelder and Pippert, 2002; La Vigne, 2003b.

10. For intellectual resistance as it relates to keeping mentally active, see Intrator, 2004; to escaping through fantasy, see Cohen and Taylor, 1992; claiming private space, see McColgan, 2005; to "resistance through distance," see Collinson, 2000; to "cognitive escape," see Page, 2011.

11. For avoidance, see Shorter-Gooden, 2004; for "resistance-through-distance," see Lutgen-Sandvik, 2006; for "avoidance protest," see Adas, 1981; Adas, 1986; Scott, 1985.

12. For a general discussion of everyday distancing strategies, see Scott, 1985; for avoidance coping, see Smyth and Yarandi, 1996; for games and gambling, see Goifman, 2002. For games' potential to establish normalcy in oppressed groups, see Eisen, 1988; and among working-class women, see Casey, 2008.

13. For prayer and stress, see Ano and Vasconcelles, 2005; Benson, 2007; Pargament, Smith, Koenig, and Perez, 1998. For prayer as a method for dealing with constraints over behavior, see Shorter-Gooden, 2004, p. 416.

14. For the use of makeup to regain autonomy, see Dellinger and Williams, 1997; for dress, see Murphy, 1998. For residents in other domestic social contexts, see McColgan, 2005.

15. See Giallombardo, 1966; Leger, 1987; Owen, 1998; Pollock, 2002; Teresa, 1999.

16. See Bowker, 1981; Giallombardo, 1966; Greer, 2000; Mark and Mary, 2001.

17. See Crawford, 2003; Downe, 1999; Gouin, 2004; Obrdlik, 1942; Sanders, 2004; Sorensen, 2008.

FOUR | C LEVEL

1. See De Leon, 1999; Schram, Koons-Witt, Williams, and McShane, 2006.

2. See Andrews and Kiessling, 1980; Andrews et al., 1990; Andrews, 1994; Andrews, Dowden, and Gendreau, 1999; Andrews, Dowden, and Gendreau, 1999.

3. For how unmet needs create institutional misconduct, see Wright et al., 2012; for failure on parole, see Schram, Koons-Witt, Williams, and McShane, 2006; for recidivism, see Grella and Rodriguez, 2011; Petersilia, 2001.

4. See Roscigno and Hodson, 2004; Adas, 1986; Scott, 1985; Scott, 1990.

5. For the relationship between confrontation and complaints/challenge, see Kolchin, 1978, and Lens, 2007; between confrontation and fighting back, Shorter-Gooden, 2004; and on confrontation with abusers, see Lutgen-Sandvik, 2006.

6. For general discussion of covert resistance, see Hollander and Einwohner, 2004. For covert strategies involving time, see Nordstrom and Martin, 1992; geography or space, see Keith and Pile, 1997; rule-bending, see Hutchinson, 1990. For probationers and parolees' use of covert resistance, see Werth, 2012.

FIVE | B AND A LEVELS

1. See Koons et al., 1997; Law, 2009; Morash, Haarr, and Rucker, 1994.

2. See Gendreau and Goggin, 1996; Makarios, Steiner, and Travis, 2010; Petersilia, 2005; Redcross, Bloom, Azurdia, Zweig, and Pindus, 2009; Solomon, Visher, La Vigne, and Osborne, 2006. On employment and recidivism of returning prisoners, see Rossman and Roman, 2003; Uggen and Staff, 2001; Visher, Debus, and Yahner, 2008.

3. See Freudenberg, Daniels, Crum, Perkins, and Richie, 2005; Solomon, Visher, La Vigne, and Osborne, 2006; Garfinkel, 1956, p. 420.

4. See Johnson and Rea, 2009; King-Jones, 2011; McKenna, Smith, Poole, and Coverdale, 2003.

REFERENCES

Abberley, P. (1987). The concept of oppression and the development of a social theory of disability. *Disability, Handicap and Society, 2*(1), 5–19.

Abramovitz, M. (1996). *Regulating the lives of women: Social welfare policy from colonial times to the present.* Cambridge, MA: South End Press.

Abu-Lughod, L. (1990). The romance of resistance: Tracing transformations of power through Bedouin women. *American Ethnologist, 17*(1), 41–55.

Acker, J. (1988). Class, gender, and the relations of distribution. *Signs, 13*(3), 473–97.

———. (1990). Hierarchies, jobs, bodies: A theory of gendered organizations. *Gender and Society, 4*(2), 139–58.

Acoca, L. (1998). Defusing the time bomb: Understanding and meeting the growing health care needs of incarcerated women in America. *Crime and Delinquency, 44*, 49–69.

———. (1999). Investing in girls: A 21st Century strategy. *Juvenile Justice, 6*(1), 3–13.

Acoca, L., and Dedel, K. (1998). *No place to hide: Understanding and meeting the needs of girls in the California juvenile justice system.* San Francisco: National Council on Crime and Delinquency.

Adas, M. (1981). From avoidance to confrontation: Peasant protest in precolonial and colonial Southeast Asia. *Comparative Studies in Society and History, 23*(2), 217–47.

———. (1986). From footdragging to flight: The evasive history of peasant avoidance protest in south and South-East Asia. *The Journal of Peasant Studies, 13*(2), 64–86.

Agarwal, B. (1997). "Bargaining" and gender relations: Within and beyond the household. *Feminist Economics, 3*(1), 1–51.

Alsop, E. (2012). Refusal to tell: Withholding heroines in Hawthorne, Wharton, and Coetzee. *College Literature, 39*(3), 84–105.

Anda, R. F., Croft, J. B., Felitti, V. J., Nordenberg, D., Giles, W. H., Williamson, D. F. et al. (1999). Adverse childhood experiences and smoking during adolescence and adulthood. *JAMA: The Journal of the American Medical Association, 282*(17), 1652–58.

Anderson, B. J. (2000). *Doing the dirty work? The global politics of domestic labour.* New York: Zed Books.

Anderson, P., Davoli, C. R., and Moriarty, L. (1985). Private corrections: Feast or fiasco? *The Prison Journal, 65*(2), 32–41.

Anderson, T. L. (2003). Issues in the availability of health care for women prisoners. In S. F. Shart and R. Muraskin (Eds.), *The incarcerated woman: Rehabilitative programming in women's prisons* (pp. 49–60). New York: Prentice Hall.

———. (2005). Dimensions of women's power in the illicit drug economy. *Theoretical Criminology, 9*(4), 371–400.

Andrews, D. A. (1994). An overview of treatment effectiveness: Research and clinical principles. Unpublished manuscript. Ottowa: Carleton University.

Andrews, D. A., and Kiessling, J. J. (1980). Program structure and effective correctional practices: A summary of the CaVIC research. In R. R. Ross and P. Gendreau (Eds.), *Effective correctional treatment* (pp. 439–63). Toronto: Butterworth.

Andrews, D. A., Zinger, I., Hoge, R. D., Bonta, J., Gendreau, P., and Cullen, F. T. (1990). Does correctional treatment work? A clinically relevant and psychologically informed meta-analysis. *Criminology, 28*(3), 369–404.

Andrews, D. A., Dowden, C., and Gendreau, P. (1999). Clinically relevant and psychologically informed approaches to reduced re-offending: A meta-analytic study of human service, risk, need, responsivity, and other concerns in justice contexts. Unpublished manuscript. Ottowa: Carleton University.

Annandale, E. (2003). Gender and health status: Does biology matter? In G. Bendelow, L. Birke, and S. Williams (Eds.), *Debating biology: Sociological reflections on health, medicine, and society* (pp. 84–95). New York: Routledge.

Ano, G. G., and Vasconcelles, E. B. (2005). Religious coping and psychological adjustment to stress: A meta-analysis. *Journal of Clinical Psychology, 61*(4), 461–80.

Arkles, G. (2012). Correcting race and gender: Prison regulation of social hierarchy through dress. *New York University Law Review, 87*, 12–49.

Armstrong, N., and Murphy, E. (2012). Conceptualizing resistance. *Health: An Interdisciplinary Journal for the Social Study of Health, Illness and Medicine, 16*(3), 314–26.

Ash, J. (2009). *Dress behind bars: Prison clothing as criminality.* New York: IB Tauris and Company.

Ashforth, B. (1994). Petty tyranny in organizations. *Human Relations, 47*(7), 755–78.

Austin, J. (2001). Prisoner reentry: Current trends, practices, and issues. *Crime and Delinquency, 47*(3), 314–34.

Baernstein, P. R. (1994). In widow's habit: Women between convent and family in sixteenth-century Milan. *The Sixteenth Century Journal*, 787–807.

Barak, G., Leighton, P., and Flavin, J. (2010). *Class, race, gender, and crime: The social realities of justice in America.* Lanham, MD: Rowman.

Barreca, G. (2013). *They used to call me Snow White, but I drifted: Women's strategic use of humor.* Lebanon, NH: University Press of New England.

Barrett, M. (1980). Women's oppression today: Problems in Marxist feminist analysis. London: Verso.

Barrett, M., and McIntosh, M. (1998). The anti-social family. In K. V. Hansen and A. I. Garey (Eds.), *Families in the US: Kinships and domestic politics* (pp. 219–29). Philadelphia: Temple University Press.

Barry, E. M. (2001). Bad medicine: Health care inadequacies in women's prisons. *Criminal Justice, 16*, 38–43.

Bartky, S. L. (1990). *Femininity and domination: Studies in the phenomenology of oppression.* New York: Routledge.

Bartlett, K. T. (1994). Only girls wear barrettes: Dress and appearance standards, community norms, and workplace equality. *Michigan Law Review, 92*(8), 2541–82.

Batchelder, J. S., and Pippert, J. M. (2002). Hard time or idle time: Factors affecting inmate choices between participation in prison work and education programs. *The Prison Journal,* *82*(2), 269–80.

Becker, H. (1963). *Outsiders*. New York: Free Press.

Becker, H. S. (1966). Whose side are we on? *Social Problems, 14*, 239–47.

Belknap, J. (2007). *The invisible woman: Gender, crime, and justice* (3rd ed.). Belmont, CA: Wadsworth.

Belknap, J., and Holsinger, K. (1998). An overview of delinquent girls: How theory and practice have failed and the need for innovative changes. In R. T. Zaplin (Ed.), *Female offenders: Critical perspectives and effective interventions* (pp. 31–64). Gaithersburg, MD: Aspen.

———. (2006). The gendered nature of risk factors for delinquency. *Feminist Criminology, 1*(1), 48–71.

Benson, D. (2007). *Utilization of religious coping in a homeless population*. Malibu, CA: Pepperdine University Press.

Berman, C. N. (2006). *Wayward nuns, randy priests, and women's autonomy:" Convent abuse" and the threat to Protestant patriarchy in Victorian England*. Saint Paul, MN: Macalester College.

Bianchi, S. M., Milkie, M. A., Sayer, L. C., and Robinson, J. P. (2000). Is anyone doing the housework? Trends in the gender division of household labor. *Social Forces, 79*(1), 191–228.

Bibars, I. (2001). *Victims and heroines: Women, welfare and the Egyptian state*. New York: Zed Books.

Billow, R. M. (2007). On refusal. *International Journal of Group Psychotherapy, 57*(4), 419–49.

Blackwelder, J. K. (1978). Women in the work force: Atlanta, New Orleans, and San Antonio, 1930 to 1940. *Journal of Urban History, 4*(3), 331–58.

Blair, K. J. (1980). *The clubwoman as feminist: True womanhood redefined, 1868–1914*. New York: Holmes and Meier Publishers.

Blanchette, K., and Brown, S. L. (2006). *The assessment and treatment of women offenders: An integrative perspective*. West Sussex, UK: John Wiley.

Blitz, C. L., Wolff, N., Pan, K.-Y., and Pogorzelski, W. (2005). Gender-specific behavioral health and community release patterns among New Jersey prison inmates: Implications for treatment and community reentry. *American Journal of Public Health, 95*(10), 1741–46.

Block, K. J., and Potthast, M. J. (1998). Girl scouts beyond bars: Facilitating parent-child contact in correctional settings. *Child Welfare, 77*, 561–78.

Bloom, B. (1995). Imprisoned mothers. In K. Gabel and D. Johnston (Eds.), *Children of incarcerated parents* (pp. 21–30). New York: Lexington Books.

———. (1999). Gender-responsive programming for women offenders: Guiding principles and practices. *Forum on Corrections Research, 11*(3), 22–27.

Bloom, B., and Covington, S. (1998). *Gender-specific programming for female offenders: What is it and why is it important?* Proceedings from 50th Annual meeting of the American Society of Criminology, Washington, DC.

Bloom, B., Owen, B., and Covington, S. (2002). *A theoretical basis for gender-responsive strategies in criminal justice*. Proceedings from annual meeting of the American Society of Criminology, Chicago.

———. (2003). Gender-responsive strategies. *Research, practice and guiding principles for women offenders*. Washington, DC: US Department of Justice, National Institute of Corrections.

———. (2004). Women offenders and the gendered effects of public policy. *Review of Policy Research, 21*(1), 31–48.

———. (2005). *Gender-responsive strategies for women offenders: A summary of research, practice, and guiding principles for women offenders.* Washington, DC: US Department of Justice, National Institute of Corrections.

Bloom, B., Owen, B., Deschenes, E. P., and Rosenbaum, J. (2002). Moving toward justice for female juvenile offenders in the new millennium: Modeling gender-specific policies and programs. *Journal of Contemporary Criminal Justice, 18*(1), 37–56.

Bloom, B., Owen, B., Rosenbaum, J., and Deschenes, E. P. (2003). Focusing on girls and young women. *Women and Criminal Justice, 14*(2–3), 117–36.

Bosworth, M. (1999). Engendering resistance: Agency and power in women's prisons. Aldershot, UK: Ashgate.

Bosworth, M., and Carrabine, E. (2001). Reassessing resistance race, gender and sexuality in prison. *Punishment and Society, 3*(4), 501–15.

Bouffard, J. A., and Taxman, F. S. (2000). Client gender and the implementation of jail- based therapeutic community programs. *Journal of Drug Issues*, 881–900.

Bourgois, P., and Dunlap, E. (1993). Exorcising sex-for-crack: An ethnographic perspective from Harlem. In M. Ratner (Ed.), *Crack pipe as pimp: An ethnographic investigation of sex-for-crack exchanges* (pp. 97–132). New York: Lexington Books.

Bowker, L. H. (1981). Gender differences in prisoner subcultures. In L. H. Bowker (Ed.), *Women and crime in America* (pp. 409–19). New York: Macmillan.

———. (1983). *Beating wife-beating.* Lexington, MA: Lexington Books.

Boydston, J. (1990). *Home and work: Housework, wages, and the ideology of labor in the early republic* (55). New York: Oxford.

Braz, R. (2006). Kinder, gentler, gender-responsive cages: Prison expansion is not prison reform. *Women, Girls and Criminal Justice*, 87–91.

Brenner, J., and Laslett, B. (1986). Social reproduction and the family. *Sociology from Crisis to Science, 2*, 116–31.

Britton, D. M. (1999). Cat fights and gang fights. *The Sociological Quarterly, 40*(3), 455–74.

———. (2000). The epistemology of the gendered organization. *Gender and Society, 14*(3), 418–34.

———. (2003). *At work in the iron cage: The prison as gendered organization.* New York: New York University Press.

Brock, M. P. (2010). Resisting the Catholic Church's notion of the nun as self-sacrificing woman. *Feminism and Psychology, 20*(4), 473–90.

Broman, C. L. (1996). Coping with personal problems. In H. W. Neighbors and J. S. Jackson (Eds.), *Mental health in Black America* (pp. 117–29). Thousand Oaks, CA: Sage Publications.

Brown, J. C., and Bohn, C. R. (1989). *Christianity, patriarchy, and abuse: A feminist critique.* Cleveland, OH: Pilgrim Press.

Brown, L. M., and Gilligan, C. (1993). Meeting at the crossroads: Women's psychology and girls' development. *Feminism and Psychology, 3*(1), 11–35.

Brown, V. B., Sanchez, S., Zweben, J. E., and Aly, T. (1996). Challenges in moving from a traditional therapeutic community to a women and children's TC model. *Journal of Psychoactive Drugs, 28*(1), 39–46.

Bryant, J., Carveth, R. A., and Brown, D. (1981). Television viewing and anxiety: An experimental examination. *Journal of Communication, 31*(1), 106–19.

Burgess-Proctor, A. (2006). Intersections of race, class, gender, and crime future directions for feminist criminology. *Feminist Criminology, 1*(1), 27–47.

Burling, T. A., and Ziff, D. C. (1988). Tobacco smoking: A comparison between alcohol and drug abuse inpatients. *Addictive Behaviors, 13*(2), 185–90.

Burstow, B. (1992). Radical feminist theory: Working in the context of violence. Cambridge, UK: Polity Press.

Buzzanell, P. M. (1994). Gaining a voice feminist organizational communication theorizing. *Management Communication Quarterly, 7*(4), 339–83.

Caputo, G. A. (2004). *Intermediate sanctions in corrections.* Denton: University of North Texas Press.

———. (2008). *Out in the storm: Drug-addicted women living as shoplifters and sex workers.* Lebanon, NH: University Press of New England.

Carlen, P. (1983). *Women's imprisonment: A study in social control.* New York: Routledge and Kegan Paul.

Carson, E. A., and Sabol, W. J. (2012). Prisoners in 2011. Washington DC: US Department of Justice, Bureau of Justice Statistics.

Casarjian, R. (1995). *Houses of healing : A prisoner's guide to inner power and freedom* (5th ed.). Boston, MA: Lionheart Foundation.

Casey, E. (2008). *Women, pleasure and the gambling experience.* Burlington, VT: Ashgate Publishing.

Celinska, K., and Siegel, J. A. (2010). Mothers in trouble: Coping with actual or pending separation from children due to incarceration. *The Prison Journal, 90*(4), 447–74.

Chandy, J. M., Blum, R. W., and Resnick, M. D. (1996). Gender-specific outcomes for sexually abused adolescents. *Child Abuse and Neglect, 20*(12), 1219–31.

Charvet, J. (1982). *Feminism.* London: J. M. Dent and Sons.

Chesler, P., and Goodman, E. J. (1976). *Women, money and power.* New York: Morrow.

Chesney-Lind, M. (1997). Patriarchy, prisons, and jails: A critical look at trends in women's incarceration. In M. D. McShane and F. P. Williams (Eds.), *The philosophy and practice of corrections* (pp. 71–88). New York: Routledge.

———. (2006). Patriarchy, crime, and justice feminist criminology in an era of backlash. *Feminist Criminology, 1*(1), 6–26.

Chesney-Lind, M., and Mauer, M. (2011). *Invisible punishment: The collateral consequences of mass imprisonment.* New York: The New Press.

Chesney-Lind, M., and Pasko, L. (2012). *The female offender: Girls, women, and crime* (3rd ed.). Thousand Oaks, CA: Sage Publications.

Chesney-Lind, M., and Rodriguez, N. (1983). Women under lock and key: A view from the inside. *The Prison Journal, 63*, 47–65.

Chesney-Lind, M., and Shelden, R. G. (2004). *Girls, delinquency, and juvenile justice* (3rd ed.). Belmont, CA: Wadsworth.

Clair, R. P. (1998). *Organizing silence: A world of possibilities*. Albany: State University of New York Press.

Cobas, J. A., and Feagin, J. R. (2008). Language oppression and resistance: The case of middle-class Latinos in the United States. *Ethnic and Racial Studies, 31*(2), 390–410.

Cohen, S., and Taylor, L. (1992). *Escape attempts: The theory and practice of resistance in everyday life*. New York: Routledge.

Collins, P. H. (2000). *Black feminist thought: Knowledge, consciousness, and the politics of empowerment*. New York: Routledge.

Collinson, D. L. (1992). *Managing the shopfloor: Subjectivity, masculinity and workplace culture*. Berlin: Walter de Gruyter.

———. (2000). Strategies of resistance: Power, knowledge and subjectivity in the workplace. In K. Grint (Ed.), *Work and society: A reader* (pp. 163–98). Bristol, UK: Polity Press.

Comfort, M. L. (2002). Papa's House': The prison as domestic and social satellite. *Ethnography, 3*(4), 467–99.

Condelli, W. S., and Hubbard, R. L. (1994). Client outcomes from therapeutic communities. In F. M. Tims, G. De Leon, Nancy, and (Eds.), *Therapeutic community: Advances in research and application* (pp. 80–98). Rockville, MD: National Institute on Drug Abuse.

Condren, M. (1989). *The serpent and the goddess: Women, religion, and power in Celtic Ireland*. San Francisco: Harper and Row.

Conklin, T. J., Lincoln, T., and Tuthill, R. W. (2000). Self-reported health and prior health behaviors of newly admitted correctional inmates. *American Journal of Public Health, 90*(12), 1939.

Connell, R. W. (1990). The state, gender and sexual politics: Theory and appraisal. *Theory and Society, 19*(5), 507–44.

Covington, S. (1998). The relational theory of women's psychological development: Implications for the criminal justice system. In R. T. Zaplin (Ed.), *Female offenders: Critical perspectives and effective interventions* (pp. 113–31). Gaithersburg, MD: Aspen.

Covington, S. (2004). *A Woman's journey home: Challenges for female offenders and their children*. Washington, DC: The Urban Institute.

Covington, S. S., and Bloom, B. E. (2007). Gender responsive treatment and services in correctional settings. *Women and Therapy, 29*(3–4), 9–33.

Cox, D. R. (1989). *Welfare practice in a multicultural society*. Sydney, Australia: Prentice Hall.

Crawford, M. (2003). Gender and humor in social context. *Journal of Pragmatics, 35*(9), 1413–30.

Crenshaw, K. (1989). Demarginalizing the intersection of race and sex: A Black feminist critique of antidiscrimination doctrine, feminist theory and antiracist politics. *University of Chicago Legal Forum*, 139–67.

———. (1991). Mapping the margins: Intersectionality, identity politics, and violence against women of color. *Stanford Law Review*, 1241–99.

Crewe, B. (2007). Power, adaptation and resistance in a late-modern men's prison. *British Journal of Criminology, 47*(2), 256–75.

Crockett, D., and Wallendorf, M. (1998). Sociological perspectives on imposed school dress codes: Consumption as attempted suppression of class and group symbolism. *Journal of Macromarketing, 18*(2), 115–31.

Cropsey, K., Eldridge, G. D., and Ladner, T. (2004). Smoking among female prisoners: An ignored public health epidemic. *Addictive Behaviors, 29*(2), 425–31.

Cullen, F. T., and Gendreau, P. (2000). Assessing correctional rehabilitation: Policy, practice, and prospects. *Criminal Justice, 3*, 109–75.

Dalla, R. L., Xia, Y., and Kennedy, H. (2003). "You just give them what they want and pray they don't kill you": Street-level sex workers' reports of victimization, personal resources, and coping strategies. *Violence Against Women, 9*(11), 1367–94.

Dallaire, D. H. (2007). Children with incarcerated mothers: Developmental outcomes, special challenges and recommendations. *Journal of Applied Developmental Psychology, 28*(1), 15–24.

Daly, K. (1992). Women's pathways to felony court: Feminist theories of lawbreaking and problems of representation. *Southern California Review of Law and Women's Studies, 2*, 11–52.

Daly, M. (1985). *The church and the second sex.* Boston: Beacon Press.

Davidson, J. T., and Chesney-Lind, M. (2009). Discounting women: Context matters in risk and need assessment. *Critical Criminology, 17*(4), 221–45.

Davis, F. (1994). *Fashion, culture, and identity.* Chicago: University of Chicago Press.

Davis, K. (2008). Intersectionality as buzzword. *Feminist Theory, 9*(1), 67–85.

DeKeseredy, W. S. (2003). *Under siege: Poverty and crime in a public housing community.* Lexington, MA: Lexington Books.

DeKeseredy, W. S., and Dragiewicz, M. (2012). *Handbook of Critical Criminonlogy.* New York: Routledge.

DeKeseredy, W. S., and Kelly, K. (1993). Woman abuse in university and college dating relationships: The contribution of the ideology of familial patriarchy. *The Journal of Human Justice, 4*(2), 25–52.

DeKeseredy, W. S., and Schwartz, M. D. (1998). *Woman abuse on campus: Results from the Canadian national survey.* Thousand Oaks, CA: Sage Publications.

———. (2009). *Dangerous exits: Escaping abusive relationships in rural America.* New Brunswick, NJ: Rutgers University Press.

De Leon, G. (1989). Therapeutic communities for substance abuse: Overview of approach and effectiveness. *Psychology of Addictive Behaviors, 3*(3), 140–47.

———. (1995). Therapeutic communities for addictions: A theoretical framework. *Substance Use and Misuse, 30*(12), 1603–45.

———. (1997). *Community as method: Therapeutic communities for special populations and special settings.* Westport, CT: Praeger.

———. (1999). The therapeutic community treatment model. In B. S. McCrady and E. E. Epstein (Eds.), *Addictions: A comprehensive guidebook* (pp. 306–27). New York: Oxford University Press.

———. (2000). *The therapeutic community: Theory, model, and method.* New York: Springer Publishing Company.

De Leon, G., and Wexler, H. (2009). The therapeutic community for addictions: An evolving knowledge base. *Journal of Drug Issues, 39*(1), 167–77.

Dell, C. (1999). Crimes of violence: An examination of the identification of women as "violent" offenders in the Canadian criminal justice system. In M. Corsianos and K. Train (Eds.), *Interrogating social justice: Politics, culture and identity* (pp. 109–42). Toronto: Canadian Scholars' Press.

Dellinger, K., and Williams, C. L. (1997). Makeup at work: Negotiating appearance rules in the workplace. *Gender and Society, 11*(2), 151–77.

Delphy, C. (1988). Patriarchy, domestic mode of production, gender and class. In C. Nelson and L. Grossberg (Eds.), *Marxism and the Interpretation of Culture* (pp. 259–69). Urbana: University of Illinois Press.

Delphy, C., and Leonard, D. (1984). *Close to home: A materialist analysis of women's oppression.* London: Hutchinson.

De Paermentier, E. (2008). Experiencing space through women's convent rules: The rich Clares in medieval Ghent (Thirteenth to Fourteenth Centuries). *Medieval Feminist Forum, 44*(1), 53–68.

Deschenes, E. P., Owen, B., and Crow, J. (2006). Recidivism among female prisoners: Secondary analysis of the 1994 BJS recidivism data set. Washington, DC: US Department of Justice, National Institute of Justice.

Dinnerstein, D. (1976). The mermaid and the minotaur: Sexual arrangements and human nature. New York: Harper and Row.

Dobash, R. E., and Dobash, R. (1979). *Violence against wives: A case against the patriarchy.* New York: Free Press.

Dobash, R., Dobash, R. E., and Gutteridge, S. (1986). *The imprisonment of women.* Oxford, UK: B. Blackwell.

Dodge, M., and Pogrebin, M. R. (2001). Collateral costs of imprisonment for women: Complications of reintegration. *The Prison Journal, 81*(1), 42–54.

Dovidio, J. F., Brigham, J. C., Johnson, B. T., and Gaertner, S. L. (1996). Stereotyping, prejudice, and discrimination: Another look. In C. N. Macrae, C. Stangor, and M. Hewstone (Eds.), *Stereotypes and Stereotyping* (pp. 276–19). New York: Guilford Press.

Dow, B. J., and Wood, J. T. (2006). *The SAGE handbook of gender and communication.* Thousand Oaks, CA: Sage Publications.

Downe, P. J. (1999). Laughing when it hurts: Humor and violence in the lives of Costa Rican prostitutes. *Women's Studies International Forum, 22*(1), 63–78.

Dragiewicz, M. (2011). *Equality with a vengeance: Men's rights groups, battered women, and antifeminist backlash.* Lebanon, NH: University Press of New England.

Dubberley, W. S. (1988). Humor as resistance. *Internation Journal of Qualitative Studies in Education, 1*(2), 109–23.

Duffy, E. (1995). Horizontal violence: A conundrum for nursing. *Collegian, 2*(2), 5–17.

Duffy, M. (2005). Reproducing labor inequalities: Challenges for feminists conceptualizing care at the intersections of gender, race, and class. *Gender and Society, 19*(1), 66–82.

Ebaugh, H. R. F. (1977). *Out of the cloister: A study of organizational dilemmas.* Austin: University of Texas Press.

Eberhardt, J. L., Goff, P. A., Purdie, V. J., and Davies, P. G. (2004). Seeing Black: Race, crime, and visual processing. *Journal of Personality and Social Psychology, 87*, 876–93.

Edmondson Bell, E. L. J., and Nkomo, S. M. (1998). Armoring: Learning to withstand racial oppression. *Journal of Comparative Family Studies*, 285–95.

Edwards, P., Collinson, D., and Della Rocca, G. (1995). Workplace resistance in western

Europe: A preliminary overview and a research agenda. *European Journal of Industrial Relations, 1*(3), 283–16.

Eisen, G. (1988). *Children and play in the Holocaust: Games among the shadows.* Amherst: University of Massachusetts Press.

Eisenberg, E. M., Goodall Jr., H. L., and Trethwey, A. (2010). *Organizational communication: Balancing creativity and constraint.* New York: Macmillan.

Eisenhauer, E. (2001). In poor health: Supermarket redlining and urban nutrition. *GeoJournal, 53*(2), 125–33.

Eisikovits, R. (1983). Socialization behind convent gates. *Religious Education, 78*(1), 62–75.

Epstein, B. L. (1981). *The politics of domesticity: Women, evangelism, and temperance in nineteenth-century America.* Middletown, CT: Wesleyan University Press.

Evangelisti, S. (2007). *Nuns: A history of convent life 1450–1700.* Oxford, UK: Oxford University Press.

Evans, T., and Harris, J. (2004). Street-level bureaucracy, social work and the (exaggerated) death of discretion. *British Journal of Social Work, 34*(6), 871–95.

Faith, K. (1994). Resistance: Lessons from Foucault and feminism. In H. L. Radtke and H. J. Stam (Eds.), *Power/gender: Social relations in theory and practice* (pp. 36–66). Thousand Oaks, CA: Sage Publications.

Federal Bureau of Prisons (2007). *Statement of work: Residential Reentry Center.* Washington, DC: US Department of Justice: Federal Bureau of Prisons.

———. (nd). *Residential Reentry Management.* Washington, DC: US Department of Justice: Federal Bureau of Prisons.

Feinman, C. (1983). An historical overview of the treatment of incarcerated women: Myths and realities of rehabilitation. *The Prison Journal, 63*(2), 12–26.

Ferguson, K. E. (1985). *The feminist case against bureaucracy.* Philadelphia: Temple University Press.

Fergusson, D. M., John Horwood, L., and Ridder, E. M. (2005). Show me the child at seven: The consequences of conduct problems in childhood for psychosocial functioning in adulthood. *Journal of Child Psychology and Psychiatry, 46*(8), 837–49.

Ferszt, G. G., Salgado, D., DeFedele, S., and Leveillee, M. (2009). Houses of healing: A group intervention for grieving women in prison. *The Prison Journal, 89*(1), 46–64.

Fetterman, D. M. (2010). *Ethnography: Step-by-step* (17). Thousand Oaks, CA: Sage Publications.

Few, M. (1995). Women, religion, and power: Gender and resistance in daily life in late-Seventeenth-Century Santiago de Guatemala. *Ethnohistory,* 627–37.

Fine, G. A., and Holyfield, L. (1996). Secrecy, trust, and dangerous leisure: Generating group cohesion in voluntary organizations. *Social Psychology Quarterly,* 22–38.

Finkelhor, D. (1993). Epidemiological factors in the clinical identification of child sexual abuse. *Child Abuse and Neglect, 17*(1), 67–70.

———. (1994). Current information on the scope and nature of child sexual abuse. *The Future of Children,* 31–53.

Firestone, S. (2003). *The dialectic of sex: The case for feminist revolution.* New York: Farrar, Straus and Giroux.

Fleming, P., and Sewell, G. (2002). Looking for the good soldier, Švejk: Alternative modalities of resistance in the contemporary workplace. *Sociology, 36*(4), 857–73.

Fletcher, B. R., Shaver, L. D., Moon, D. G., and Billy, L. J. (1993). *Women prisoners: A forgotten population*. Westport, CT: Praeger.

Fletcher, J. K. (2001). *Disappearing acts: Gender, power and relational practice at work*. Cambridge, MA: The MIT Press.

Flowers, R. B. (2001). *Runaway kids and teenage prostitution: America's lost, abandoned, and sexually exploited children*. Westport, CT: Praeger.

Foster, J. A., Gore, S. A., and West, D. S. (2006). Altering TV viewing habits: An unexplored strategy for adult obesity intervention? *American Journal of Health Behavior, 30*(1), 3–14.

Foucault, M. (1977). *Discipline and punish*. New York: Knopf Doubleday Publishing Group.

———. (1990). The history of sexuality, Vol. 1: An introduction. New York: Random House.

Freedman, E. B. (1984). *Their sisters' keepers: Women's prison reform in America, 1830–1930*. Ann Arbor: University of Michigan Press.

Freeman, A. (2007). Fast food: Oppression through poor nutrition. *California Law Review, 95*(6), 2221–59.

French, J. R. P., and Raven, B. (1959). The bases of social power. *Studies in Social Power*, 150–67.

Freudenberg, N. (2002). Adverse effects of US jail and prison policies on the health and well-being of women of color. *American Journal of Public Health, 92*(12), 1895–99.

Freudenberg, N., Daniels, J., Crum, M., Perkins, T., and Richie, B. E. (2005). Coming home from jail: The social and health consequences of community reentry for women, male adolescents, and their families and communities. *American Journal of Public Health, 95*(10), 1725–36.

Fromm, E. (2012). *The sane society*. New York: Routledge.

Fullilove, M. T., Lown, E. A., and Fullilove, R. E. (1992). Crack 'hos and skeezers: Traumatic experiences of women crack users. *Journal of Sex Research, 29*(2), 275–87.

Garfinkel, H. (1956). Conditions of successful degradation ceremonies. *American Journal of Sociology, 61*(5), 420–24.

Gavazzi, S. M., Yarcheck, C. M., and Chesney-Lind, M. (2006). Global risk indicators and the role of gender in a juvenile detention sample. *Criminal Justice and Behavior, 33*(5), 597–612.

Geertz, C. (1988). *Works and lives: The anthropologist as author*. Palo Alto, CA: Stanford University Press.

Gehring, K., Van Voorhis, P., and Bell, V. (2010). "What works" for female probationers? An evaluation of the Moving On program. *Women, Girls, and Criminal Justice, 11*(1), 6–10.

Gendreau, P. (1996). *The principles of effective intervention with offenders*. Thousand Oaks, CA: Sage Publications.

Gendreau, P., and Goggin, C. (1996). Principles of effective correctional programming. *Forum on Corrections Research, 8*, 38–41.

Gengler, A. M. (2012). Defying (dis)empowerment in a battered women's shelter: Moral rhetorics, intersectionality, and processes of control and resistance. *Social Problems, 59*, 501–21.

Gerami, S., and Lehnerer, M. (2001). Women's agency and household diplomacy: Negotiating fundamentalism. *Gender and Society, 15*(4), 556–73.

Gerstein, D. R., and Lewin, L. S. (1990). Treating drug problems. *New England Journal of Medicine, 323*(12), 844–48.

Giallombardo, R. (1966). *Society of women: A study of a women's prison*. New York: Wiley.

Gilbert, J. (2004). *Performing marginality: Humor, gender, and cultural critique*. Detroit: Wayne State University Press.

Gilfus, M. E. (2002). *Women's experiences of abuse as a risk factor for incarceration*. VaWNet Applied Research Forum. Harrisburg, PA: National Resource Center on Domestic Violence

Gilligan, C. (1982). *In a different voice: Psychological theory and women's development*. Cambridge, MA: Harvard University Press.

Gilligan, C., Rogers, A. G., and Tolman, D. L. (1991). *Women, girls and psychotherapy: Reframing resistance*. New York: Routledge.

Gilligan, C., Ward, J. V., McLean Taylor, J., and Bardige, B. E. (Eds.). (1988). *Mapping the moral domain: A contribution of women's thinking to psychological theory and education*. (Vol. 2). Cambridge, MA: Harvard University Press.

Gilliom, J. (2001). *Overseers of the poor: Surveillance, resistance, and the limits of privacy*. Chicago: University of Chicago Press.

———. (2005). Resisting surveillance. *Social Text, 23*(2), 71–83.

Gillooly, E. (1991). Women and humor. *Feminist Studies, 17*, 472–92.

Gilson, E. (2011). Vulnerability, ignorance, and oppression. *Hypatia, 26*(2), 308–32.

Ginsberg, E. K. (1966). Introduction: The politics of passing. In E. K. Ginsberg (Ed.), *Passing and the fictions of identity* (pp. 1–18). Durham, NC: Duke University Press.

Girshick, L. B. (1999). *No safe haven: Stories of women in prison*. Lebanon, NH: University Press of New England.

Glaze, L. E. (2011). *Correctional populations in the United States, 2010*. Washington, DC: US Department of Justice, Bureau of Justice Statistics.

Glaze, L. E., and Parks, E. (2012). *Correctional populations in the United States, 2011*. Washington, DC: US Department of Justice, Bureau of Justice Statistics.

Glenn, E. N. (1992). From servitude to service work: Historical continuities in the racial division of paid reproductive labor. *Signs, 18*(1), 1–43.

Goffman, E. (1961). Asylums: Essays on the social situation of mental patients and other inmates. New York: Anchor Books.

———. (1989). On fieldwork. *Journal of Contemporary Ethnography, 18*, 123–32.

Goifman, K. (2002). Killing time in the Brazilian slammer. *Ethnography, 3*(4), 435–41.

Golden, S. (1992). *The women outside: Meanings and myths of homelessness*. Berkeley: University of California Press.

Gouin, R. R. (2004). What's so funny? Humor in women's accounts of their involvement in social action. *Qualitative Research, 4*(1), 25–44.

Greaves, L. (2003). Smoke screen: The cultural meaning of women's smoking. In A. Alexander and M. S. Roberts (Eds.), *High culture: Reflections on addiction and modernity* (pp. 261–78). Albany: State University of New York Press.

Greer, K. R. (2000). The changing nature of interpersonal relationships in a women's prison. *The Prison Journal, 80*(4), 442–68.

Grella, C. E. (1999). Women in residential drug treatment: Differences by program type and pregnancy. *Journal of Health Care for the Poor and Underserved*, 216–29.

Grella, C. E., and Rodriguez, L. (2011). Motivation for treatment among women offenders in prison-based treatment and longitudinal outcomes among those who participate in community aftercare. *Journal of Psychoactive Drugs, 43*(sup1), 58–67.

Griffin, M. A. (1975). *The courage to choose: An American nun's story*. Boston: Little, Brown.

Griffin, S. M. (1996). Awful disclosures: Women's evidence in the escaped nun's tale. *PLMA: Publications of the Modern Language Association of America*, 93–107.

Guerino, P., Harrison, P. M., and Sabol, W. J. (2011). *Prisoners in 2010*. Washington, DC: US Department of Justice, Bureau of Justice Statistics.

Hackman, M. Z., Furniss, A. H., Hills, M. J., and Paterson, T. J. (1992). Perceptions of gender-role characteristics and transformational and transactional leadership behaviours. *Perceptual and Motor Skills, 75*(1), 311–19.

Hairston, C. F. (1991). Family ties during imprisonment: Important to whom and for what. *Journal of Sociology and Social Welfare, 18*, 87–104.

Hairston, C. F., Rollin, J., and Jo, H. (2004). Family connections during imprisonment and prisoners' community reentry. *Children, Families, and the Criminal Justice System*. Chicago: University of Illinois at Chicago.

Halliwell, E., Malson, H., and Tischner, I. (2011). Are contemporary media images which seem to display women as sexually empowered actually harmful to women? *Psychology of Women Quarterly, 35*(1), 38–45.

Hammersley, M., and Atkinson, P. (1995). *Ethnography: Principles in practice* (2nd ed.). New York: Routgedge.

Hancock, A.-M. (2007). Intersectionality as a normative and empirical paradigm. *Political Science and Politics, 37*(1), 41–45.

Handler, J. F. (1992). Postmodernism, protest, and the new social movements. *Law and Society Review, 26*, 697–732.

Hannah-Moffat, K. (1999). Moral agent or actuarial subject: Risk and Canadian women's imprisonment. *Theoretical Criminology, 3*(1), 71–94.

———. (2001). *Punishment in disguise: Penal governance and federal imprisonment of women in Canada*. Toronto: University of Toronto Press.

———. (2009). Gridlock or mutability: Reconsidering "gender" and risk assessment. *Criminology and Public Policy, 8*(1), 209–19.

———. (2010). Sacrosanct or flawed: Risk, accountability and gender-responsive penal politics. *Current Issues in Criminal Justice, 22*, 193–215.

Hanson, G. R. (2002). *Therapeutic community*. Rockville, MD: National Institute on Drug Abuse.

Hardyman, P. L., and Van Voorhis, P. (2004). *Developing gender-specific classification systems for women offenders*. Washington, DC: US Department of Justice, National Institute of Corrections.

Harlow, C. W. (2003). *Education and correctional populations*. Washington, DC: US Department of Justice, Bureau of Justice Statistics.

Harm, N. J., and Phillips, S. D. (2000). You can't go home again: Women and criminal recidivism. *Journal of Offender Rehabilitation, 32*(3), 3–21.

Harman, L. D. (1989). *When a hostel becomes a home: Experiences of women*. Toronto: Garamond Press.

Hartmann, H. (1976). Capitalism, patriarchy, and job segregation by sex. *Signs, 1*(3), 137–69.

Hartmann, H. I. (1981). The family as the locus of gender, class, and political struggle: The example of housework. *Signs, 6*(3), 366–94.

Hartwell, S. (2001). Female mentally ill offenders and their community reintegration needs: An initial examination. *International Journal of Law and Psychiatry.*

Harvey, D. (1993). From space to place and back again: Reflections on the condition of post-modernity. In J. Bird, B. Curtis, T. Putnam, G. Robertson, and L. Tickner (Eds.), *Mapping the futures: Local cultures, global change* (pp. 2–29). New York: Routledge.

Hearn, J. (2004). Personal resistance through persistence to organizational resistance through distance. In R. Thomas, A. J. Mills, and J. Helms Mills (Eds.), *Identity politics at work: Resisting gender, gendering resistance* (pp. 40–63). London: Routledge.

Hearn, J., and Parkin, P. W. (1986). Women, men, and leadership: A critical review of assumptions, practices, and change in the industrialized nations. *International Studies of Management and Organization, 16*(3/4), 33–60.

Helgesen, S. (1990). *The female advantage: Women's ways of leadership.* New York: Doubleday.

Henriques, Z. W., and Manatu-Rupert, N. (2001). Living on the outside: African American women before, during, and after imprisonment. *The Prison Journal, 81*(1), 6–19.

Hensley, C., Tewksbury, R., and Koscheski, M. (2002). The characteristics and motivations behind female prison sex. *Women and Criminal Justice, 13*(2–3), 125–39.

Hodson, R. (1995). Worker resistance: An underdeveloped concept in the sociology of work. *Economic and Industrial Democracy, 16*(1), 79–110.

Hollander, J. A. (2002). Resisting vulnerability: The social reconstruction of gender in interaction. *Social Problems, 49*(4), 474–96.

———. (2009). The roots of resistance to women's self-defense. *Violence Against Women, 15*(5), 574–94.

Hollander, J. A., and Einwohner, R. L. (2004). *Conceptualizing resistance. Sociological Forum, 19*(4), 533–54.

Holtfreter, K., and Morash, M. (2003). The needs of women offenders. *Women and Criminal Justice, 14*(2–3), 137–60.

Holzer, H. J., Raphael, S., and Stoll, M. A. (2003). *Employment barriers facing ex-offenders.* Proceedings from Reentry Roundtable, The Employment Dimensions of Prisoner Reentry: Understanding the Nexus between Prisoner Reentry and Work, New York.

hooks, b. (1984). *Feminist theory: From margin to center.* Boston: South End Press.

Houston, M., and Kramarae, C. (1991). Speaking from silence: Methods of silencing and of resistance. *Discourse and Society, 2*(4), 387–99.

Hughes, E. C. (1945). Dilemmas and contradictions of status. *American Journal of Sociology,* 353–59.

Hughes, T. A., and Wilson, D. J. (2003). *Reentry trends in the United States.* Washington, DC: US Department of Justice, Bureau of Justice Statistics.

Hughes, T. A., Wilson, D. J., and Beck, A. J. (2001). *Trends in state parole, 1990–2000.* Washington, DC: US Department of Justice, Bureau of Justice Statistics.

Hunnicutt, G. (2009). Varieties of patriarchy and violence against women resurrecting "patriarchy" as a theoretical tool. *Violence Against Women, 15*(5), 553–73.

Hutchinson, M., Vickers, M., Jackson, D., and Wilkes, L. (2006). Workplace bullying in nursing: Towards a more critical organisational perspective. *Nursing Inquiry, 13*(2), 118–26.

Hutchinson, S. A. (1990). Responsible subversion: A study of rule-bending among nurses. *Research and Theory for Nursing Practice, 4*(1), 3–17.

Inciardi, J. A., Martin, S. S., and Butzin, C. A. (2004). Five-year outcomes of therapeutic community treatment of drug-involved offenders after release from prison. *Crime and Delinquency, 50*(1), 88–107.

Inciardi, J. A., Martin, S. S., and Surratt, H. L. (2001). Therapeutic communities in prisons and work release: Effective modalities for drug involved offenders. In B. Rawlings and R. Yates (Eds.), *Therapeutic communities for the treatment of drug users* (pp. 241–56). London: Jessica Kingsley.

Inciardi, J. A., and Surratt, H. L. (2001). Drug use, street crime, and sex-trading among cocaine-dependent women: Implications for public health and criminal justice policy. *Journal of Psychoactive Drugs, 33*(4), 379–89.

Intrator, M. (2004). Avenues of intellectual resistance in the ghetto theresienstadt: Escape through the central library, books, and reading. *Libri, 54*(4), 237–46.

Jacobson, B. (1981). *The ladykillers: Why smoking is a feminist issue.* London: Pluto Press.

James, D. J., and Glaze, L. E. (2006). *Mental health problems of prison and jail inmates.* Washington, DC: US Department of Justice, Bureau of Justice Statistics.

Jermier, J. M., Knights, D. E., and Nord, W. R. (Eds.). (1994). *Resistance and power in organizations.* New York: Routledge.

Jewkes, Y. (2002). The use of media in constructing identities in the masculine environment of men's prisons. *European Journal of Communication, 17*(2), 205–25.

Johnson, M. P. (1995). Patriarchal terrorism and common couple violence: Two forms of violence against women. *Journal of Marriage and the Family,* 283–94.

———. (2010). *A typology of domestic violence: Intimate terrorism, violent resistance, and situational couple violence.* Lebanon, NH: University Press of New England.

Johnson, S. L., and Rea, R. E. (2009). Workplace bullying: Concerns for nurse leaders. *Journal of Nursing Administration, 39*(2), 84–90.

Jurik, N. C., Cavender, G., and Cowgill, J. (2009). Resistance and accommodation in a post-welfare social service organization. *Journal of Contemporary Ethnography, 38*(1), 25–51.

Kalish, C. B. (1981). *Prisoners in 1980.* Washington, DC: US Department of Justice, Bureau of Justice Statistics.

Kamphoff, C. S. (2010). Bargaining with patriarchy: Former women coaches' experiences and their decision to leave collegiate coaching. *Research Quarterly for Exercise and Sport, 81,* 360–72.

Kandiyoti, D. (1988). Bargaining with patriarchy. *Gender and Society, 2*(3), 274–90.

———. (1998). Gender, power and contestation: Rethinking bargaining with patriarchy. In C. Jackson and R. Pearson (Eds.), *Feminist visions of development: Gender analysis and policy* (pp. 135–52). London: Routledge.

Kann, M. E. (2005). *Punishment, prisons, and patriarchy: Liberty and power in the early American republic.* New York: New York University Press.

Kanuha, V. K. (1999). The social process of 'passing' to manage stigma: Acts of internalized oppression or acts of resistance? *Journal of Sociology and Social Welfare, 26,* 27–46.

Kärreman, D., and Alvesson, M. (2009). Resisting resistance: Counter-resistance, consent and compliance in a consultancy firm. *Human Relations, 62*(8), 1115–44.

Kassebaum, P. (1999). *Substance abuse treatment for women offenders: Guide to promising practices*. Rockville, MD: US Department of Health and Human Services.

Katila, S., and Meriläinen, S. (2002). Metamorphosis: From 'nice girls' to 'nice bitches': Resisting patriarchal articulations of professional identity. *Gender, Work and Organization, 9*(3), 336–54.

Keith, M., and Pile, S. (1997). *Geographies of resistance*. New York: Routledge.

Kelley, M. S. (2003). The state-of-the-art in substance abuse programs for women in prison. In S. F. Sharp (Ed.), *The incarcerated woman: Rehabilitative programming in women's prisons* (pp. 119–48). Upper Saddle River, NJ: Prentice Hall.

Kelly, L. (1988). *Surviving sexual violence*. Cambridge, UK: Polity.

Kennedy, E. L., and Davis, M. D. (1993). *Boots of leather, slippers of gold: The history of a lesbian community*. New York: Routledge.

Kenning, M., Merchant, A., and Tomkins, A. (1991). Research on the effects of witnessing parental battering: Clinical and legal policy implications. In M. Steinman (Ed.), *Woman battering: Policy responses* (pp. 237–61). Cincinnati, OH: Anderson.

Kilpatrick, D. G., Acierno, R., Saunders, B., Resnick, H. S., Best, C. L., and Schnurr, P. P. (2000). Risk factors for adolescent substance abuse and dependence: Data from a national sample. *Journal of Consulting and Clinical psychology, 68*(1), 19–30.

Kilty, J. M. (2006). Under the barred umbrella: Is there room for a women-centered self-injury policy in Canadian corrections? *Criminology and Public Policy, 5*(1), 161–82.

———. (2012). 'It's like they don't want you to get better': Psy control of women in the carceral context. *Feminism and Psychology, 22*(2), 162–82.

King-Jones, M. (2011). Horizontal violence and the socialization of new nurses. *Creative Nursing, 17*(2), 80–86.

Klare, K. E. (1991). Power/Dressing: Regulation of employee appearance. *New England Law Review, 26*, 1395–1451.

Knight, K., Dwayne, S. D., Chatham, L. R., and Camacho, L. M. (1997). An assessment of prison-based drug treatment: Texas' in-prison therapeutic community program. *Journal of Offender Rehabilitation, 24*(3–4), 75–100.

Koenig, L. A. (2007). Financial literacy curriculum: The effect on offender money management skills. *Journal of Correctional Education, 58*(1), 43–56.

Kolchin, P. (1978). The process of confrontation: Patterns of resistance to bondage in nineteenth-century Russia and the United States. *Journal of Social History, 11*(4), 457–90.

Koons, B. A., Burrow, J. D., Morash, M., and Bynum, T. (1997). Expert and offender perceptions of program elements linked to successful outcomes for incarcerated women. *Crime and Delinquency, 43*(4), 512–32.

Koss, M. P., Koss, P. G., and Woodruff, W. J. (1991). Deleterious effects of criminal victimization on women's health and medical utilization. *Archives of Internal Medicine, 151*(2), 342–47.

Kruttschnitt, C., Gartner, R., and Miller, A. (2000). Doing her own time? Women's responses to prison in the context of the old and the new penology. *Criminology, 38*(3), 681–718.

Kuhns, E. (2003). *The habit: A history of the clothing of Catholic nuns*. New York: Doubleday.

La Vigne, N. G. (2003a). *A portrait of prisoner reentry in Illinois*. Washington, DC: US The Urban Institute.

————. (2003b). *A portrait of prisoner reentry in Maryland.* Washington, DC: US The Urban Institute.

————. (2009). *Women on the outside: Understanding the experiences of female prisoners returning to Houston, Texas.* Washington, DC: The Urban Institute.

Lahm, K. F. (2000). Equal or equitable: An exploration of educational and vocational program availability for male and female offenders. *Federal Probation, 64,* 39–46.

Langan, P. A., and Levin, D. J. (2002). Recidivism of prisoners released in 1994. *Federal Sentencing Reporter, 15,* 58–65.

Last, M. (1970). Aspects of administration and dissent in Hausaland, 1800–1968. *Africa,* 345–57.

Lattimore, P. K., Brumbaugh, S., Visher, C., Lindquist, C., Winterfield, L., Salas, M. et al. (2004). National Portrait of SVORI: Serious and Violent Offender Reentry Initiative. Washington, DC: The Urban Institute.

Lattimore, P. K., Steffey, D. M., and Visher, C. A. (2010). Prisoner reentry in the first decade of the twenty-first century. *Victims and Offenders, 5*(3), 253–67.

Law, V. (2009). *Resistance behind bars: The struggles of incarcerated women.* Oakland, CA: Pm Press.

Lawston, J. (2013). Prisons, gender responsive strategies and community sanctions. In M. Malloch and G. McIvor (Eds.), *Women, Punishment and Social Justice: Human Rights and Penal Practices* (pp. 109–20). New York: Routledge.

Leap, N. (1997). Making sense of 'horizontal violence' in midwifery. *British Journal of Midwifery, 5*(11), 689–89.

Leblanc, L. (2000). *Pretty in punk: Resistance in a boy's subculture.* New Brunswick, NJ: Rutgers University Press.

Leger, R. G. (1987). Lesbianism among women prisoners: Participants and nonparticipants. *Criminal Justice and Behavior, 14*(4), 448–67.

Lens, V. (2007). In the fair hearing room: Resistance and confrontation in the welfare bureaucracy. *Law and Social Inquiry, 32*(2), 309–32.

Lerner, G. (1986). *The creation of patriarchy* (1). New York: Oxford University Press.

Lester, D., and Van Voorhis, P. (1997). Cognitive therapies. In P. Van Voorhis, M. Braswell, and D. Lester (Eds.), *Correctional Counseling and Rehabilitation* (pp. 109–26). Cincinnati: Anderson Publishing Company.

Leverentz, A. M. (2006). *People, places, and things: The social process of reentry for female ex-offenders.* Washington, DC: US Department of Justice, National Institute of Justice.

Lewis, M. (1990). Interrupting patriarchy: Politics, resistance, and transformation in the feminist classroom. *Harvard Educational Review, 60*(4), 467–89.

Liebling, A. (2001). Whose side are we on? Theory, practice and allegiances in prisons research. *British Journal of Criminology, 41*(3), 472–84.

Lim, L. (1983). Capitalism, imperialism, and patriarchy: The dilemma of third world women workers in multinational factories. In J. Nash and M. P. Fernandez-Kelly (Eds.), *Women, men and the international division of labor* (pp. 70–91). Albany: State University of New York Press.

Lipsky, M. (1980). *Street-level bureaucracy: Dilemmas of the individual in public services.* New York: Russell Sage Foundation.

Lipton, D. S. (1998). *Principles of correctional therapeutic community treatment programming for drug abusers.* Proceedings from ONDCP Consensus Meeting on Treatment in the Criminal Justice System, New York.

Listwan, S. J., Cullen, F. T., and Latessa, E. J. (2006). How to prevent prisoners re-entry programs from failing: Insights from evidence-based corrections. *Federal Probation, 70,* 19–25.

Lockwood, D., McCorkel, J., and Inciardi, J. A. (1998). Developing comprehensive prison-based therapeutic community treatment for women. *Drugs and Society, 13*(1–2), 193–212.

Lorber, J. (1994). *Paradoxes of gender.* New Haven, CT: Yale University Press.

Lussier, J. P., Heil, S. H., Mongeon, J. A., Badger, G. J., and Higgins, S. T. (2006). A meta-analysis of voucher-based reinforcement therapy for substance use disorders. *Addiction, 101*(2), 192–203.

Lutgen-Sandvik, P. (2006). Take this job and . . . : Quitting and other forms of resistance to workplace bullying. *Communication Monographs, 73*(4), 406–33.

Lykes, M. B. (1983). Discrimination and coping in the lives of Black women: Analyses of oral history data. *Journal of Social Issues, 39*(3), 79–100.

Lynch, J. P., and Sabol, W. J. (2001). Prisoner reentry in perspective. Washington, DC: The Urban Institute.

Maher, L. (1997). *Sexed work: Gender, race, and resistance in a Brooklyn drug market.* New York: Oxford University Press.

Makarios, M., Steiner, B., and Travis, L. F. (2010). Examining the predictors of recidivism among men and women released from prison in Ohio. *Criminal Justice and Behavior, 37*(12), 1377–91.

Mallik-Kane, K., and Visher, C. (2008). *Health and prisoner reentry: How physical, mental, and substance abuse conditions shape the process of reintegration.* Washington, DC: The Urban Institute.

Mark, R. P., and Mary, D. (2001). Women's accounts of their prison experiences: A retrospective view of their subjective realities. *Journal of Criminal Justice, 29*(6), 531—541.

Maruschak, L. M. (2008). *Medical problems of prisoners.* Washington, DC: US Department of Justice, Bureau of Justice Statistics.

Maruschak, L. M., and Parks, E. (2012). *Probation and Parole in the United States, 2011.* Washington, DC: US Department of Justice, Bureau of Justice Statistics.

Massey, D. B. (1994). *Space, place, and gender.* Minneapolis: University of Minnesota Press.

McClain, L. (2003). Using what's at hand: English Catholic reinterpretations of the rosary, 1559–1642. *Journal of Religious History, 27*(2), 161–76.

McColgan, G. (2005). A place to sit resistance strategies used to create privacy and home by people with dementia. *Journal of Contemporary Ethnography, 34*(4), 410–33.

McCorkel, J. A. (1998). Going to the crackhouse: Critical space as a form of resistance in total institutions and everyday life. *Symbolic Interaction, 21*(3), 227–52.

———. (2003). Embodied surveillance and the gendering of punishment. *Journal of Contemporary Ethnography, 32*(1), 41–76.

McKenna, B. G., Smith, N. A., Poole, S. J., and Coverdale, J. H. (2003). Horizontal violence: Experiences of registered nurses in their first year of practice. *Journal of Advanced Nursing, 42*(1), 90–96.

McKim, A. (2008). "Getting gut-level": Punishment, gender, and therapeutic governance. *Gender and Society, 22*(3), 303–23.

McNamara, B. W. (1994). All dressed up with no place to go: Gender bias in Oklahoma federal court dress codes. *Tulsa Law Journal, 30*, 395–423.

Messina, N., Calhoun, S., and Warda, U. (2012). Gender-responsive drug court treatment: A randomized controlled trial. *Criminal Justice and Behavior*, 1539–58.

Messina, N., and Grella, C. (2006). Childhood trauma and women's health outcomes in a California prison population. *American Journal of Public Health, 96*(10), 1842–48.

Messina, N., Grella, C. E., Cartier, J., and Torres, S. (2010). A randomized experimental study of gender-responsive substance abuse treatment for women in prison. *Journal of Substance Abuse Treatment*, 97–107.

Michelman, S. O. (1997). Changing old habits: Dress of women religious and its relationship to personal and social identity. *Sociological Inquiry, 67*(3), 350–63.

Mies, M. (1998). *Patriarchy and accumulation on a world scale: Women in the international division of labour.* New York: Zed Books.

Miller, E. M. (1987). *Street woman.* Philadelphia: Temple University Press.

Miller, K. M. (2006). The impact of parental incarceration on children: An emerging need for effective interventions. *Child and Adolescent Social Work Journal, 23*(4), 472–86.

Millett, K. (1970). *Sexual politics.* Champaign: University of Illinois Press.

Minton, T. D. (2011). *Jail inmates at midyear 2010-Statistical tables.* Washington, DC: US Department of Justice, Bureau of Justice Statistics.

Morash, M. (2010). *Women on probation and parole: A feminist critique of community programs and services.* Lebanon, NH: University Press of New England.

Morash, M., Haarr, R. N., and Rucker, L. (1994). A comparison of programming for women and men in US prisons in the 1980s. *Crime and Delinquency, 40*(2), 197–221.

Moses, M. C. (2006). Does parental incarceration increase a child's risk for foster care placement. *National Institute of Justice Journal, 255*, 12–15.

Motsemme, N. (2004). The mute always speak: On women's silences at the truth and reconciliation commission. *Current Sociology, 52*(5), 909–32.

Moyer, I. L. (1984). Deceptions and realities of life in women's prisons. *The Prison Journal, 64*(1), 45–56.

Mumby, D. K. (2005). Theorizing resistance in organization studies A dialectical approach. *Management Communication Quarterly, 19*(1), 19–44.

Mumola, C. J. (2000). *Incarcerated parents and their children.* Washington, DC: US Department of Justice, Bureau of Justice Statistics.

Murphy, A. G. (1998). Hidden transcripts of flight attendant resistance. *Management Communication Quarterly, 11*(4), 499–535.

Nakano Glenn, E. (1985). Racial ethnic women's labor: The intersection of race, gender and class oppression. *Review of Radical Political Economics, 17*(3), 86–108.

Nardi, B. A., and Whittaker, S. (2002). The place of face-to-face communication in distributed work. In P. J. Hinds and S. Kiesler (Eds.), *Distributed work* (pp. 83–110). Cambridge, MA: MIT Press.

Natalle, E. (1996). Gendered issues in the workplace. In J. T. Wood (Ed.), *Gendered relationships* (pp. 253–74). Mountain View, CA: National Communication Association.

Nordstrom, C., and Martin, J. (1992). *The paths to domination, resistance and terror.* Berkeley: University of California Press.

Northouse, P. G. (2012). *Leadership: Theory and practice.* Thousand Oaks, CA: Sage Publications.

O'Brien, P. (2001a). " Just like baking a cake": Women describe the necessary ingredients for successful reentry after incarceration. *Families in Society: The Journal of Contemporary Social Services, 82*(3), 287–95.

———. (2001b). *Making it in the" free world": Women in transition from prison.* Albany: SUNY Press.

Obrdlik, A. J. (1942). "Gallows humor": A sociological phenomenon. *American Journal of Sociology,* 709–16.

Ogle, R. S., and Batton, C. (2009). Revisiting patriarchy: Its conceptualization and operationalization in criminology. *Critical Criminology, 17*(3), 159–82.

Ottenberg, D. J. (1982). Therapeutic community and the danger of the cult phenomenon. *Marriage and Family Review, 4*(3–4), 151–73.

Owen, B. A. (1998). *"In the mix": Struggle and survival in a women's prision.* Albany: SUNY Press.

Owen, B., and Bloom, B. (1995). Profiling women prisoners: Findings from national surveys and a California sample. *The Prison Journal, 75*(2), 165–85.

Page, D. (2011). From principled dissent to cognitive escape: Managerial resistance in the English further education sector. *Journal of Vocational Education and Training, 63*(1), 1–13.

Pargament, K. I., Smith, B. W., Koenig, H. G., and Perez, L. (1998). Patterns of positive and negative religious coping with major life stressors. *Journal for the Scientific Study of Religion,* 710–24.

Pateman, C. (1988). The fraternal social contract. In J. Keane (Ed.), *Civil society and the state: New European perspectives* (pp. 101–27). London: Verso.

Paules, G. F. (1991). *Dishing it out: Power and resistance among waitresses in a New Jersey restaurant.* Philadelphia: Temple University Press.

Pennsylvania Department of Corrections. (nd). *Reentry and community transition.* www.portal.state.pa.us/portal/server.pt/community/reentry___community_transition/17857.

Petersilia, J. (2001). Prisoner reentry: Public safety and reintegration challenges. *The Prison Journal, 81*(3), 360–75.

———. (2004). What works in prisoner reentry: Reviewing and questioning the evidence. *Federal Probation, 68,* 4–8.

———. (2005). Hard time: Ex-offenders returning home after prison. *Corrections Today, 67*(2), 66–71.

———. (2009). *When prisoners come home: Parole and prisoner reentry.* New York: Oxford University Press.

Peugh, J., and Belenko, S. (1999). Substance-involved women inmates: Challenges to providing effective treatment. *The Prison Journal,* 23–44.

Pheterson, G. (1986). Alliances between women: Overcoming internalized oppression and internalized domination. *Signs, 12*(1), 146–60.

Pickering, S. (2000). Women, the home and resistance in Northern Ireland. *Women and Criminal Justice, 11*(3), 49–82.

Pitts, V. L. (1998). 'Reclaiming' the female body: Embodied identity work, resistance and the grotesque. *Body and Society, 4*(3), 67–84.

Pleck, J. H. (1984). Men's power with women, other men, and society: A men's movement analysis. In P. P. Rieker and E. H. Carmen (Eds.), *The gender gap in psychotherapy* (pp. 79–89).
Springer.

Pollack, S. (2004). Anti-oppressive social work practice with women in prison: Discursive re-
constructions and alternative practices. *British Journal of Social Work, 34*(5), 693–707.

———. (2007). I'm just not good in relationships: Victimization discourses and the gendered
regulation of criminalized women. *Feminist Criminology, 2*(2), 158–74.

———. (2013). An imprisoning gaze Practices of gendered, racialized and epistemic violence.
International Review of Victimology, 19(1), 103–14.

Pollock, J. M. (2002). *Women, prison and crime* (2nd ed.). Belmont, CA: Wadsworth.

Prasad, P., and Prasad, A. (2000). Stretching the iron cage: The constitution and implications of
routine workplace resistance. *Organization Science, 11*(4), 387–403.

Prendergast, M., Podus, D., Finney, J., Greenwell, L., and Roll, J. (2006). Contingency management for treatment of substance use disorders: A meta-analysis. *Addiction, 101*(11), 1546–60.

Prendergast, M. L. (2009). Interventions to promote successful re-entry among drug-abusing
parolees. *Addiction Science and Clinical Practice, 5*(1), 4–13.

Prendergast, M. L., Messina, N. P., Hall, E. A., and Warda, U. S. (2011). The relative effectiveness of women-only and mixed-gender treatment for substance-abusing women. *Journal of
Substance Abuse Treatment, 40*, 336–84.

Prendergast, M. L., Wellisch, J., and Wong, M. M. (1996). Residential treatment for women
parolees following prison-based drug treatment: Treatment experiences, needs and services,
outcomes. *The Prison Journal*, 253–74.

Pringle, R., and MacDowell, L. (Eds.). (1992). *Defining women: Social institutions and gender
divisions*. Cambridge, UK: Polity.

Profitt, N. J. (1996). " Battered women" as" victims" and" survivors" creating space for resistance. *Canadian Social Work Review/Revue Canadienne de Service Social*, 23–38.

Propper, A. M. (1978). Lesbianism in female and coed correctional institutions. *Journal of
Homosexuality, 3*(3), 265–74.

Purpora, C., and Blegen, M. A. (2012). Horizontal violence and the quality and safety of patient
care: A conceptual model. *Nursing Research and Practice, 2012*, 5 pages, 306948. Epub 2012.

Radford, J., and Stanko, E. A. (1991). Violence against women and children: The contradictions
of crime control under patriarchy. In K. Stenson and D. Cowell (Eds.), *The politics of crime
control* (pp. 1888–1202). Thousand Oaks, CA: Sage Publications.

Rafaeli, A., Dutton, J., Harquail, C. V., and Mackie-Lewis, S. (1997). Navigating by attire: The
use of dress by female administrative employees. *Academy of Management Journal, 40*(1),
9–45.

Ramazanoglu, C. (2012). *Feminism and the contradictions of oppression*. New York: Routledge.

Ramdas, S. M., Manan, S. A., and Sabapathy, E. (2010). Resistance and oppression in Su-Chen
Christine Lim's Novels: A radical feminist analysis. *Studies in Literature and Language, 1*(7),
89–97.

Redcross, C., Bloom, D., Azurdia, G., Zweig, J., and Pindus, N. (2009). Transitional jobs for
ex-prisoners: Implementation, two-year impacts, and costs of the Center for Employment
Opportunities (CEO) Prisoner Reentry Program. Washington, DC: The Urban Institute.

Reed, M. I. (1992). *The sociology of organizations: Themes, perspectives and prospects* (301).
Hampstead: Harvester Wheatsheaf.

Reisig, M. D., Holtfreter, K., and Morash, M. (2006). Assessing recidivism risk across female pathways to crime. *Justice Quarterly, 23*(3), 384–405.

Renzetti, C. M. (1992). *Violent betrayal: Partner abuse in lesbian relationships.* Thousand Oaks, CA: Sage Publicatins.

———. (2013). *Feminist Criminology (Key Ideas in Criminology).* New York: Routledge.

Rich, A. (1980). Compulsory heterosexuality and lesbian existence. *Signs, 5*(4), 631–60.

Richie, B. (1996). *Compelled to crime: The gender entrapment of battered Black women.* New York: Routledge.

Richie, B. E. (2001). Challenges incarcerated women face as they return to their communities: Findings from life history interviews. *Crime and Delinquency, 47*(3), 368–89.

Ridgeway, C. L. (1997). Interaction and the conservation of gender inequality: Considering employment. *American Sociological Review,* 218–35.

Riessman, C. K. (2000). Stigma and everyday resistance practices childless women in South India. *Gender and Society, 14*(1), 111–35.

Roberts, D. E. (1993). Racism and patriarchy in the meaning of motherhood. *American University Journal of Gender and the Law, 1,* 1–38.

Robinson, G., and McNeill, F. (2008). Exploring the dynamics of compliance with community penalties. *Theoretical Criminology, 12*(4), 431–49.

Rollins, J. (1987). *Between women: Domestics and their employers.* Philadelphia: Temple University Press.

Romero, M. (2002). *Maid in the USA.* New York: Routledge.

Roscigno, V. J., and Hodson, R. (2004). The organizational and social foundations of worker resistance. *American Sociological Review, 69*(1), 14–39.

Rosener, J. B. (1990). Ways women lead. *Harvard Business Review,* 3–10.

Ross, L. (1998). *Inventing the savage: The social construction of Native American criminality.* Austin: University of Texas Press.

Ross, L., Anderson, D. R., and Wisocki, P. A. (1982). Television viewing and adult sex-role attitudes. *Sex Roles, 8*(6), 589–92.

Rossman, S. B., and Roman, C. G. (2003). Case-managed reentry and employment: Lessons from the Opportunity to Succeed Program. *Justice Research and Policy, 5*(2), 75–100.

Rubenstein, C., and Shaver, P. (1982). The experience of loneliness. In L. T. Peplau and D. Perlman (Eds.), *Loneliness: A sourcebook of current theory, research and therapy* (pp. 206–23). New York: Wiley.

Russell, K., Wilson, M., and Hall, R. (2011). *The color complex: The politics of skin color among African Americans.* New York: Anchor.

Russell-Brown, K. (1998). *The color of crime: Racial hoaxes, white fear, Black protectionism, police harassment, and other macroaggressions.* New York: New York University Press.

Ryan, R. M., and Deci, E. L. (2000). Self-determination theory and the facilitation of intrinsic motivation, social development, and well-being. *American Psychologist, 55*(1), 68–78.

Sacks, K. B. (1989). Toward a unified theory of class, race, and gender. *American Ethnologist, 16*(3), 534–50.

Sacks, S., Sacks, J. Y., McKendrick, K., Banks, S., and Stommel, J. (2004). Modified TC for MICA offenders: Crime outcomes. *Behavioral Sciences and the Law, 22*(4), 477–501.

Sainsbury, D. (1996). *Gender, equality and welfare states.* New York: Cambridge University Press.

Salisbury, E. J., Van Voorhis, P., and Spiropoulos, G. V. (2009). The predictive validity of a gender-responsive needs assessment an exploratory study. *Crime and Delinquency, 55*(4), 550–85.

Sanders, T. (2004). Controllable laughter managing sex work through humour. *Sociology, 38*(2), 273–91.

Sarat, A. (1990). The law is all over: Power, resistance and the legal consciousness of the welfare poor. *Yale Journal of Law and the Humanities, 2*, 343–79.

Schirmer, S., Nellis, A., and Mauer, M. (2009). *Incarcerated parents and their children: Trends 1991–2007*. Washington, DC: The Sentencing Project.

Schram, P. J., Koons-Witt, B. A., Williams, F. P., and McShane, M. D. (2006). Supervision strategies and approaches for female parolees: Examining the link between unmet needs and parolee outcome. *Crime and Delinquency, 52*(3), 450–71.

Schwartz, M. D., and DeKeseredy, W. S. (1997). *Sexual assault on the college campus: The role of male peer support*. Thousand Oaks, CA: Sage Publications.

Scott, J. C. (1985). *Weapons of the weak: Everyday forms of peasant resistance*. New Haven, CT: Yale University Press.

———. (1990). *Domination and the arts of resistance: Hidden transcripts*. New Haven, CT: Yale University Press.

Scraton, S. (2001). Reconceptualizing race, gender and sport. In B. Carrington and I. McDonald (Eds.), *"Race," Sport, and British Society* (pp. 170–87). New York: Routledge.

Seiter, R. P., and Kadela, K. R. (2003). Prisoner reentry: What works, what does not, and what is promising. *Crime and Delinquency, 49*(3), 360–88.

Sen, A. (1985). Well-being, agency and freedom: The Dewey lectures 1984. *The Journal of Philosophy, 82*(4), 169–221.

Sen, P. (1999a). *Development as freedom*. New York: Oxford University Press.

———. (1999b). Enhancing women's choices in responding to domestic violence in Calcutta: A comparison of employment and education. *The European Journal of Development Research, 11*(2), 65–86.

Shaylor, C. (1998). It's like living in a black hole: Women of color and solitary confinement in the prison industrial complex. *New England Journal on Criminal and Civil Confinement, 24*, 385–416.

———. (2009). Neither kind nor gentle: The perils of 'gender responsive justice.' In P. Scranton and J. McCollouch (Eds.), *The violence of incarceration* (pp. 145–63). New York: Routledge.

Shelton, B. A., and John, D. (1996). The division of household labor. *Annual Review of Sociology, 299–322.

Shorter-Gooden, K. (2004). Multiple resistance strategies: How African American women cope with racism and sexism. *Journal of Black Psychology, 30*(3), 406–25.

Sibley, D., and Hoven, B.,van. (2009). The contamination of personal space: Boundary construction in a prison environment. *Area, 41*(2), 198–206.

Siegel, J. (2011). *Disrupted childhoods: Children of women in prison*. New Brunswick, NJ: Rutgers University Press.

Skidmore, P. L. (1999). Dress to impress: Employer regulation of gay and lesbian appearance. *Social and Legal Studies, 8*(4), 509–29.

Smith–McLallen, A., Johnson, B. T., Dovidio, J. F., and Pearson, A. R. (2006). Black and white: The role of color bias in implicit race bias. *Social Cognition, 24*(1), 46–73.

Smyth, K., and Yarandi, H. N. (1996). Factor analysis of the ways of coping questionnaire for African American women. *Nursing Research, 45*(1), 25–29.

Sokoloff, N. J. (2005). Women prisoners at the dawn of the 21st century. *Women and Criminal Justice, 16*(1–2), 127–37.

Solomon, A. L., Visher, C., La Vigne, N. G., and Osborne, J. (2006). *Understanding the challenges of prisoner reentry: Research findings from the Urban Institute's prisoner reentry portfolio.* Washington, DC: The Urban Institute.

Sonn, C. C., and Fisher, A. T. (1998). Sense of community: Community resilient responses to oppression and change. *Journal of Community Psychology, 26*(5), 457–72.

Sorensen, M. J. (2008). Humor as a serious strategy of nonviolent resistance to oppression. *Peace and Change, 33*(2), 167–90.

Sotirin, P., and Gottfried, H. (1999). The ambivalent dynamics of secretarial 'bitching': Control, resistance, and the construction of identity. *Organization, 6*(1), 57–80.

Spjeldnes, S., and Goodkind, S. (2009). Gender differences and offender reentry: A review of the literature. *Journal of Offender Rehabilitation, 48*(4), 314–35.

Spradley, J. (2003). Asking descriptive questions. In M. Pogrebin (Ed.), *Qualitative approaches to criminal justice; perspectives from the field* (pp. 44–53). Thousand Oaks, CA: Sage Publications.

St Martin, L., and Gavey, N. (1996). Women's bodybuilding: Feminist resistance and/or femininity's recuperation? *Body and Society, 2*(4), 45–57.

Steele, F. (1973). *Physical settings and organizational development.* Reading, MA: Addison-Wesley

Steffensmeier, D. J., and Terry, R. M. (1986). Institutional sexism in the underworld: A view from the inside. *Sociological Inquiry, 56*(3), 304–23.

Sullivan, C. J., Sullivan, C. J., McKendrick, K., Sacks, S., and Banks, S. (2007). Modified therapeutic community treatment for offenders with MICA disorders: Substance use outcomes. *The American Journal of Drug and Alcohol Abuse, 33*(6), 823–32.

Sullivan, M. A. (2002). Current perspectives on smoking cessation among substance abusers. *Current Psychiatry Reports, 4*(5), 388–96.

Sullivan, R. (2005). *Visual habits: Nuns, feminism, and American postwar popular culture.* Toronto: University of Toronto Press.

Sutherland, D. E. (1981). *Americans and their servants: Domestic service in the United States from 1800 to 1920.* Baton Rouge: Louisiana State University Press.

Taxman, F. S. (1998). *Reducing recidivism through a seamless system of care: Components of effective treatment, supervision, and transition services in the community.* College Park: University of Maryland.

———. (2004). The offender and reentry: Supporting active participation in reintegration. *Federal Probation, 68,* 31–35.

Taxman, F. S., Young, D., Byrne, J. M., Holsinger, A., and Anspach, D. (2002). *From prison safety to public safety: Innovations in offender reentry.* College Park: University of Maryland.

Teresa, D. (1999). Carceral spaces in South Africa: A case study of institutional power, sexuality and transgression in a women's prison. *Geoforum, 30*(1), 71–83.

Thompson, C. J., and Haytko, D. L. (1997). Speaking of fashion: Consumers' uses of fashion discourses and the appropriation of countervailing cultural meanings. *Journal of Consumer Research, 24*(1), 15–42.

Tonry, M. H. (1995). *Intermediate sanctions in overcrowded times.* Lebanon, NH: University Press of New England.

Travis, J. (2002). *Invisible punishment: An instrument of social exclusion.* Washington, DC: The Urban Institute.

———. (2005). *But they all come back: Facing the challenges of prisoner reentry.* Washington, DC: The Urban Insitute.

Travis, J., Keegan, S., and Cadora, E. (2003). *A portrait of prisoner reentry in New Jersey.* Washington, DC: The Urban Institute.

Travis, J., and Petersilia, J. (2001). Reentry reconsidered: A new look at an old question. *Crime and Delinquency, 47*(3), 291–313.

Travis, J., Solomon, A. L., and Waul, M. (2001). *From prison to home: The dimensions and consequences of prisoner reentry.* Washington, DC: The Urban Institute.

Trethewey, A. (1997). Resistance, identity, and empowerment: A postmodern feminist analysis of clients in a human service organization. *Communications Monographs, 64*(4), 281–301.

Treuthart, M. P. (1990). Adopting a more realistic definition of family. *Gonzaga Law Review, 26*, 91.

Tuerk, E. H., and Loper, A. B. (2006). Contact between incarcerated mothers and their children: Assessing parenting stress. *Journal of Offender Rehabilitation, 43*(1), 23–43.

Turiel, E. (2003). Resistance and subversion in everyday life. *Journal of Moral Education, 32*(2), 115–30.

Turnbull, S., and Hannah-Moffat, K. (2009). Under these conditions gender, parole and the governance of reintegration. *British Journal of Criminology, 49*(4), 532–51.

Uggen, C., and Staff, J. (2001). Work as a turning point for criminal offenders. *Corrections Management Quarterly, 5*, 1–16.

Ullman, S. E., and Knight, R. A. (1992). Fighting back: Women's resistance to rape. *Journal of Interpersonal Violence, 7*(1), 31–43.

———. (1993). The efficacy of women's resistance strategies in rape situations. *Psychology of Women Quarterly, 17*(1), 23–38.

US General Accounting Office. (1991). *Prison alternatives: Crowded federal prisons can transfer more inmates to halfway houses.* Washington, DC: US General Accounting Office.

Van Dieten, M. 2008. *Women Offender Case Management Model.* Washington, DC: U.S. Department of Justice, National Institute of Corrections.

Van Dijk, T. A. (1993). Principles of critical discourse analysis. *Discourse and Society, 4*(2), 249–83.

Van Doorn-Harder, P. (1995). *Contemporary coptic nuns.* Columbia: University of South Carolina Press.

Van Maanen, J. (2011). *Tales of the field: On writing ethnography.* Chicago: University of Chicago Press.

Van Voorhis, P. (2012). On behalf of women offenders: Women's place in the science of evidence-based practice. *Criminology and Public Policy, 11*(2), 111–45.

Van Voorhis, P., Salisbury, E., Wright, E., and Bauman, A. (2008). *Achieving accurate pictures of risk and identifying gender responsive needs: Two new assessments for women offenders.* Washington, DC: US Department of Justice, National Institute of Corrections.

Van Voorhis, P., Wright, E. M., Salisbury, E., and Bauman, A. (2010). Women's risk factors and their contributions to existing risk/needs assessment the current status of a gender-responsive assessment. *Criminal Justice and Behavior, 37*(3), 261–88.

Van Wormer, K. (2010). *Working with female offenders: A gender sensitive approach.* Hoboken, NJ: John Wiley and Sons.

Vandebosch, H. (2000). Research note: A captive audience? The media use of prisoners. *European Journal of Communication, 15*(4), 529–44.

———. (2009). Media use as an adaptation or coping tool in prison. *Communications, 26*(4), 371–88.

Vaughn, M. S., and Carroll, L. (1998). Separate and unequal: Prison versus free-world medical care. *Justice Quarterly, 15*(1), 3–40.

Vaughn, M. S., and Smith, L. G. (1999). Practicing penal harm medicine in the United States: Prisoners' voices from jail. *Justice Quarterly, 16*(1), 175–231.

Visher, C., Debus, S., and Yahner, J. (2008). Employment after prison: A longitudinal study of releasees in three states.

Visher, C. A., and Travis, J. (2003). Transitions from prison to community: Understanding individual pathways. *Annual Review of Sociology, 29*, 89–113.

Wacquant, L. (2010). Prisoner reentry as myth and ceremony. *Dialectical Anthropology, 34*(4), 605–20.

Wade, A. (1997). Small acts of living: Everyday resistance to violence and other forms of oppression. *Contemporary Family Therapy, 19*(1), 23–39.

Walby, S. (1986). *Patriarchy at work: Patriarchal and capitalist relations in employment.* Cambridge: Polity Press.

———. (1990). *Theorizing patriarchy.* Cambridge, MA: B. Blackwell.

———. (1997). *Gender transformations.* New York: Routledge.

Walker, C. (1999). Combining Martha and Mary: Gender and work in seventeenth-century English cloisters. *The Sixteenth Century Journal, 30*(2), 397–418.

Walker, E. A., Gelfand, A., Katon, W. J., Koss, M. P., Von Korff, M., Bernstein, D. et al. (1999). Adult health status of women with histories of childhood abuse and neglect. *The American Journal of Medicine, 107*(4), 332–39.

Walsh, D. C., Sorensen, G., and Leonard, L. (1995). Gender, health, and cigarette smoking. In B. C. Amick, S. Levine, A.R. Tarloy, and D. C. Walsh (Eds.), *Society and Health* (pp. 131–71). New York: Oxford University Press.

Ward, D. A., and Kassebaum, G. G. (1964). Homosexuality: A mode of adaptation in a prison for women. *Social Problems, 12*(2), 159–77.

Watson, R., Stimpson, A., and Hostick, T. (2004). Prison health care: A review of the literature. *International Journal of Nursing Studies, 41*(2), 119–28.

Watt, S. K. (2003). Come to the river: Using spirituality to cope, resist, and develop identity. *New Directions for Student Services, 2003*(104), 29–40.

Weitz, R. (2001). Women and their hair: Seeking power through resistance and accommodation. *Gender and Society, 15*(5), 667–86.

Wells, T. (1973). The covert power of gender in organizations. *Journal of Contemporary Business, 2*, 53–68.

Welsh, W. N. (2007). A multisite evaluation of prison-based therapeutic community drug treatment. *Criminal Justice and Behavior, 34*(11), 1481–98.

Werth, R. (2012). I do what I'm told, sort of: Reformed subjects, unruly citizens, and parole. *Theoretical Criminology, 16*(3), 329–46.

West, C., and Zimmerman, D. H. (1987). Doing gender. *Gender and Society, 1*(2), 125–51.

West, H. C. (2010). *Prison inmates at midyear 2009—Statistical Tables.* Washington, DC: US Department of Justice, Bureau of Justice Statistics.

Wexler, H. K., Falkin, G. P., and Lipton, D. S. (1990). Outcome evaluation of a prison therapeutic community for substance abuse treatment. *Criminal Justice and Behavior, 17*(1), 71–92.

Wexler, H. K., Falkin, G. P., Lipton, D. S., and Rosenblum, A. B. (1992). Outcome evaluation of a prison therapeutic community for substance abuse treatment. *National Institute on Drug Abuse Research Monograph Series,* 156–56.

Whisner, M. (1982). Gender-specific clothing regulation: A study in patriarchy. *Harvard Women's Law Journal, 5,* 73–78.

Wijndaele, K., Brage, S., Besson, H., Khaw, K.-T., Sharp, S. J., Luben, R. et al. (2011). Television viewing time independently predicts all-cause and cardiovascular mortality: The EPIC Norfolk Study. *International Journal of Epidemiology, 40*(1), 150–59.

Willcocks, D., Peace, S., and Kellaher, L. (1987). Private lives in public places: Research-based critique of residential life in local authority old people's homes. New York: Tavistock.

Wills, G. (2006). *The rosary.* New York: Penguin Books.

Wilper, A. P., Woolhandler, S., Boyd, J. W., Lasser, K. E., McCormick, D., Bor, D. H. et al. (2009). The health and health care of US prisoners: Results of a nationwide survey. *American Journal of Public Health, 99*(4), 666–72.

Wilsnack, S. C., Vogeltanz, N. D., Klassen, A. D., and Harris, T. R. (1997). Childhood sexual abuse and women's substance abuse: National survey findings. *Journal of Studies on Alcohol and Drugs, 58*(3), 264–71.

Wilson, E. (1977). *Women and the welfare state.* New York: Routledge.

Wilson, M. K., and Anderson, S. C. (1997). Empowering female offenders: Removing barriers to community-based practice. *Affilia, 12*(3), 342–58.

Witz, A. (2003). *Professions and patriarchy.* New York: Routledge.

Wolf, M. (1972). *Women and the family in rural Taiwan.* Redwood City, CA: Stanford University Press.

Woshinsky, B. R. (2010). *Imagining Women's Conventual Spaces in France, 1600–1800: The Cloister Disclosed.* Burlington, VT: Ashgate Publishing Company.

Yuval-Davis, N. (2006). Intersectionality and feminist politics. *European Journal of Women's Studies, 13*(3), 193–209.

Zahn, G. L. (1991). Face-to-face communication in an office setting: The effects of position, proximity, and exposure. *Communication Research, 18*(6), 737–54.

Zoller, H. M., and Fairhurst, G. T. (2007). Resistance leadership: The overlooked potential in critical organization and leadership studies. *Human Relations, 60*(9), 1331–60.

INDEX